Romantic Days and Nights®

IN BOSTON

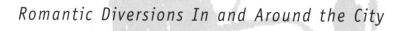

Romantic Diversions In and Around the City

THIRD EDITION

*by Patricia Harris
and David Lyon*

The Globe Pequot Press

GUILFORD, CONNECTICUT

Cover illustration, text design, and interior illustrations by M.A. Dubé
Spot Art by www.ArtToday.com
Maps by Mary Ballachino

Romantic Days and Nights is a registered trademark of The Globe Pequot Press.

Library of Congress Cataloging-in-Publication Data
Harris, Patricia, 1949-
    Romantic days and nights in Boston : romantic diversions in and
around the city / by Patricia Harris and David Lyon.—3rd ed.
        p.cm.—(Romantic days and nights series)
    Includes index.
    ISBN 0-7627-0890-5
    1. Boston (Mass.)—Guidebooks. 2.
Couples—Travel—Massachusetts—Boston—Guidebooks. I. Lyon, David,
1949- II. Title. III. Series.

F73.18 .H375 2001
917.44'610444—dc21   00-066269

Manufactured in the United States of America
Third Edition/First Printing

To generous friends

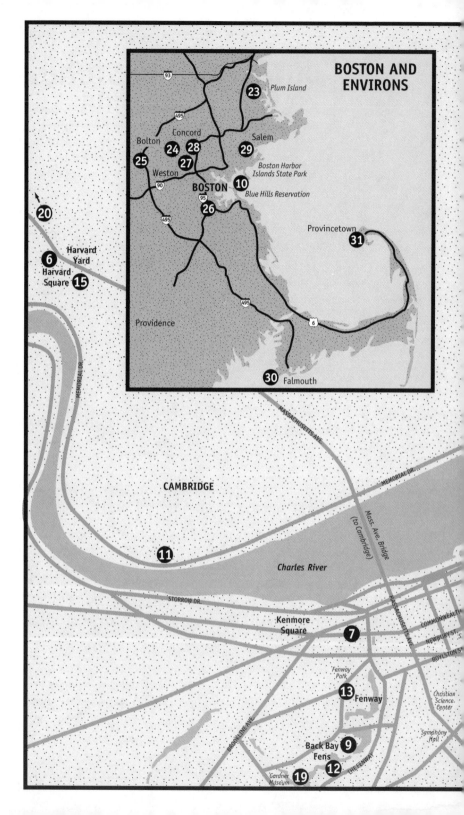

BOSTON AND ENVIRONS

23 Plum Island

Concord
Bolton
24 28
25
27
Weston
BOSTON
10
Salem
29

Boston Harbor
Islands State Park
Blue Hills Reservation

26

Provincetown
31

20

6 Harvard
Yard

Harvard
Square 15

Providence

30 Falmouth

CAMBRIDGE

11

Charles River

STORROW DR.

MEMORIAL DR.

MASSACHUSETTS AVE.

Mass. Ave. Bridge
(to Cambridge)

MEMORIAL DR.

Kenmore
Square

7

COMMONWEALTH

NEWBURY ST.

BOYLSTON ST.

Fenway
Park

13 Fenway

Christian
Science
Center

BROOKLINE AVE.

Back Bay
Fens

9

Symphony
Hall

12

Gardner
Museum

19

THE FENWAY

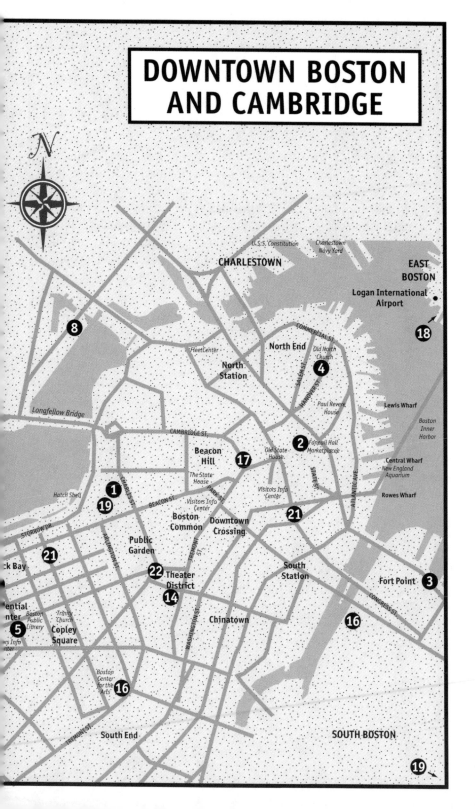

Acknowledgments

WE WOULD LIKE TO THANK our editor, Laura Strom, for bringing us into this exciting new series of guides; Karen Ingebretsen for her supportive and clear-headed copyediting; the research staff of the Boston and Cambridge public libraries; the curators, directors, and spokespeople of innumerable museums and historical societies; the rangers of the National Park Service and the Metropolitan District Commission; and our many friends and colleagues who shared their own romantic secrets about Boston.

Contents

Introduction   xi

HEARTS OF THE CITY

1. When Harry Met Sally
   (on Beacon Hill)   3
2. One If by Land
   *The Heart of Old
   Boston*   10
3. Two If by Sea
   On the Waterfront   18
4. The Snug North End   25
5. Cozy in Back Bay
   A Winter Idyll   33
6. In the Groves of
   Academe   39

GOOD SPORTS

7. Take Me Out to the
   Ball Game   49
8. A River Runs Through It
   Boating on the Charles   54
9. Budget Boston
   Biking Through the Parks   61
10. On a Desert Island in
    Your Dreams   70
11. Brewpubs and
    Flashing Blades   75

THE MUSES

12. The Painters' Passion
    A Fine Arts Weekend   85
13. Ode to Joy
    Classical Weekend   94
14. A Stage for Romance   101
15. Poetry and All
    That Jazz
    Cambridge Coolest   108
16. The Artist's Touch
    *Two Autumn
    Weekends*   116

OCCASIONS

17. Anniversary Recharge   129
18. The Right Foot
    First Night   135
19. Hearts and Flowers
    *A Celebration of
    Spring*   141
20. Echoes of Camelot
    *Irish Roots of
    American Royalty*   148
21. Laissez Les Bon
    Temps Rouler
    Bastille Day in Boston   155
22. Holiday Shopping in
    the Hub   162

Well-Seasoned Day Trips

23. Bird-Watching at
    Plum Island   173

24. Literary Concord
    *The Lives of the
    Authors*   179

25. Nashoba Valley
    Apple Picking   185

26. A Foliage Hike in
    the Blue Hills   189

27. A Cross-Country
    Outing   194

28. Design for Living:
    *Domesticity
    West of the City*   198

Out-of-Town Sleepovers

29. Salem When It Ruled
    the Waves   207

30. Sweet Seclusion on
    Old Cape Cod   215

31. Provincetown by
    Ferry   222

Appendix

Recommended Annual
Events   229

Indexes

Special Indexes
    Romantic Restaurants   233
    Romantic Lodgings   238
    Evening Diversions   239
General Index   243

About the Authors   255

*The prices and rates listed
in this guidebook were confirmed at press time.
We recommend, however, that you call establishments
before traveling to obtain current
information.*

Speaking of prices . . . The budget icon (look for the piggy bank in the margins) indicates less expensive activities. Also, many of the attractions we recommend, especially government-related buildings, parks, monuments, and museums, are open to the public at no charge.

Introduction

E HAPPEN TO THINK THAT BOSTON is an intensely romantic city, but then, we're biased because this is where we played out the scenes of our courtship. Even so, it makes a terrific backdrop for personal drama. Let us tell you why.

For starters, Boston is Boston because even as it matures, it never forgets. The colonial wellspring of American passion lies embedded in a vibrant, modern city. Its legendary winding streets weren't laid out by cows (despite what the fanciful trolley driver might say), but by meandering men and women delightfully unencumbered by modern ideas about businesslike pace.

Boston is a city on a human, even intimate, scale where life won't pass you by. It's a place where men and women engage one another, where the life of the mind and the passion for beauty find direct expression in the architecture, the art, the music—and the explosion of culinary genius of the restaurant scene. (It's nearly as hard to eat a bad meal in Boston as in Paris.) Boston is also a sports town par excellence, where you can cheer professional sports teams or engage in outdoor activity of your own without leaving the confines of the city.

Boston never goes stale, never fails to surprise and delight. Classical music fans know the dynamic acoustics of Symphony Hall—but few suspect that Jordan Hall, a block away, is a Victorian gem that rings like a fine violin. Between Back Bay and the South End stretches an unanticipated string of small parks and a bicycle path that links downtown with the western suburban parks. At the heart of the public library you suddenly stumble on a hidden courtyard. With three and a half centuries to build up a storehouse of wit, the city never fails to have a story to tell.

Yet, unlike so many other cities, Boston still has wide, green spaces in its parks, islands, and revitalized waterfront. It is a city directly in touch with the natural world, which spells great opportunities for outdoor activities in all seasons. (And we do have seasons—four gorgeous ones.) To make sure that you really enjoy them, this book takes you hiking, skiing, bird-watching, sunbathing, and apple picking at spots near Boston that become truly perfect for a sweet, short season each year.

Boston has elegant grand hotels the way old-time Boston matrons had their hats. But the Hub also holds small hotel hide-aways and intimate B&Bs. It's a city where you can spend a winter weekend hopping from fireplaced room to fireplaced room—or a summer idyll almost entirely al fresco. It's a great place for a couple to be alone together—or to dissolve into a sea of activity.

Boston is a great city for falling in love. We did.

THE ITINERARIES

To borrow a line from a country-and-western tune, we think that many couples are "looking for love in all the wrong places." A full-blown loving relationship is built on a lot more than the sentiments of a greeting card, a box of candy, and a bouquet of flowers (although they're all nice). Serious romance is about sharing new experiences or adventures together, about engaging yourselves in activities that are stimulating, that open new horizons. The important part is that you're sharing them. In that same vein, while we offer many suggestions for luxury accommodations and dining, other itineraries acknowledge that romance can bloom in less indulgent surroundings as well.

So these itineraries supply ways for you to share Boston. Each takes advantage of some characteristic of the city—the charm of a district, a festival or an event, history, particular natural beauty. Many of the itineraries are compact and can be easily handled by walking from place to place (one of the great pleasures of Boston). But we didn't leave out something wonderful—such as Mount Auburn Cemetery—just because it's a little out of the way.

USING THIS BOOK

Most of the itineraries in this volume presume that you'll be visiting Boston on a weekend. We made that assumption because it's statistically true; the majority of weekday visitors come on business. If you do come on weekdays (and a few itineraries suggest that you do), you may have to make a few adjustments, such as substituting breakfast and lunch for brunch.

As always, we have tried to be as accurate as possible in giving dates and prices, but they're always subject to change. Maybe we don't need to remind you, but be sure to call ahead to check. Hotel specials, in particular, are always subject to availability.

We're sorry to say that as the millennium unfolds, Boston's excellent economy has spelled substantial inflation in hotel rooms, so be aggressive in asking about promotional rates or discounts for organizational memberships such as AAA or AARP. This same booming economy means that tables at premium restaurants must often be reserved weeks ahead, though a table may be available at the last minute if you ask.

If you're coming to Boston for more than a few days, it's fairly easy to link one itinerary to another. For example, either of the weekends devoted to visiting artists' studios ("The Artist's Touch") might easily be linked to the museum visits of "The Painters' Passion,"—or to the day hike in the Blue Hills or to the weekend of brewpubs and skating. The two different weekends in Cambridge ("In the Groves of Academe" and "Poetry and All That Jazz") fit together quite nicely— and both mesh well with the sailing and canoeing of "A River Runs Through It." So experiment and look through the chapters to find a second choice that would make a good extension. If you're spending a few days, consider purchasing a Boston CityPass for savings on several attractions. The $30.50 pass provides admission to the New England Aquarium, the John F. Kennedy Library and Museum, the Museum of Fine Arts, the Museum of Science, the Isabella Stewart Gardner Museum, and the John Hancock Observatory. It's available at all participating institutions. The day trips—which also make good activities for a first date—are explicitly intended to be added on to any other itinerary. If your primary choice is an activity with which you're already familiar, supplement it with activities you've never tried. Variety is the spice of romance.

We happen to agree with M. F. K. Fisher that "gastronomy has always been connected with its sister art of love," so the dining in this book tends to emphasize really good food in places with good service and romantic decor. Eating well is also an art worth cultivating. Fortunately, Boston offers places where you can eat a great plate of ribs or a bucket of clams as well as superb filet mignon. As a general guideline, we have indicated approximate prices for each restaurant based on the price per person for an appetizer, entree, and dessert but not including drinks, tax, and tip. "Inexpensive" indicates less than $25, "moderate" between $25 and $50, "expensive" more than $50.

Getting Here and Getting Around

Boston is served by more than forty airlines via Logan International Airport. Public transportation—either the Blue Line subway for $1.00 or the water shuttle for $10.00—is the easiest and least expensive way to get into the city. Amtrak pulls directly into downtown Boston at South Station several times daily.

Most pleasure travelers, however, come to Boston by automobile—an approach that requires patience and forbearance. I–93 enters Boston from the south as the Southeast Expressway, which becomes the Central Artery when it gets into town. (The Central Artery is currently undergoing the equivalent of bypass surgery, a process not due for completion until at least 2004.) Slightly easier access from the west is by the Massachusetts Turnpike, also known as I–90. Before you get into town, we suggest calling SmartRoutes at (617) 374–1234 to learn road conditions.

Once you're here, you can park your car unless the "Practical notes" say otherwise. Whenever possible, we believe in taking public transportation or walking. After all, it's hard (and unsafe) to hold hands while one of you is driving.

The subway and bus system (called the "T") uses tokens, which cost $1.00 each, with some surcharges on trolley and bus lines that reach far into the suburbs. The Visitor Passport provides token-free passage for one day ($6.00), three days ($11.00), or seven days ($22.00). It is sold at the T office at Downtown Crossing and in the Greater Boston Convention and Visitors Bureau locations on the Boston Common and at Prudential Center.

For More Information

**Greater Boston Convention
and Visitors Bureau**
2 Copley Place, Suite 105
Boston, MA 02116-6501
(888) 733–2678
(617) 536–4100
www.bostonusa.com

**Cambridge Office
for Tourism**
18 Brattle Street
Cambridge, MA 02138
(617) 441–2884
www.ci.cambridge.
ma.us/info/

Most Romantic Places in Boston

MOST ROMANTIC CHEAP DATES

Jazz, classical, or pop concert on the **Esplanade,** Boston

Ice-skating on the **Frog Pond,** Boston

Selecting verses at the **Grolier Poetry Book Shop,** Cambridge

Concert at **Jordan Hall** (New England
Conservatory of Music), Boston

Beach-basking on the **Harbor Islands,** Boston

MOST GLAMOROUS SPOTS FOR ROMANCE

Moonlight Tango on the **Weeks Footbridge,** Cambridge

Oak Bar at the Fairmont Copley Plaza Hotel, Boston

The **Federalist restaurant** at XV Beacon Hotel, Boston

Brunch on the **Liberty schooner** *Clipper,* Boston

Balcony seats at the **Colonial Theatre,** Boston

Most Romantic Places to Be Photographed Together

In front of **Trinity Church** as reflected in
Hancock Tower, Boston

Courtyard of **Isabella Stewart Gardner Museum,** Boston

On the rail of **harbor ferry** approaching
Long Wharf, Boston

Aboard **Swan Boats,** Public Garden, Boston

In front of the **murals** at **Boston Public Library,** Boston

Holding hot dogs at **Fenway Park,** Boston

Most Romantic Restaurants

L'Espalier, Boston

Salts, Cambridge

Icarus, Boston

Torch, Boston

Martin House, Provincetown

Most Romantic Lodgings

Charles Street Inn, Boston

Gryphon House, Boston

"Suite Seclusion" at **Palmer House Inn,** Falmouth

Eliot Hotel, Boston

XV Beacon Hotel, Boston

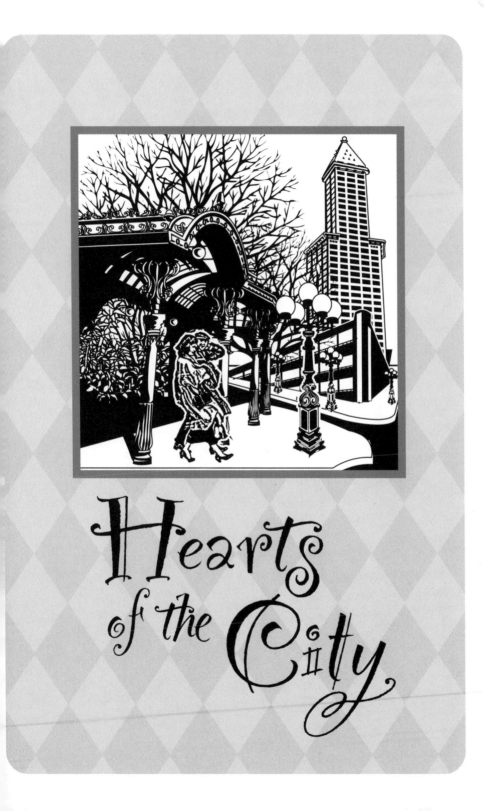

Hearts of the City

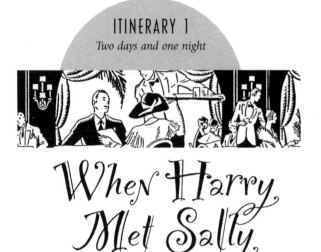

When Harry Met Sally
(ON BEACON HILL)

FOR TWO DAYS YOU'LL BE LIVING ATOP BEACON HILL as you're transported back two centuries to trace the footsteps of Boston's first perfect couple. In the 1790s, few Bostonians showed such vision of the good life as young Harrison Gray Otis, lawyer and member of Congress, and his savvy wife, Sally. They were instrumental in establishing what quickly became Boston's best address—Beacon Hill—and in promoting their architect friend, Charles Bulfinch, who was to define the American Federal style. This sojourn along graceful streets created from a bramble-strewn cow pasture follows Harry and Sally's ascent across Beacon Hill from the North Slope to the sunny South Slope and their social ascent to become *the* host and hostess of the city.

PRACTICAL NOTES: The Nichols House Museum is closed in January.

DAY ONE: morning

Urban hideaways don't get much more romantic than the **Charles Street Inn** (94 Charles Street; 617–371–0008 or 888–321–0008; $200–$295). Built in the 1870s as a "display house" to show prospective Back Bay buyers the level of luxury they could expect in their custom-built homes, this eight-room property was completely modernized as an inn in 2000 to the tune of $2.5 million. But such twenty-first-century touches as Sub-Zero refrigerators, high-speed

Romance AT A GLANCE

◆ Enjoy a nightcap of tawny port beside the marble fireplace in your room at the **Charles Street Inn** (94 Charles Street; 617–371–0008 or 888–321–0008). If the evening is cool, offer a toast to true love by toasty firelight.

◆ Visit the opulent first home of Harry and Sally Otis for a glimpse of how the cream of Boston society entertained in the generation after the American Revolution: the **Harrison Gray Otis House** (141 Cambridge Street; 617–227–3956).

◆ Drop in for a taste of Beacon Hill eccentricity at the house museum established by the strong-minded Rose Nichols, one of America's first authors on landscape gardening: **Nichols House Museum** (55 Mount Vernon Street; 617–227–6993).

◆ Dine at a window table at **Torch** (26 Charles Street; 617–723–5939), where chef Evan Deluty's Parisian bistro cooking could make you believe you're in the City of Light.

◆ Select from the finest in contemporary American cooking as you brunch sumptuously in the book-lined **Library Grill at the Hampshire House** (84 Beacon Street; 617–227–9600) overlooking the picture-perfect Public Garden.

◆ Seek out the hidden treasures—or simply the curios that amuse you both—from the multitude of **antiques dealers** on Charles Street, where the American antiques industry got its start more than a century ago.

Internet access, and Thermo Spa tub-showers are gorgeously balanced by the original marble fireplaces in each room and the period furnishings.

All the rooms at the Charles Street Inn are named for Boston artistic or literary figures. The most classically romantic of the lot is the Henry James room with its soaring ceilings, king-size canopy bed and Victorian opulence expressed in antique gold and forest green.

While you may be loath to leave your perfect 1870s town house, you should head down Joy Street to Harry and Sally's first house, the **Harrison Gray Otis House** (141 Cambridge Street; 617–227–3956), which they built in 1796 from a design by their friend, architect Charles Bulfinch. It's now a house museum and the headquarters of the Society for the Preservation of New England Antiquities, aka SPNEA. In the mid-1790s, many of the successful merchant types were leaving Boston for what would become the suburbs. But Sally Otis was a confirmed urbanite, reportedly telling her husband that she would have "rather an attic in the city than a mansion in the countryside." Instead, she ended up with a succession of three mansions—in the city.

From Wednesday through Sunday from 11:00 A.M. to 5:00 P.M., the house is open for tours, which cost $4.00. The classical exterior bespeaks a kind of modesty that the colorful and opulent interior belies. Decorated with oriental carpets, vibrantly painted and papered walls, dozens of paintings and lithographs, and separate post-dinner sitting rooms for men and women, this was probably the house where Harry and three friends hatched their plans to turn John Copley's cow pasture into the most select neighborhood in Boston. (At 11:00 A.M. and 3:00 P.M. on Saturday from May through October, SPNEA also offers an excellent walking tour of Beacon Hill for $10; reservations are recommended.)

You may prefer to take the Hill at your own pace. Cross Cambridge Street and head up Joy Street. About halfway up on the right is Smith Court. **The African Meeting House** here is a key stop on the Black Heritage Trail (see "For More Romance"). Near the crest of the hill, Joy Street intersects Mount Vernon, which novelist Henry James called "the most civilized street in America." With its handsome brick town houses, brick sidewalks, and tall shade trees, it is indeed a picture-perfect neighborhood. This was where Otis and his fellow investors, the Mount Vernon Proprietors, chose to build once they had laid roads. As you walk down Mount Vernon, note the house at number 55—you'll return here later.

Number 85 Mount Vernon was the second Otis mansion, built in 1800. Even its grand turnaround for carriages survives at this private residence. Like the other Otis houses, it was designed by Charles Bulfinch, who built number 87 for himself. A poor businessman, he never lived at number 87 because he had to sell it to settle debts.

Farther downhill you'll come to the inner sanctum of Beacon Hill cachet, the collection of town houses known as **Louisburg Square**. It's the last private square in the city (the on-street parking spaces are deeded!) and home to such luminaries as Senator John Kerry and heiress Teresa Heinz, who purchased a former convent, and blockbuster author Robin Cook, who comments that some people spend as much as $2 million to buy one of these town houses, whereas others spend that sum and more in renovations alone.

Keep walking down Mount Vernon and turn left on West Cedar

Street. You'll pass one end of Acorn Street, a colorful but narrow cobbled way where tradesmen and coachmen once lived. (Its modern occupants are hardly so strapped.) Turn up Chestnut Street, pausing to admire some of the original purple glass panes at 31 Chestnut, dating from a shipment of manganese-contaminated glass from Germany in the early 1800s. Turn right onto Spruce Street to emerge on Beacon Street.

Just a few houses uphill is 45 Beacon Street—the final home of Sally and Harry Otis, which they built in 1805. When they lived here, Harry served as mayor of Boston as well as in other posts. The punch bowl on a small table at a landing halfway up the stairs was always kept full for guests; among the dignitaries the Otises entertained were President James Monroe and, during his farewell tour of America in 1825, the Marquis de Lafayette.

DAY ONE: afternoon

LUNCH

Hungry? You should have worked up quite an appetite tramping up and down the Hill. Descend Beacon Street to its foot, which is Charles Street. One of the smallest but most stylish nooks for Charles Street dining is **Figs** (42 Charles Street; 617–742–3447). We recommend sharing one of owner Todd English's signature fig and prosciutto grilled pizzas and a salad.

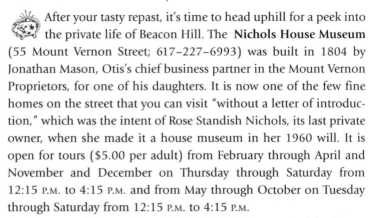

After your tasty repast, it's time to head uphill for a peek into the private life of Beacon Hill. The **Nichols House Museum** (55 Mount Vernon Street; 617–227–6993) was built in 1804 by Jonathan Mason, Otis's chief business partner in the Mount Vernon Proprietors, for one of his daughters. It is now one of the few fine homes on the street that you can visit "without a letter of introduction," which was the intent of Rose Standish Nichols, its last private owner, when she made it a house museum in her 1960 will. It is open for tours ($5.00 per adult) from February through April and November and December on Thursday through Saturday from 12:15 P.M. to 4:15 P.M. and from May through October on Tuesday through Saturday from 12:15 P.M. to 4:15 P.M.

Rose was thirteen when the Nichols family acquired the house in 1885, and she spent her life there as a Beacon Hill paragon. Aided by a little family money (a common Beacon Hill tale), she invented a genteel career as a landscape designer, was a prominent social activist, and generally adapted the world around her to suit her tastes and interests. Rose Nichols adored good conversation but considered serving dinner to be too much trouble—so she invited interesting people, sometimes two dozen at a time, to tea.

Resident curator Bill Pear is a fount of information about the house and Rose's life on the Hill. He explains the eclectic mix of furnishings acquired during Ms. Nichols' many travels: "She was of the opinion that an excellent piece of any era went with an excellent piece of any other—as long as it wasn't Victorian, which she loathed because that's what she had grown up with."

Armed with Mr. Pear's tales, you might wish to wander about the neighborhood a bit, or maybe just enjoy your own proper Beacon Hill house back at the B&B.

DINNER

For a tête-à-tête dinner, we suggest the wonderful French cooking of Evan Deluty at **Torch** (26 Charles Street; 617–723–5939; moderate). With two small rooms, one on the street and another in back, Torch feels like a classic Parisian bistro—a local family restaurant owned by a couple where she runs the reservations and he operates the kitchen. The

A Nightingale Sings

Number 20 on Louisburg Square was the site of one of the great celebrity weddings in 1852, when the "Swedish Nightingale," soprano Jenny Lind, wed her accompanist at the town house of banker Samuel Grey Ward. (Ward was the man who raised the money for "Seward's Folly"—America's purchase of Alaska from Russia.) Lind was such a sensation on her one hundred–concert tour of America, promoted by P. T. Barnum, that an auction of seats at her first performance at Boston's Tremont Temple in 1850 brought a bid of $625 for one seat!

menu changes with the seasons, but it's hard to go wrong with Deluty's delectable treatments of duck breast. You won't be able to watch the passersby on Charles Street, as the tiny windows are set high above your heads, but that contributes to the cozy air.

Stop off at **Beacon Hill Spirits** (63 Charles Street) for a nice sipping wine. If you'd like to get into the feel of Beacon Hill, you might try a tawny port—an old-time favorite of Beacon Hill types going back to the days when the neighborhood made its money in overseas trade. (Actually, Otis and his friends probably preferred Madeira, but a good Madeira is getting awfully hard to find and a bad Madeira is better not found at all.) Properly fortified, you can spin away the rest of the evening by sipping your port next to your fireplace.

DAY TWO: morning

Your B&B offers a continental breakfast, but we'd suggest sticking to some juice and coffee or tea, then taking a stroll around the top of Beacon Hill before a sumptuous brunch. Walk to the head of Beacon Street to get a good look at the **Massachusetts State House.** The central portion is the original building as designed by Charles Bulfinch. This grand example of his public architecture prefigures his work on the U.S. Capitol building in Washington and remains one of the most architecturally influential buildings of the late eighteenth century. The gilding on the golden dome is not original; it was added over the copper sheathing applied by Boston's jack-of-all-trades (and famed equestrian) Paul Revere.

Directly across Beacon Street from the State House steps, the **Robert Gould Shaw Memorial** by Augustus Saint-Gaudens (Rose Nichols's uncle by marriage) is easily the best memorial sculpture in the city. You may know Colonel Shaw's story from the stirring movie *Glory,* or Robert Lowell's elegiac poem, "For the Union Dead." The young abolitionist "of gentle birth and breeding" commanded the first African-American regiment in the Civil War, the 54th Massachusetts. He and half his men died for freedom in the mud outside Fort Wagner in the harbor of Charleston, South Carolina. It is a somber story, yet Saint-Gaudens's dramatic bas-relief catches all its valor without wallowing in the sorrow.

BRUNCH

You'll head downhill for brunch at **The Library Grill at the Hampshire House** (84 Beacon Street; 617–227–9600; moderate). This very classy dining room stands above the Bull & Finch Tavern (the model for the TV show *Cheers!*), which, we suppose, makes it "Melville's." Except it isn't. The Library Grill serves a top-of-the-line à la carte jazz brunch in a wood-paneled, book-lined room on the second floor that feels for all the world like a posh library in a fine Beacon Hill home. Request a window table so that you can look out on the Public Garden.

Before you depart for home, spend a few hours poking into the shops of what has been called the first antiquing district in America: **Charles Street.** You could look for a memento of Beacon Hill—a silver salt cellar, perhaps, at **Antiques at 80 Charles** (617–742–8006), a fine old print of the early days of Beacon Hill from **Eugene Galleries** (76 Charles Street; 617–227–3062), or some fine art pottery from **Boston Antique Cooperative No. 1** (119 Charles Street; 617–227–9810).

FOR MORE ROMANCE

Trace the **Black Heritage Trail**—mostly on or near Beacon Hill—with a tour from the National Park Service (617–742–5415). Lasting approximately two hours, these free tours leave from the Robert Gould Shaw Memorial from Memorial Day to Labor Day.

If you love private gardens, schedule your visit to coincide with the **Hidden Gardens of Beacon Hill** on the third Thursday in May. This one-day self-guided tour of gardens that cannot be seen from the sidewalk has been sponsored since 1929 by the Beacon Hill Garden Club (617–227–4392).

☆One If by Land
THE HEART OF OLD BOSTON

E LOVE BOOKS, BUT HISTORY is a lot more exciting on the streets—especially as you intersperse the lessons with modern pleasures and comforts. Downtown Boston's buildings are taller than those of the eighteenth century, but the streets are the same ones where the characters from history books carried on their ordinary lives—and where they rose to the challenges of extraordinary circumstances. The street patterns have changed so little that feisty Sam Adams and crafty John Hancock could still stumble from countinghouse to alehouse, though today they'd be going from Fidelity Investments to Trattoria Il Panino rather than from a private money man to one of the market taverns replaced by the Faneuil Hall Marketplace shopping center. The battle for the rights of "life, liberty and the pursuit of happiness" began in this part of the city. So prepare to do some pursuing of your own for a few days as you wander through history that remains very much alive. And fear not—there's no quiz on Monday.

DAY ONE: morning

You'll be in a lot of heady company when you sign the register at the **Omni Parker House** (60 School Street; 617–227–8600 or 800–THE–OMNI; $229–435; a dizzying array of romance packages range from $210 to $329). Harvey Parker opened this hotel in 1855, though the current building of more than 500 rooms dates from 1927. (When the 1927 addition and entrance opened, the keys were dropped ceremoniously into Boston Harbor to symbolize that the

♦ Ensconce yourselves at the **Omni Parker House** (60 School Street; 617–227–8600 or 800–THE–OMNI), the oldest continuously operating hotel in America and the historic meeting place for some of America's most prominent nineteenth-century writers.

♦ If time permits, take the tour of the majestic **Custom House** (3 McKinley Square; 617–310–6300), literally topped by stepping out on the twenty-fifth-story outdoor observation deck.

♦ Kindle your passion by visiting **Faneuil Hall,** where orators of the eighteenth century lit the fires of revolution, giving the building its nickname "the cradle of liberty." Afterward, explore the shops of **Faneuil Hall Marketplace.**

♦ Sit down with strangers at the family-style long tables at **Durgin-Park** (340 Faneuil Hall Marketplace; 617–227–2038), "established before you were born" as the dining hall of the waterfront's laborers and sailors.

♦ Quaff a refreshing afternoon drink with a commanding view of the city and the long reach of Boston Harbor from the pinnacle of **The Bay Tower** (60 State Street; 617–723–1666).

♦ Dine in the elegance of Old City Hall at **Maison Robert** (45 School Street; 617–227–3370) and return to the Parker House for a nightcap in the softly lit bar.

doors would never be closed.) The Parker House is one of the most historic hotels in America and sits in one of the most historic sections of Boston. Who has stayed here over the years? Everyone from Charles Dickens and Mark Twain to Kurt Vonnegut, from the Swedish Nightingale Jenny Lind to the Material Girl Madonna. And now those famous lovers: the two of you.

In 1998, the Parker House completed a full-scale, $50-million renovation of all guest rooms and public areas. The lobby is the very picture of everything a gracious hotel should be—elevated ceilings, chandeliers, rich wood and gilt, and deep carpeting. Glass display cases recount the fascinating stories of people—from the famous to the unknown—who chose the Parker House for their reunions, their honeymoons, their great dinners.

Because so much of Boston's history belongs to the whole nation, many sites in the downtown area are part of a National Park.

Visit the **Boston National Historical Park Visitor Center** across from the Old State House on State Street (open daily 9:00 A.M. to 6:00 P.M. during the summer, 9:00 A.M. to 5:00 P.M. the rest of the year; 617–242–5642) to gather information and a map of historic sites, most of which are part of the Freedom Trail.

As you continue down State Street toward the harbor, you'll be following the purposeful march of many a colonial Boston merchant, for the Old State House was a trading center and the foot of the street was the main dock for mercantile vessels. Down near the bottom, Boston's first skyscraper suddenly rises: the 1913 addition to the fine Greek Revival **Custom House** (3 McKinley Square; 617–310–6300). It's now a suite hotel, but the twenty-fifth-floor open-air observation deck is the highlight of twice-daily free tours at 10:00 A.M. and 4:00 P.M. While you're waiting, be sure to walk around the first three floors to check out the art on loan from the Peabody Essex Museum in Salem.

If the timing doesn't work, veer left at Congress Street to visit **Faneuil Hall** (open daily 9:00 A.M. to 5:00 P.M.; free; no phone). This 1742 building was the city's first centralized market (until then, vendors sold food door to door from pushcarts) as well as its first assembly hall. Town Meetings made Faneuil Hall the focal point of Revolutionary rhetoric. The hall was enlarged in 1805 to double its size under the oversight of Charles Bulfinch, and it continued to nurture free speech. William Lloyd Garrison spoke here against slavery in the mid-nineteenth century, and in 1903 Susan B. Anthony addressed the New England Woman Suffrage Association. Climb the stairs to this second-floor hall, laid out much like a Federal-period church, to appreciate the hush above the market's hubbub. Because ground-floor merchants have always paid rent, Faneuil Hall may be the only self-supporting monument in the country.

DAY ONE: afternoon

Faneuil Hall anchors America's first festival marketplace development, which also incorporates the solid, stately market buildings constructed in the 1820s. Festival marketplaces—historic buildings reborn as entertainment and shopping areas—are found all over the country now, but **Faneuil Hall Marketplace** was the original, celebrating its twenty-fifth anniversary in August 2001.

LUNCH

The North Market building contains your luncheon spot: **Durgin-Park** (340 Faneuil Hall Marketplace; 617–227–2038), which was established in 1826. The restaurant's motto is "Your grandfather and perhaps your Great-Grandfather dined with us too!" Legend has it that the wait staff is surly, but that's one tradition that disappeared generations ago. Although Durgin-Park has become a tourist attraction, it has kept its old-time feel and menu of simple fare from the days when Boston was "the home of the bean and the cod." So be seated at a long table with a mix of visitors and locals and strike up a conversation. It's that kind of friendly place. And be sure to order Indian pudding for dessert.

More than 14 million people per year visit Faneuil Hall Marketplace, making it the perfect place to be alone together in a crowd. People speaking a dozen different languages pass by, and jugglers, musicians, acrobats, and magicians hold forth in the brick and cobblestone plazas. The development also revived the now widely emulated pushcart shopping. Unless you're dedicated shoppers (in which case, see "Holiday Shopping in the Hub"), the pushcarts offer the most enjoyable way to browse and even buy. The vendors frequently carry unique items such as tapestry designer bags, watercolor prints of Boston, or New England gourmet foods. Pose at **MPC Caricatures** in front of Marketplace Center for a memento of your visit. Although some larger chain stores have gained a foothold at Faneuil Hall Marketplace, you'll find quirky and unusual shopping, too. For example, **Whippoorwill Crafts** stocks the work of American craftspeople and specializes in kaleidoscopes. The **Bill Rodgers Running Center** carries shoes and all kinds of runners' paraphernalia; it also has an informal museum of medals and running gear owned by Rodgers (four-time winner of the Boston Marathon) and other great marathoners.

When you've had enough of the ongoing bazaar, take a rest on the benches in the little park between Union and Congress Streets. The seated bronze statue depicts **James Michael Curley,** one of Boston's more colorful modern characters. Ask a passerby to photograph the two of you with this flamboyant politician who was so popular at the polls that he won reelection in the 1940s from a jail cell.

JFK's Hotel

The Parker House has hosted many illustrious figures in its long history, but one in particular made the Parker House "his" hotel: John F. Kennedy. A lobby case shows a World War II–era photo of Kennedy attending a birthday party for his grandfather (Rose Kennedy's father), John F. "Honey Fitz" Fitzgerald. JFK chose the Press Room to tell his closest associates and supporters that he would run for the U.S. Congress in 1946, and he proposed to Jacqueline Bouvier in Parker's Restaurant. A party for Jack and Jackie took place in the Press Room the night before their 1953 Newport society wedding.

Before you retire to the Parker House, have a relaxing drink in **The Bay Tower** on the thirty-third floor of 60 State Street (617–723–1666). This office building is the workplace of some of the city's most powerful bankers and lawyers, and The Bay Tower gives the impression of being literally on top of the world, or at least the world of Boston. Settle in at a window table for the most sweeping view of Boston Harbor in any public place in the city and pretend you are royalty, rulers of all you survey.

DINNER

By the looks of the building, you'd expect royalty to dine at **Maison Robert** (45 School Street; 617–227–3370; moderate to expensive). This elaborate French Second Empire building used to be Boston's City Hall, constructed on the site of the first public school in the city, Boston Latin School (1635). A statue of Boston Latin's most famous dropout, Benjamin Franklin, stands out front. (A bronze of Boston's second mayor and builder of Quincy Market, Josiah Quincy, completes the symmetry on the other side.)

If the weather cooperates, you may even want to sit outdoors near the statue of Franklin (who was considered quite the epicure) in the casual Ben's Café section of Maison Robert, where you can take advantage of the prix fixe dinners of appetizer, entree, and dessert for $18 or $25. Otherwise, the formal dining room inside manifests an air of momentous decorum to celebrate the grand food of chef Jacky Robert, who began his career here, left to train for several years in France, and set the foodie scene afire in San Francisco before coming home to

Maison Robert in 1996. Robert's all-American twists on classic French cuisine are approachable yet intense. Decide by your mood: Do you prefer a secluded and dreamy table for two in the bistro-like cafe or would you rather dine like modern aristocrats of high gastronomy?

After dinner, stroll back across the street to the Parker House, but before you head to your room, turn upstairs to your left in the lobby for **Parker's Bar** to enjoy a martini nightcap.

DAY TWO: morning
BREAKFAST

The elegant, wood-paneled **Parker's Restaurant** has been a Boston social (and business) center since it opened in 1855. It's a grand place to enjoy the Sunday breakfast buffet. Chef Joseph Ribas has a creative way in the kitchen, but sometimes you just don't mess with tradition. Among the bakery items will be Parker House rolls, a creation of this restaurant (which also concocted Boston cream pie).

DAY TWO: afternoon

Boston's ancient burial grounds provide a means to touch the lives of those who also passed this way. Walk together down the narrow rows to seek out the famous and the anonymous, the legendary and the forgotten. Their names are written on weathered stone, sometimes obscured by lichen and moss. Their markers were not made for them, but for us—that we might look upon these resting places and speak their names again.

From the Parker House walk toward State Street on Tremont Street to **King's Chapel Burying Ground,** Boston's first cemetery, established in 1631. Some of the first to perish in the new colony are buried here, including the first governor, John Winthrop, and an "immigrant" from Plymouth, Mary Chilton, the first Pilgrim to touch Plymouth Rock. Mr. Revere's companion rider in raising the alarm to every Middlesex village and farm also rests here: William Dawes. Just for the record, the strange octagonal cage-like features in this graveyard have nothing to do with burials. They are ventilation shafts for the subway.

Take special note of the gravestone of Elizabeth Pain, whom many scholars have suggested was Nathaniel Hawthorne's inspiration

Romantic Days and Nights in Boston

for Hester Prynne of *The Scarlet Letter*, perhaps the greatest heroine in American literature. Not to dash the romance, but otherwise anonymous Pain was no Prynne; nonetheless, Hester is so seared into our literary memory as love's quintessential martyr that we keep seeking a real-life inspiration for her character.

Retrace your steps on Tremont Street and cross to the **Granary Burying Ground,** which dates from 1660. Among its illustrious markers are those for patriots John Hancock and Samuel Adams (first and second governors of Massachusetts, respectively) as well as the famous silversmith, jack-of-all-trades, and excellent horseman, Paul Revere. Revere lived so long that he almost lost his chance to be laid to rest with his compatriots, for the burying ground had been declared full. Elizabeth Foster Goose, Boston's candidate for the Mother Goose of nursery rhyme fame, is not buried here—but her husband Isaac's first wife Mary is. (Some scholars claim Elizabeth wrote the children's stories; others say "Mother Goose" was a fictional character given credit for folk tales.) The Granary Burying Ground (so-called because a grain storage facility stood next door where the church now stands) is a serene and ordered place. The tidiness of the stones is a modern phenomenon; straightening up the rows was a Depression-era public works job.

Wind up your trip in the **Boston Common,** the green heart of the city that has been used for everything from public punishment in the stocks to kite-flying since it was set aside in 1634. The long diagonal path across the Common has been popularly known as "the Lovers' Walk" since the first gaslights were installed in the nineteenth century. And it's still a popular site for strolling hand in hand, pausing to watch a pickup game on the ball fields or small children splashing at the edges of the Frog Pond's fountain jets.

FOR MORE ROMANCE

If you're still hungry for the romance of Boston's past, several other historic sites lie near your hotel:

Old South Meeting House (310 Washington Street; 617-482-6439) was colonial Boston's largest meeting hall and hosted the Town Meeting that led to the Boston Tea Party. Among the many displays is one that relates the life of Phillis Wheatley, a former African slave who became Boston's first African-American poet in the 1770s. Old South is open from April 1 to October 31 daily from 9:30 A.M. to 5:00 P.M. and from November 1 to March 31 daily from 10:00 A.M. to 4:00 P.M. Admission is $3.00.

Old State House (206 Washington Street; 617-720-3290) was the center of public life in colonial Boston. The plaza in front, destined for makeover in the coming years, is the site of the Boston Massacre. The Declaration of Independence was read from the balcony. Since 1881 the Old State House has been a museum of Boston and Revolutionary War history, of which it is its own greatest artifact. It is open daily from 9:00 A.M. to 5:00 P.M.; adults pay $3.00.

The first Anglican church in Boston was **King's Chapel** (corner of School and Tremont Streets; 617-523-1749), founded in 1686 to serve the British officers dispatched to the city by the king. As the present stone building was constructed from 1749 to 1754, it was built around an older one, which was then dismantled and thrown through the windows. The King's Chapel bell, cast in 1816 by Paul Revere, at one time tolled the deaths of major figures, including Revere himself two years after he made it. The chapel is open Memorial Day to Labor Day, Tuesday and Wednesday from 1:00 to 4:00 P.M., Thursday, Friday, Saturday, and Monday from 10:00 A.M. to 4:00 P.M. A musical recital is held on Tuesday from 11:00 A.M. to 1:00 P.M. From Labor Day to October 31 hours are Friday, Saturday, and Monday from 10:00 A.M. to 4:00 P.M.; November through March 14, Saturday 10:00 A.M. to 4:00 P.M. A donation is requested.

Two If by Sea
ON THE WATERFRONT

OSTON'S WATERFRONT IS WHERE the primal pull of the sea meets the civilized city as a dynamic backdrop for the dance of desire. Boston was born at the edge of the ocean and in recent years has reclaimed its birthright with delightful redevelopment that makes the waterfront one of the most exciting sections of the city. On this summer weekend, you'll capitalize on the new amenities of Boston's proud maritime appointments and relish the enduring lure of the meeting of land and sea.

PRACTICAL NOTES: To take advantage of all the attractions and to enjoy the harbor and waterfront at their best, this itinerary should be done in July or August. For information and a schedule of FleetBoston Pavilion performances, call (617) 728–1600; to purchase tickets in advance, call (617) 931–2000. The box office is open on show days only, but you may be disappointed if you wait until the last minute.

DAY ONE: morning

Check in at the **Seaport Hotel** (1 Seaport Lane; 617–385–4000 or 877–SEAPORT; summer packages begin at $169 per night), convenient to the piers of the South Boston Waterfront and a hop and a skip (or a reasonable water taxi ride) from downtown Boston. Built as a convention hotel adjunct to the World Trade Center, the Seaport is large, spacious, and gracious. While it's walking distance from the waterfront, the Seaport stands outside the hubbub, making it a perfect retreat from busy Boston. Piers at the World Trade

Romance AT A GLANCE

◆ Stay at the spacious and convenient **Seaport Hotel** (1 Seaport Lane; 617–385–4000 or 877–SEAPORT), the key lodging for the exciting new district known as the South Boston Waterfront

◆ Pick your picnic table on the deck, pick up your shell-cracking rock, and prepare to pick succulent meat from your crustaceans at the **Barking Crab** (88 Sleeper Street; 617–426–2722), Boston's only in-town shellfish shack.

◆ Stroll down the edge of the South Boston Waterfront toward an early dinner at the legendary **Anthony's Pier 4** (140 Northern Avenue; 617–482–6262), where niceties of big-night dining from the 1950s (popovers at every table, for example) are de rigueur.

◆ Catch a rising star or one of the leading lights of popular music in a waterfront concert under the billowing sail-like tent of **FleetBoston Pavilion**, literally just steps from your hotel.

◆ Linger at the rail in the moonlight or stay below to dance the night away on a dinner cruise aboard the cruising yacht **Spirit of Boston** (World Trade Center Pier; 617–748–1450).

◆ Sail aboard the Liberty schooner **Clipper** (Long Wharf; 617–742–0333) for a festive Sunday brunch while you bid adieu to lovely Boston Harbor from the wooden decks of this tall ship.

Center—just across an elevated walkway—are home to many of Boston's best harbor tour boats. Aura, the elegant Seaport Hotel restaurant, ranks among the city's leading fine dining venues, especially for fresh seafood, and the window tables are particularly pleasant places to start the day with the breakfast buffet included in several room packages. Ask about both the Bed & Breakfast package and the *Spirit of Boston* Cruise package. You'll want to combine the two for your two-night stay.

DAY ONE: afternoon

LUNCH

Stroll along the waterfront walk to Fort Point Channel, then cross the Northern Avenue bridge for lunch at the **Barking Crab** (88 Sleeper Street; 617–426–2722), the only real fish shack on the harbor. This is the place for a classic summer feast of steamed clams, mussels, crab claws, and peel-and-eat shrimp. Grab a seat on the city side so you can look up now and then to see the contrast of the pristine, modern architecture of the Financial District across the channel.

One of the waterfront's prime attractions is just one wharf over from your hotel: the **New England Aquarium** (Central Wharf; 617–973–5200). The Aquarium really celebrates its location. The plaza in front features brightly colored flags, a 45-foot wind sculpture, and a hubbub of family activity, especially clustered around the outdoor pool usually filled with cavorting harbor seals. Marine mammals also make a big splash in daily presentations aboard *Discovery*, the Aquarium's unique floating pavilion. Inside the main structure, the 187,000–gallon Giant Ocean Tank spirals to the ceiling as huge sea turtles, tropical fish, streamlined sharks, and sleek moray eels glide with the current.

The aquarium is open July 1 through Labor Day on Monday, Tuesday, and Friday from 9:00 A.M. to 6:00 P.M., Wednesday and Thursday until 8:00 P.M., Saturday and Sunday until 7:00 P.M. From the day after Labor Day through June 30, it is open on Monday through Friday from 9:00 A.M. to 5:00 P.M., Saturday and Sunday until 6:00 P.M. Admission is $14.00 for adults on summer weekends and $12.50 otherwise. Get in line before 9:00 A.M. on summer weekends and your tickets will be half price.

DAY ONE: evening
DINNER

From your hotel you can see the FleetBoston Pavilion, a dramatic sail-like structure right on the water where you'll be going later for entertainment. Stroll over that way and past the pavilion to **Anthony's Pier 4** (140 Northern Avenue; 617–482–6262; moderate). You'll want to plan an early dinner as concerts begin at 7:30 P.M. Anthony's is a legend, and like all legends it has its supporters and detractors, but no one faults the exquisite view of the harbor and the downtown skyline. To a great extent, it's an expense-account restaurant where power brokers often go to seal deals. But ask for a table near the windows and stick to seafood basics, and you'll have a grand time. The style, decor, and service conspire to give dining at Anthony's a sense of occasion. Select the catch of the day grilled, or stick with broiled scrod or broiled bay scallops, if they're available. Anthony's has a deep, deep wine list. A California viognier or a French muscadet will complement the fish but be light enough so you won't doze off during the concert. If you'd rather have a far more casual experience of dining at a real Fish Pier restaurant, keep walking up Northern Avenue to the **Daily Catch** (261 Northern Avenue; 617-338-3093; moderate).

FleetBoston Pavilion is the city's summer concert venue and attracts well-known artists throughout the summer to this beautiful setting on the water. Performers run the gamut from such soft-rockers as Jackson Browne to crooning legends such as Tony Bennett and Julio Iglesias. Jazz buffs relish the likes of Cassandra Wilson while fans of oldies might find Ray Charles more to their liking. When the music stops, you're only steps from home. Since the walk is so short (maybe ten minutes if the crowds are thick and you dawdle), why not stop for a nightcap at the hotel bar?

DAY TWO: morning

After a buffet breakfast at the Aura restaurant in your hotel, stroll over to Haymarket Square along Atlantic Avenue. Pass Faneuil Hall Marketplace and cross to the MBTA bus terminal. Here you can pick up either bus #92 or #93 to the Charlestown Navy Yard and the USS *Constitution*. Fare is 75 cents each. This will place you at the farthest point in today's itinerary, allowing you to work your way back along the waterfront.

The **Charlestown Navy Yard** (Boston National Historic Park; 617-242-5601) was one of six navy yards established in 1800 by President John Adams, who certainly chose a glorious— and strategic—location. From this point of land, you can see from the docks across the harbor all the way out to Boston Light on a clear day. When the yard was decommissioned in 1974, thirty acres were preserved under the National Park Service to interpret the art and history of naval shipbuilding.

Open to visitors daily from 9:00 A.M. to 5:00 P.M., the Yard offers free ranger-led tours daily at 11:00 A.M. mid-June through Labor

An Aquatic Epiphany

The New England Aquarium can be a very moving experience. In his memoir of faith, Returning: A Spiritual Journey, *writer Dan Wakefield recounts this revelation. "I cannot pinpoint any particular time when I suddenly believed in God again. I only know that such belief came to seem as natural as for all but a few stray moments of twenty-five or more years it had been inconceivable. I realized this while looking at fish.*

"I had gone with my girl friend to the New England Aquarium, and as we gazed at the astonishingly brilliant colors of some of the small tropical fish—reds and yellows and oranges and blues that seemed to be splashed on by some innovative artistic genius—and watched the amazing lights of the flashlight fish that blinked on like the beacons of some creature of a sci-fi epic, I wondered how anyone could think that all this was the result of some chain of accidental explosions."

Day. The tours emphasize the innovation and ingenuity of the Navy Yard in meeting the needs of the growing Navy. Of all the innovations, the most clever might be Drydock #1, the second drydock on America's Atlantic coast when it was built in 1802. Essentially a giant bathtub, the drydock is opened to the ocean and a ship is floated in. Then the drydock is sealed and drained while the ship is braced in place. When the hull is repaired, the drydock is refilled and the ship floats again. The first, and most recent, occupant of Drydock #1 was the venerable USS *Constitution*.

The **USS *Constitution*** (Charlestown Navy Yard; 617–242–5670) is a name to conjure with—the oldest commissioned naval vessel afloat, flagship of America's North Atlantic fleet. She won her stripes battling the Barbary pirates at the turn of the nineteenth century, and she won her nickname during the War of 1812. During her first upset victory—over the *Guerriere*, a former French ship recommissioned in the British Navy—legend has it that a sailor who saw cannonballs bounce off the *Constitution*'s oak planks cried out, "Huzza! Her sides are made of iron." During eighty-four years of active service this "overbuilt and oversailed" floating fortress won forty-two battles, lost none, captured twenty vessels, and was never boarded by an enemy.

Old Ironsides received a major overhaul for her 1997 bicentennial. Artisans from around the world worked to refit the *Constitution* from her keel up, using live oak cut from South Carolina and the Georgia sea islands. Free tours are offered daily from 9:30 A.M. to 3:50 P.M. They are conducted by inordinately polite Navy personnel, who seem genuinely excited by the symbolic and historic significance of the vessel on which they serve.

DAY TWO: afternoon

DINNER

Have a relaxing light lunch at **Tavern on the Water** (1 Pier 6 in the Charlestown Navy Yard; 617-242-0050). You'll have the breeze at your back and the city straight ahead.

Walk up the streets of Charlestown to **Bunker Hill Monument** (Boston National Historic Park; 617-242-5641), which commemorates the Revolutionary War battle that took place here. Open daily at no charge from 9:00 A.M. to 5:00 P.M., this was America's first monument built by public subscription and may have been the first touted as a tourist attraction. The tall shaft popularized the obelisk style, inspiring countless imitations around the country. Bunker Hill Monument, however, remained the tallest until the Washington Monument was erected. The monument presents a challenge to get your hearts pounding—that is, the 294 steps that spiral to the top. That's right: no elevator. When you get there, however, you're rewarded with a fabulous sweeping view of the city and the harbor. No wonder the British so badly wanted to take this height.

DAY TWO: evening

DINNER

By booking a dinner cruise on the *Spirit of Boston* (World Trade Center Pier; 617-748-1450; $65-$80 per person) as part of your hotel package, you'll have saved yourselves enough to justify splurging on a nice bottle of champagne during your three-hour sail aboard this mammoth and elegant yacht. Shipboard dining is shipboard dining, which is to say that the choices are somewhat limited but the portions are up to you. Dinners are prepared in rather large quantities, and you'll find that the sliced ham or roast beef entrees tend to hold up better than the stuffed chicken breasts or filet of sole.

Part of the fun on a *Spirit of Boston* cruise is shaking a leg to the live dance bands both above- and belowdecks. If you're too tired to move, hang around for the lively musical revue inside the cabin. Otherwise, it's hard to imagine a more romantic spot on a summer eve than on the rail of a ship with a city's bright lights twinkling across the water. You'll be delivered practically to your door well before midnight—leaving time for a nightcap in the big, comfortable armchairs of the Seaport's downstairs lobby bar.

DAY THREE: morning

Have a leisurely morning enjoying your hotel room before heading over to Long Wharf to catch the Sunday brunch sailing of the **Liberty schooner *Clipper*** from 11:00 A.M. to 1:30 P.M. This 125-foot modern replica of a mid-nineteenth-century coastal schooner features a festive brunch, coffee, and tea beneath unfurled sails. The brunch tour is $45 per person. Call (617) 742–0333 for reservations.

FOR MORE ROMANCE

If you want to stay right *on* the water, book **Boston's Bed & Breakfast Afloat** (781–545–2845; $165) aboard the *Golden Slipper*, a refurbished 40-foot wooden boat docked at Lewis Wharf. The interior of the maroon and white boat features a main salon decorated with white wicker, floral cushions, and lace doilies. Your private stateroom has a double bed, an attached bath, and a fully equipped galley kitchen. You'll have the boat to yourselves, with breakfast arriving in a basket.

The Snug North End

HE NARROW, WINDING STREETS of the North End have a way of enforcing a leisurely pace for exploration. Once the home of historical figures such as Paul Revere and the Mather dynasty of preacher-politicians, today's North End is a predominantly Italian neighborhood of churches, cafes, greengrocers, and trattorias. During the saints' festivals in July and August, the streets are filled with music and confetti. The rest of the year they merely bustle with a lively cafe life and the red, white, and green of an Italian identity. Visiting this part of the city is an instant vacation from Yankee Boston, an escape to a gentler pace to savor *la dolce vita*.

PRACTICAL NOTES: The choice is yours. Some people believe the North End shines brightest on July and August weekends when festivals to honor patron saints fill the neighborhood with religious processions, music and dancing, and food vendors. Others prefer quieter times when the streets are less crowded and it's easier to sample the easygoing neighborhood camaraderie and local color. This itinerary is set up for a Friday and Saturday, as much of the North End (except the churches) closes down on Sunday mornings. Make reservations well in advance for private dining room "Number 99" at Mamma Maria restaurant.

DAY ONE: morning

Check in at the **Regal Bostonian Hotel** (corner of Blackstone and North Streets; 617–523–3600 or 800–343–0922; $275–$425, weekend rates begin at $245). Just across North Street from Faneuil Hall Marketplace, the Bostonian sits at the gateway from the market district into the geographically isolated North End. This gem of a small luxury hotel incorporates a fully renovated former warehouse building.

Romance AT A GLANCE

♦ Stay at the polished **Regal Bostonian Hotel** (Blackstone and North Streets; 617–523–3600 or 800–343–0922) with the edge of the North End on one side, Faneuil Hall Marketplace on the other. Select one of the extremely comfortable corner rooms in the "traditional" wing with fireplace and Jacuzzi tub.

♦ Welcome yourselves to the North End by sharing a huge plate of pasta for lunch in tiny, hospitable **Pomodoro** (319 Hanover Street; 617–367–4348).

♦ After exploring the North End, dine in your own semi-private little room for two (Number 99) overlooking historic North Square at **Mamma Maria** (3 North Square; 617–523–0077). Savor the contemporary Italian cuisine, seemingly miles from the red-sauce Italian of ages past.

♦ Visit historic **Old North Church** (193 Salem Street; 617–523–6676), the beacon that lit the fires of Revolution, and be sure to contemplate the church's modern gardens and the somber history of nearby **Copp's Hill Burial Ground.**

♦ Lunch on delectable roasted lamb and a cold roasted vegetable salad at **Artù** (6 Prince Street; 617–742–4336), then catch some competitive bocce at **Waterfront Park.**

♦ For your concluding dinner, enjoy the bright and delectable Provençal cuisine of **Sel de la Terre** (255 State Street; 617–720–1300), where you'll never go wrong with the city's best restaurant breads and the ever-changing bouillabaisse.

In fact, we suggest requesting a room in the "traditional" wing. Rooms in the corner (230, 330, 430, etc.) feature a fireplace, a Jacuzzi tub, beamed ceilings, and a side view of Faneuil Hall Marketplace from the narrow balcony. Rooms 235 and 535 have canopy beds. The hotel sits on a very historic site—the center of commerce in seventeenth-century Boston. A lobby display explains some of the archaeological finds unearthed when the hotel was constructed, and the concierge can lend you a book detailing the discoveries if you want to dig deeper into the past.

DAY ONE: afternoon

As you go out the front of the hotel, turn left and then left again to walk through **Haymarket,** Boston's outdoor produce market. It may be but a faint echo of the busy market that once occupied the district, but it's still a colorful sight and a good spot to pick up some fresh fruit for munching. At the light where you encounter the Freedom Trail red stripe, go under the highway and you will emerge in the North End. Cross the street, turn right, then left onto Hanover Street. You're bound for one of the smallest and most intimate places in the district for lunch.

LUNCH

Don't let the diminutive size of **Pomodoro** (319 Hanover Street; 617-367-4348) fool you. The flavors (and the portions) are as big as the room is small. Order a big plate of pasta served family style (we like the penne with chicken and broccoli served in a sage-cream sauce) and two glasses of red wine. Toast yourselves as a welcome to the neighborhood.

After lunch, wend your way around to North Square (follow the Freedom Trail markings) and the **Paul Revere House** (19 North Square; 617-523-2338). Built in 1680, this is the only surviving seventeenth-century house in Boston and was nearly a century old when it was the family home of Paul Revere and his second wife, Rachel.

This is the house from which Revere crept to make his famous midnight ride, but the interpretation focuses more on the domestic life that took place beneath its roof than the history outside. From the tales told of Rachel, she was the iron in Revere's backbone, providing the drive that made him one of Boston's most successful businessmen. Among the furnishings you'll see some of the beautiful silver fashioned by Revere. The house is open daily April 15 to October 31 from 9:30 A.M. to 5:15 P.M. and daily November through April 14 from 9:30 A.M. to 4:15 P.M., closed Mondays from January through March. Admission is $2.50.

But the North End became solidly Italian within a few generations of Revere's death, and that's the identity that gives the neighborhood its energy today. Spend some time browsing along Cross Street and the lower ends of Hanover and Salem Streets for Italian specialty foods to remind you of your trip whenever you open your home cupboards. **Salumeria Toscana** (272 Hanover Street) and **Il Fornaio** (221 Hanover Street), for example, have delectable selections of olive oils and dried pastas, while **J. Pace and Sons** (42 Cross Street) and **Polcari** (105 Salem Street) carry terrific bulk spices and other dry goods. **Martignetti Liquors** (64 Cross Street) is the retail outpost of Boston's leading importer of fine Italian wines. When your energy flags, take a break for an espresso at one of the Hanover Street cafes. There are no wrong choices, but try **Cafe Graffiti** (307 Hanover) for a daytime stop where you can check out the brightly painted walls festooned with scribbles.

You can repair to the hotel to unburden yourselves of your haul, then have a quiet drink in the **Atrium Lounge**. The plate-glass walls overlook the plaza between Faneuil Hall and Quincy Market. When snow is falling in the winter, the lounge is a front-row seat on a Christmas card.

DAY ONE: evening

DINNER

Dinner tonight is an event at **Mamma Maria** (3 North Square; 617–523–0077; moderate to expensive), where you have reserved room "Number 99." Situated in a quiet turn-of-the-twentieth-century town house at the head of North Square, Mamma Maria has several dining rooms. Snug "Number 99" is painted a deep choco-late brown and holds but a single round table illuminated by a chandelier. Classical music in the background completes the mood. Your only distractions from each other will be the stunning view down North Square and your waiter as he brings your selections from Mamma Maria's very contemporary Italian menu. Perhaps you'll have a warm pepper soup, a tart of goat cheese and smoked tomato, a potato crostini with smoked salmon salad for starters, fol-lowed by soothing ricotta and sage ravioli with wild mushrooms or pappardelle tossed with corn and house-smoked duck. Great finesse goes into the little touches; for example, fresh bread arrives with a bowl of crunchy green olives floating in a fruity olive oil. The close walls provide an intimate privacy and the twinkling lights outside a view a painter would envy.

You'll be tempted by Mamma Maria's desserts (especially the choco-late mascarpone semifreddo with raspberry sauce), but you'd be missing a quintessential North End experience if you didn't adjourn to a cafe for strong coffee and a sweet. Our favorite nighttime hangout is **Caffé Vittoria** (296 Hanover Street; 617–227–7606), instantly recognizable by the antique coffee machines in the windows. Of the two entrances, the one on the corner (the modern-looking side) is more or less nonsmoking (a rarity in the North End), while the tradition-steeped room next door has great atmosphere enhanced by old photographs almost covering the walls. Be sure to choose your favorite selections from the CD jukebox loaded with Dean Martin, Al Martino, Jerry Vale, Frank Sinatra, and every other Italian-American popular singer you can name.

A Singular Voice

In an earlier incarnation, the "modern" side of Caffè Vittoria was known as the Grotto Azura and it was Enrico Caruso's favorite dining spot when he was in town. Pressed for cash one day, he sent a check to a nearby bank. Since he had no identification, a bank officer came over to ask him to prove he was who he said he was. Caruso stood up in Grotto Azura and sang an aria. The bank took his check. His voice—in a scratchy recording—is on the jukebox.

DAY TWO: morning

Enjoy a chocolate croissant and hot chocolate at Seasons, overlooking Faneuil Hall Marketplace, in your hotel—or head out the front door to the central market building for the same breakfast at half the price at **Au Bon Pain.** Begin your day with a stroll up the North End's other thoroughfare, Salem Street, to the highest point in the neighborhood, the bluff above the river known as Copp's Hill. You'll want to stop at Christ Church, Episcopal, which is open daily from 9:00 A.M. to 5:00 P.M.; suggested donation is $2.00. Better known to schoolchildren as **Old North Church** (193 Salem Street; 617–523–6676), it's the oldest surviving church in Boston (built in 1723) and among its first bellringers was an adolescent Paul Revere. Historians largely agree that this is the church where sexton Robert Newman hung two lanterns in the belfry to alert patriots that British troops were on their way to Lexington by "sea," that is, in rowboats from the Common to Cambridge. Newman's descendants still reenact his part in the annual Patriots' Day festivities. If you want to visit the bell tower, take the "Behind the Scenes" tour for $8.00. The church's interior is classically restrained—except for the ornate trumpeting cherubim in the upper gallery, donated in 1746 by Captain Thomas James Gruchy. Gruchy, at the helm of his privateer vessel *The Queen of Hungary,* liberated the decorations from a French ship en route to a Catholic church in Quebec. To the left of the church is a tranquil hidden garden where you can find a restful seat beneath a mimosa tree.

This part of the North End has been a residential neighborhood since the spring of 1631, and many of the neighbors still lie a block from the church at Boston's second-oldest cemetery, **Copp's Hill Burial Ground.** Copp's Hill is not a particularly somber place, perhaps because it is the lightest and brightest point of land in the North End and affords great views of the harbor and Charlestown. (The views are so good that British cannon were placed here in 1776 to blow Charlestown to bits.)

Return to Hanover Street via the walkway behind Old North Church to the **Prado,** as the local residents universally refer to Paul Revere Mall. Bronze plaques along the enclosing brick walls tell brief tales of people and events in the North End. The Prado serves as a neighborhood social center in good weather: Old men hunker over tables playing cards and checkers, small children scurry about while their grandmothers look on, animated young men discuss the latest European soccer scores, teenagers cast poses. The Hanover Street end is dominated, of course, by an equestrian statue of Paul Revere.

Directly across from the Prado is the last surviving Boston church designed by Charles Bulfinch, **St. Stephen's Church** (401 Hanover Street). Actually, the church was erected in 1714, but Bulfinch did a complete overhaul between 1802 and 1804, creating a masterpiece of balance and clarity that seems the archetype of an American house of worship. St. Stephen's has been a Roman Catholic church since 1862, when the Irish and Italian immigrants began to outnumber their Yankee neighbors. Rose Fitzgerald Kennedy (matriarch of the political family) was baptized here on July 23, 1890, and she was buried from here on January 24, 1995.

DAY TWO: afternoon

LUNCH

With all the cafes and trattorias around, you may have spotted one that catches your fancy. If not, let us suggest **Artù** (6 Prince Street; 617–742–4336), a restaurant as small as Pomodoro. Feast on the cold salad of grilled vegetables (a house specialty) and a leg of lamb sandwich.

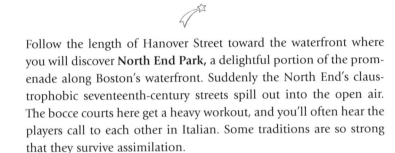

Follow the length of Hanover Street toward the waterfront where you will discover **North End Park,** a delightful portion of the prom-enade along Boston's waterfront. Suddenly the North End's claus-trophobic seventeenth-century streets spill out into the open air. The bocce courts here get a heavy workout, and you'll often hear the players call to each other in Italian. Some traditions are so strong that they survive assimilation.

The waterfront walk affords great views of the harbor and prob-ably the best view in the city of Old Ironsides, the USS *Constitution.* You can follow this path around the perimeter of the North End's thumb-like peninsula until you reach the green fields and cool arbor of **Christopher Columbus Park,** where the rose garden hon-ors Rose Kennedy. The adjacent Long Wharf is the terminus of State Street, which leads under the highway back to Faneuil Hall Marketplace. If you'd like to spend a few hours browsing and even buying, we won't tell. (See "One if by Land: The Heart of Old Boston.")

At this point you could go home, but wouldn't it be better to stretch your getaway for a few more hours?

DAY TWO: evening

DINNER

Sel de la Terre (255 State Street; 617–720–1300) is a newcomer to the Boston scene, but chef and co-owner Geoff Gardner's skills make it seem like an Old Master. Gardner is, in fact, the acknowl-edged master among Boston chefs of hearty and deeply textured breads, which makes waiting for your order to arrive just one of the great pleasures of dining in this Provençal restaurant just across Atlantic Avenue from Faneuil Hall Marketplace. Gardner seeks to embolden diners, offering such dazzling dishes as grilled squid in red wine with capers and tomatoes as mere appetizers and classic delights like lamb and eggplant with artichokes and green olives as main dishes. The good buys on wines help keep the cost down, and you can imagine you've been transported to a fine village bistro in the countryside of Provence.

FOR MORE ROMANCE

The North End has a phenomenal selection of excellent small restaurants, most of which seat only a few people, don't take reservations or credit cards, and send you to the neighboring cafes for coffee and dessert. They're all moderately priced. Among the best of these small, chef-run operations along Hanover Street are **Giacomo's, Maurizio's**, and the **Daily Catch/Calamari Cafe**. For a brighter, louder scene, we recommend **Villa Francesca,** with its grand windows swung open to Richmond Street.

For an insider's look at Italian food in the old North End, follow cuisine maven Michele Topor on a three-hour walking tour through the neighborhood's markets, cheese shops, sausage makers, pastry shops, bakeries, and enotecas. Topor gives the tours on Wednesday and Saturday from 10:00 A.M. to 1:00 P.M. or 2:00 to 5:00 P.M. and on Friday from 3:00 to 6:00 P.M. Reservations are required and tours cost $38. Call L'Arte Di Cucinare at (617) 523–6032.

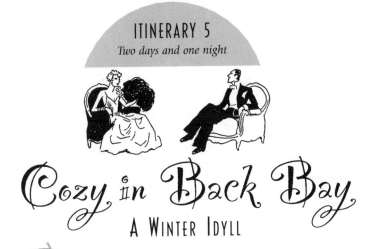

ITINERARY 5
Two days and one night

Cozy in Back Bay,
A Winter Idyll

OSTON WINTERS ARE PRECISELY RIGHT for romance— cold enough to make you want to snuggle, but not so harsh that you start humming "Lara's Theme" from *Dr. Zhivago.* Unless you're downhill ski buffs, there's no more exciting place to spend a winter getaway than in the city, where the whole life of the metropolis is close at hand. After more than three and a half centuries, Bostonians know how to enjoy winter with good food, a blazing hearth, and a judicious mix of indoor and outdoor activities. As one of Boston's finest neighborhoods, the Back Bay is just the place to find all these amenities in a compact, elegant setting.

PRACTICAL NOTES: This itinerary is geared to the winter season and requires arriving before noon on a Friday to experience some of the fun. Bring your own ice skates, if you have them. If not, don't worry; rentals are available.

DAY ONE: late morning/afternoon
In all likelihood you'll have to check your bags when you show up before noon at **The Lenox Hotel** (710 Boylston Street; 617–536–5300 or 800–225–7676; $250–$410; special promotions often available), a beautifully refurbished grande dame just a block from Copley Square. The Lenox was built in 1900 to rival New York's Waldorf-Astoria—a bit of hubris that can be forgiven because the attention to comfort and delightful ornament has worn well over the last century, especially thanks to a recent $5-million renovation. Constructed for a newly rich class accustomed to the fine rooms and elegant lobbies of European hostelries, the Lenox now

*R*om*ance* AT A GLANCE

◆ *Curl up next to your working fireplace in a spacious suite at* **The Lenox Hotel** *(710 Boylston Street; 617–536–5300 or 800–225–7676), one of the small jewels of the Back Bay.*

◆ *Let the almost subterranean bass pipes of the* **Trinity Church** *organ shake you to your bones at a Friday afternoon concert.*

◆ *Indulge in an exquisite, candlelit French gourmet meal at Boston's number-one special-occasion restaurant,* **L'Espalier** *(30 Gloucester Street; 617–262–3023).*

◆ *Whirl madly about the glossy surface of the* **Frog Pond** *on Boston Common, the city's most popular outdoor skating rink.*

◆ *Warm up by one of the fireplaces when you enjoy a rich Sunday brunch at* **The Hungry i** *(71 Charles Street; 617–227–3524).*

feels like an opulent boutique hotel. Working fireplaces in urban hotels are usually the province of the luxe of the luxe, but fifteen corner rooms in the Lenox offer this amenity. It's just the thing to provide a fireside crackle while you spark.

Postpone a visit to your room to dash across Copley Square to H. H. Richardson's architectural masterpiece, **Trinity Church,** for the free half-hour organ concert every Friday at 12:15 P.M. from mid-September through June. There's no predicting who will be sitting at the organ console, as organists from around the world vie for the chance to play Trinity's organ, which has 6,898 pipes that range from 32 feet long to less than 1 inch. Think of the dignified tones as a ceremonial opening for a weekend of togetherness. (For more details about this lovely church, see "The Painters' Passion: A Fine Arts Weekend.")

LUNCH

For lunch in one of Boston's real hideaways, head into the **Winter Garden,** a bright, plant-filled, vaulted atrium inside 222 Berkeley Street. This office building is open only during weekdays. When you arrive after the organ concert, the office workers will probably be back at their desks. Share a hearty laugh of superiority and pull up a chair to enjoy simple sandwich and salad fare in this great green garden that only a few Bostonians know.

Refreshed, you might consider walking across the street to the old
New England Life building at 501 Boylston Street for a quick introduction to the history of the Back Bay. Displayed in the soaring marble lobby are dioramas showing the prehistoric fish weir uncovered
when this building was constructed as well as picturesque depic-
tions of the immense engineering task of filling Back Bay in the
nineteenth century. (This tony neighborhood used to be a tidal
swamp.) You'll also see how they built many of the buildings,
including the *très formal* French-Academic style building constructed
in 1862 for the Museum of Natural History, which you'll visit later
in its current incarnation as the clothier Louis.

There's no better place to shop for special winter wear than
Back Bay. Look for after-Christmas specials on stylish coats, scarves,
and gloves at **Saks Fifth Avenue** (Prudential Shopping Plaza,
Boylston Street; 617–262–8500) and **Lord & Taylor** (760 Boylston
Street; 617–262–6000). The recently transformed Prudential Center
also has many superb specialty shops. Newbury Street is boutique
central, with styles ranging from the conservative and tony on the
Arlington Street end to the young and funky as you approach
Massachusetts Avenue. A good bet for leather is **The Coach Store**
(75 Newbury Street; 617–536–2777), but for an elegant sweater for
him, try **Louis** (Boylston Street at 234 Berkeley Street; 617–262–6100).
If you find yourselves flagging, take a break at **Café Louis**
(617–266–4680), the clothier's wicker-chair and yellow-walled
bistro. It's one of the choicest places in a choosy neighborhood.

DAY ONE: evening

DINNER

You'll want to dress up for dinner tonight. Tuxedo and gown would
be a bit over the top, but you're definitely dining in high style and
probably high company at **L'Espalier** (30 Gloucester Street;
617–262–3023; expensive). The Back Bay town house has three dining rooms with fireplaces (filled with candles rather than roaring
fires) as well as Frank McClelland's New French cuisine, presented
with the elegance and formality it deserves. Ask to sit at one of the
two small tables at the banquette in the Salon—a cozy place to

enjoy your meal and simultaneously survey the scene.

On weekends, L'Espalier generally offers a three-course prix fixe menu with many choices under each course. It makes for leisurely dining as you enjoy the tinkling glasses, flickering candles, impeccable service from a veritable squadron of staff in tuxedos, and food that you might not have believed could be so good. L'Espalier's wine list is nicely matched to the cuisine, and the sommelier can offer astute suggestions. With food this bold, it's hard to go wrong with a red Burgundy, perhaps a Corton.

Depending on the weather, you may or may not feel like a stroll along Newbury Street, doing a little window-shopping at the places you skipped earlier. But don't linger too long. The fireplace awaits you. . . .

DAY TWO: morning

BREAKFAST

The hour for rising and shining is entirely up to you, but even on weekends Back Bay wakes up surprisingly early. By 7:00 A.M. you can get espresso and freshly baked muffins at **Sonsie** (327 Newbury Street; 617–351–2500) and marvel at how a place that hops into the wee hours starts all over again by dawn's early light. It feels very much as a Left Bank Parisian café would—several hours later.

Will You . . . ?

Maître d' Louis Risoli, who has been with L'Espalier since 1985, says that four to five gentlemen per week choose the restaurant for formal proposals of marriage to their lady loves. He is often asked to bring the ring on a dome-covered plate, as if it were an extra course. "When I lift the dome, she will often start crying," Risoli says. "It's less popular than it used to be, but I'm still frequently asked to insert the ring into a glass of champagne." He always brings mineral water to rinse it off. "And there's always the good old-fashioned technique of the ring in the pocket," says Risoli. "Many gentlemen still get down on one knee and ask."

After fortifying yourselves, it's time to don those warm sweaters and gloves you bought yesterday and head over to Boston Common for skating on the **Frog Pond.** This was a tradition in Boston for more than a century, but the pond fell into disrepair—only to be resurrected in 1996 with a new cooling system and regular maintenance that guarantee a smooth gliding surface. Skates can be rented on the spot, if need be. Remember: Arm-in-arm pairs skating is back. A number of Zhivago-like lovers have recently become engaged on the ice. One lovestruck suitor even dropped to one knee to propose, risking the wrath of the Zamboni driver who was trying to polish the ice.

DAY TWO: afternoon

LUNCH

Come in from the cold to warm up with an à la carte lunch at **The Hungry i** (71 Charles Street; 617–227–3524) featuring brunch classics: eggs Benedict, pancakes, crepes, Belgian waffles . . . you get the idea. Ask for a table where you can bask in the warmth of one of the Hungry i's three working fireplaces.

You can spend the afternoon in Victorian Boston, an era of swelling fortunes and a civic sense that anything was possible. After all, Bostonians had just created the ultimate silk purse from a definite sow's ear by filling the malodorous marsh of Back Bay to create the elegant, Parisian-style Back Bay neighborhood. One of the pioneers who decamped from Beacon Hill to settle Back Bay was widow Catherine Hammond Gibson, who built an Italian Renaissance home for herself and her son on Beacon Street in 1859–60 on the "New Land," as it was called. Today their home is the **Gibson House Museum** (137 Beacon Street; 617–267–6338).

This bit of Victoriana survives because Catherine's grandson, Charles Hammond Jr., decided early on to keep the house just as it had been in his childhood. A poet, travel writer, horticulturalist, eccentric, and famous party-giver, Charles began roping off the furniture in 1936, inviting his guests to sit on the stairs while he mixed martinis from his own bathtub gin. Charles was a stickler for formality in other ways, however, affecting a morning coat, spats, and cane whenever he appeared in public. Winter tours ($5.00) are given on Saturday and Sunday at 1:00, 2:00, and 3:00 P.M. The leisurely tours allow plenty of opportunity to examine the details of this time capsule. Don't be surprised if you encounter scholars or filmmakers taking notes. The Gibson House has played a supporting role in many period documentaries and dramas, including the 1983 Merchant-Ivory production of *The Bostonians*.

There are grander houses in Back Bay, of course, though none so well-preserved and few open to the public. Before you head home, you can enter the **French Library** at 53 Marlborough Street, where the salon is said to be modeled on Empress Josephine's private parlor at Malmaison. You might also be able to peek into the **Boston Center for Adult Education** (5 Commonwealth Avenue). This mansion is a latecomer—1912—in the Italianate style. A 1913 wing houses the Back Bay's most glamorous ballroom (modeled after the Petit Trianon in Versailles)—built for the debut of textile industrialist Walter C. Baylies's daughter.

FOR MORE ROMANCE

It all depends on how snowy the winter has been, but both the Public Garden and the wonderful outdoorsy stretches of the Emerald Necklace (see "Budget Boston: Biking Through the Parks") support great cross-country skiing. Plan to bring your own skis.

One of the Boston area's most innovative chefs moved from his long-time digs near the Museum of Science to the heart of Copley Square. If brilliantly spiced dishes (including many modestly priced satays) intrigue you, spend an evening dining on Stan Frankenthaler's highly original creations at **Salamander Dining Room & Satay Bar** (25 Huntington Avenue; 617–451–2150; moderate to expensive).

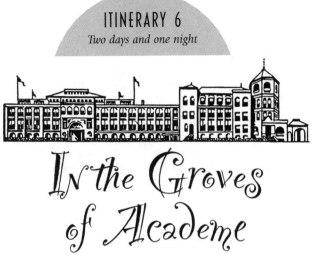

I<small>N</small> the G<small>roves</small> of A<small>cademe</small>

L OVE S<small>TORY</small> ASIDE, YOU DON'T HAVE TO be star-crossed young lovers to find romance at Harvard. The amenities of one of the world's great universities are open to every twosome, and we assure you that you won't have to spend your night studying. The accretion of art and knowledge and tradition makes for an ivy-walled set on which it's easy to play out your own less tragic tale of passion.

P<small>RACTICAL</small> N<small>OTES</small>: Don't even try to do this itinerary during the first week of June, when Harvard holds its commencement and reunions. To be sure that the American Repertory Theatre stage will be lit during your visit, call (617) 547-8300 for a schedule.

DAY ONE: morning

Begin your sojourn in the groves of academe by checking in at the **Inn at Harvard** (1201 Massachusetts Avenue, Cambridge; 617-491-2222 or 800-222-8733; $210-$310), the newest hotel in Cambridge. Harvard needed a convenient place to put up distinguished visitors, so the university built this handsome hotel at the head of Harvard Square where Massachusetts Avenue and Harvard Street converge. Although it's open to all, it's not advertised outside of Harvard publications. You'll see why they want to keep this gem a family secret, so to speak. All the rooms surround a soaring central atrium that makes a luxurious library-style lounge by day, a pleasant restaurant at night.

***R**omance* AT A GLANCE

♦ Roost in the tweedy surround of the **Inn at Harvard** (1201 Massachusetts Avenue, Cambridge; 617–491–2222 or 800–222–8733), an elegant small hotel adjacent to Harvard Yard with the atmosphere and service of a private club.

♦ Enjoy a tasty buffet lunch of delicacies from the different regions of India at **Tanjore** (18 Eliot Street, Cambridge; 617–868–1900).

♦ Marvel at the artistic treasures of **Harvard's art museums,** where emotive art ranges from lusty satyrs on ancient Greek vases to curvaceous bathing beauties in Impressionist paintings.

♦ Dine on inventive New American fare at **Harvest** (44 Brattle Street, Cambridge; 617–868–2225) before enjoying high drama at the **American Repertory Theater,** or **ART** (Loeb Drama Center, 64 Brattle Street, Cambridge; 617–547–8300).

♦ Treat yourselves to an all-American brunch in the sun-splashed dining room of **Henrietta's Table** (Charles Hotel, 1 Bennett Street, Cambridge; 617–661–5005).

♦ Visit the Botanical Museum to ooh and ahh over those triumphs of the glassblower's art, Harvard's famous **Glass Flowers**—seductive and voluptuous yet indescribably fragile.

Walk down Massachusetts Avenue into Harvard Square, stopping at the info booth at **Holyoke Center** (1350 Massachusetts Avenue) to pick up a guide to Harvard Yard or to inquire about the schedule of student-led guided tours. In near-scholarly fashion, this tour will tell you perhaps more than you care to know—but then the Yard has seen a lot of history since it was established in 1636. And while Harvard now covers 360 acres in Cambridge and Boston, the Yard is still the soul of the university. As poet-alumnus David McCord once wrote, "Other American colleges have campuses, but Harvard has always had and always will have her Yard of grass and trees and youth and old familiar ghosts."

As you cross into the Yard from Holyoke Center, you'll immediately pass the yellow clapboard **Wadsworth House,** built in 1727 and home to nine of Harvard's presidents—as well as to George Washington for a brief period in July 1775 when he first came to town to take over the Continental Army.

In front of the classical University Hall, designed by Charles Bulfinch, sits the **John Harvard Statue,** known to trivia lovers everywhere as the "statue of three lies." Its inscription reads "John Harvard, Founder, 1638." The lies? Harvard was a benefactor of the school, bequeathing it half his fortune and all his books when he died in 1638. The school was founded two years earlier. Nor is the statue a likeness of Harvard, of whom no image has survived. Sculptor Daniel Chester French (best known for the seated Lincoln in the District of Columbia Lincoln Memorial) used a generic body and modeled the head after a popular member of the class of 1882. The statue of mistaken inscription makes a curious landmark for a college whose motto is *"Veritas,"* or "Truth," but don't let that deter you from posing for a souvenir photo—as do most visitors to the Yard.

Walk around to the other side of University Hall and you are in the "New" Yard, where Commencement is held each June. The Olympian building at one end is **Widener Library.** When Harry Elkins Widener, class of '07, perished on the *Titanic* in 1912, his mother honored his wishes that his books be donated to Harvard. Then she threw in a library to house them—the largest university library in the world. Climb the grand stairs to see the John Singer Sargent murals in the entry.

DAY ONE: afternoon

LUNCH

You'll have to walk through Harvard Square and down to Eliot Street off JFK Street to find the hidden gem, **Tanjore** (18 Eliot Street; 617–868–1900; inexpensive). This classy little restaurant offers an unusually sophisticated presentation of specialties from the different geographic areas of India, with an emphasis at dinner on the roasted meats of the northwest. But at lunchtime you can enjoy a terrific buffet of regional dishes, including very fine samosas and lentil and chickpea plates.

Harvard's museums rank among the best of their kind in the world, far outshining the holdings of many big-city museums. The queen of the university's three art museums (open Monday through Saturday 10:00 A.M. to 5:00 P.M., Sunday 1:00 to 5:00 P.M.; $5.00 for entry to all three) is the **Fogg Art Museum** (32 Quincy

Street; 617–495–9400). The museums are free from 9:00 A.M. to noon on Saturday and all day on Wednesday. A plain building on the outside, its interior courtyard was modeled on a sixteenth-century church in Montepulciano, Italy. The reverential reference suits the collection, which contains work by many of the touchstone artists of the last millennium of Western art. With its collections of old masters, French art from Ingres to the Impressionists, modern painting, and English and American decorative arts (including wonderful silver), the Fogg is like a quick tour through an art history survey—except here you're looking at real works instead of color plates. The intimate scale of the Fogg also means you can get closer than many museums permit to examine the details of the maker's hand. Don't miss the Fogg's English pre-Raphaelite paintings on the second-floor balconies. These Victorian artists managed to idealize carnal love with a thousand veils of mystical reference.

Few works can measure up to the Wertheim collection for their direct emotional appeal, but Harvard has many other art treasures. Attached to the back of the Fogg is Werner Otto Hall, home of the **Busch-Reisinger Museum** of Germanic art. Be sure not to miss the breathtaking *Red Horses* by Franz

Portrait of a Lady

Gallery 17 holds the Maurice Wertheim Collection of paintings and sculpture, spanning early Impressionism to early modernism. He assembled these works—considered one of the most remarkable and focused private collections of modern European art in America—in a brief fourteen years between 1936 and 1950. Many of Wertheim's selections are intriguing portraits of women—including a double-sided Picasso from 1901 that shows the swift evolution of the artist's style, a Degas ballerina in bronze, an Eve-like portrait by Gauguin, and Renoir's voluptuous Seated Bather. Renoir wrote to his dealer about the sketches he was making on the island of Guernsey in the English Channel that inspired this work: "Here one bathes among the rocks which serve as bathing cabins, because there is nothing else; nothing can be prettier than this mixture of men and women crowded together on the rocks."

Marc, as erotic (yet nonexplicit) a piece of modern art as you'll ever see.

The **Arthur M. Sackler Museum** (485 Broadway) is directly across Broadway from the Fogg. The Sackler collections include Harvard's Asian, Islamic, and later Indian holdings as well as its ancient Greek art. Love (or lust, at any rate) is rather explicit in much of the red-and-black-figured Greek vases, though you might have to bring along a copy of *Bulfinch's Mythology* to decipher who is poised to do what with whom.

Flushed with this racy experience of the ancients, you can calm your racing pulses by returning early to the Inn at Harvard, where a very civilized tea will await you in the atrium lobby. Relax and recharge as you lean back into a love seat.

DAY ONE: evening

DINNER

But don't relax *too* long. You'll want to catch an early dinner before attending a play at the ART. Make sure you have early reservations for **Harvest** (44 Brattle Street; 617–868–2225; expensive) because you don't want to rush the experience of the chef's luscious dishes presented as startlingly beautiful compositions. Let the maître d' and your server know you have to leave for a show, and they'll coordinate service accordingly. If it's a beautiful, maybe even balmy, evening, angle for one of the casual tables in the outdoor patio for an idyllic setting open to sky. And if you think you can contain yourselves through the play, by all means indulge in the bluepoint oysters from the raw bar as an appetizer. Be sure to ask about the risotto special—it's usually a plate where the chef performs surprising feats. For example, he might decide to stud the rice with rock shrimp and serve a small peppered tuna steak on top.

The **American Repertory Theatre** (Loeb Drama Center, 64 Brattle Street; 617–547–8300), known in Cambridge as "The A-R-T," is one of the leaders in the American regional theater movement. Productions are often challenging, just as often brilliant, and usually highbrow. Every so often an ART production goes to Broadway, but it's more likely to wind up on public television.

After the show, follow the locals back to the bar at **Harvest** for a passionate discussion of the merits of the play, the playwright, the director, the actors. You get the point: Everyone at Harvard has a contrary opinion. Isn't it nice that the two of you can agree?

DAY TWO: morning

BRUNCH

Not everything at Harvard is deadly serious, and you can't help but assume a lighthearted, bright mood in the sunsplashed dining room of **Henrietta's Table** (Charles Hotel, 1 Bennett Street, Cambridge; 617–661–5005). To carve out its own culinary niche in the same hotel as the posh Rialto, Henrietta's brings a market-cuisine approach to the wonderful foods of the Northeast. Think pancakes with New England maple syrup or a selection of terrific regional cheeses. Brunch starts at noon, so if you rise early and hungry, graze on the breakfast buffet at the Inn at Harvard.

DAY TWO: afternoon

The sand is running out in the hourglass of your Harvard excursion, but before you bid farewell, you should see Harvard's marvels in glass—the stained-glass windows of **Memorial Hall** between Cambridge and Kirkland Streets and the famous **Glass Flowers** at the **Botanical Museum,** one of the **Harvard Museums of Natural and Cultural History** (26 Oxford Street; 617–495–3045). The Botanical Museum is open Monday through Saturday from 9:00 A.M. to 5:00 P.M. and on Sunday from 1:00 to 5:00 P.M. Admission is $5.00, but is free on Saturday from 9:00 A.M. to noon.

Memorial Hall is a looming Ruskin Gothic building modeled roughly on a medieval cathedral. Built to pay tribute to the Harvard men who perished defending the Union in the Civil War, its twenty-one stained-glass windows include several by the Tiffany Company and by John LaFarge. You may have to view the windows from outside, as Memorial Hall is open on weekends only when an event is taking place inside. Otherwise, it's open 10:00 A.M. to 6:00 P.M. on weekdays.

The Glass Flowers attract both artists and lovers of botany to behold this unique collection that is a triumph of the glassblower's art. Between 1887 and 1936, Leopold and Rudolph Blaschka created 3,000 models of 850 plant species. Each species is illustrated with a scientifically accurate life-size model and magnified parts—the wonder of art re-creating true wonders of nature.

FOR MORE ROMANCE

If you can linger, your $5.00 admission to the Botanical Museum also lets you into the other Harvard Museums of Cultural and Natural History in the same building. If you're thinking about rings, be sure to examine the rough and cut stones in the **Mineralogical and Geological Museum.**

On Wednesday, you can catch an evening of politically charged cabaret with rock-oriented music and even some dancing (sometimes). The show starts at 9:00 P.M. at the **Lizard Lounge** (1667 Massachusetts Avenue; 617–497–9215; $5.00).

The **Harvard Film Archive** offers screenings of classic, rare, and other films of artistic interest almost every night at Carpenter Center on Quincy Street. Call (617) 495–4700 to find out what's playing.

For an equally comfortable lodging experience (especially if the Inn at Harvard is full), by all means try the **Isaac Harding House** (288 Harvard Street; 617–876–2888; $85–$175; some rooms with shared bath). This lovely Victorian, a few blocks from the Inn at Harvard, became an ultra-elegant and delightfully modern B&B in a recent renovation. Situated halfway between Harvard Square and somewhat funkier Central Square, it's a good base for walking around both neighborhoods. And unlike many B&Bs, the public rooms and several guest rooms are fully wheelchair accessible.

See "Poetry and All That Jazz: Cambridge Coolest."

Good Sports

Take Me Out to the Ball Game

EMEMBER *BULL DURHAM*, the Kevin Costner–Susan Sarandon movie? That was minor league stuff. Now come up to The Show at Major League Baseball's most hallowed field, Fenway Park. If both of you already love the National Pastime, you need no further convincing. If only one of you is a fan, what better place to introduce the other to this particular passion than Fenway, where legends continue to haunt the oldest professional park still standing?

Sometimes romance means excluding the rest of the world so you can focus entirely on each other. But this weekend opts for the rush of the crowd, the adrenaline of action. Together you'll partake of the sporting life in Boston, where the Red Sox have broken more hearts than Julia Roberts and Brad Pitt combined. And where true lovers keep coming back for more.

PRACTICAL NOTES: This itinerary is based on a weekend when the Boston Red Sox are playing Saturday and Sunday home games. Since the Sox play only April through September (and, once in a while, into October), this limits the season. Call ahead for ticket availability: (617) 267–1700.

DAY ONE: afternoon

Set on an elegant and quiet street just outside Kenmore Square, **The Gryphon House** (9 Bay State Road; 617–375–9003; $179–$279) is an 1895 brownstone town house converted with impeccable taste

Romance AT A GLANCE

♦ You won't believe your good fortune to discover the elegant brownstone inn, **The Gryphon House** (9 Bay State Road; 617–375–9003), a short walk from Fenway Park.

♦ Baseball—it's our national game and the one sport about which poets wax eloquent. See a Saturday afternoon game from the box seats at **Fenway Park**—and return for another on Sunday.

♦ Chalk your cue and quaff some microbrews at **Boston Billiards Club** (126 Brookline Avenue; 617–536–POOL), one of the country's top-rated billiards parlors.

♦ Have a soulful meal at **Bob the Chef's** (604 Columbus Avenue; 617–536–6204), then stick around for a night of jazz by Boston's coolest combos.

♦ Amble through the rose and Victory gardens of the **Back Bay Fens,** one of the least-known gems in Frederick Law Olmsted's "Emerald Necklace."

into an inn with just eight huge and luxuriously appointed rooms. Every room is about the size of a studio apartment, and they've been decorated in a range of striking styles, all in keeping with the late Victorian architecture of the house. If you like to enjoy your breakfast in a sun-splashed room, ask about Morningside, with its east-facing capacious bay windows. The best views of the Charles River are from the North Tower room. For classically Victorian romance, the Victoria is decorated with a mural that quotes Seurat's big-bustled lady from his famous Parisian picnic painting. All rooms have gas fireplaces, wet bars, and (if you must) high-speed Internet access.

LUNCH

Stroll up Commonwealth Avenue into Kenmore Square, veering up Brookline Avenue, the left-most of three streets leading out of the square. Don't be put off by appearances. Kenmore is Boston University student territory—a bit funky, very young. Grab a bite to eat before the game at **Boston Beer Works** (61 Brookline Avenue; 617–536–BEER), an open and airy hall where you can get a real table if you're dining. The fare is traditional pub grub, but BBW has Boston's best selection of beers crafted on premises. The Red Sox have suffered from the Curse of the Bambino since trading Babe

Ruth to the Yankees. Brewmaster Brian House creates a sharply hopped summer beer he calls Bambino Ale. Since you already have each other, order two Bambinos to take the bitter with the sweet.

The exterior of **Fenway Park** (Yawkey Way; 617–267–1700 for tickets) is honestly dowdy, but don't judge the book by its cover. The interior is the most intimate park in the major leagues. Many of the seats are so close to the play that you could get sprinkled when a fielder wipes his brow. On a summer day, you can smell the freshly cut grass at Fenway.

Whatever your team loyalties, Fenway Park may be the last place in the majors where the pure spirit of Baseball with a capital "B" still transcends overpaid players and greedy owners. (Preservationists have twice sought to make Fenway a National Historic Landmark but were stymied by team owners, who want a larger, more lucrative facility and don't want Fenway protected.) At 1:05 P.M. (on weekend home games), the umpire barks the time-honored conclusion of "The Star Spangled Banner": "Play ball!"

After the game, wet your whistle and chalk your cue at **Boston Billiards Club** (126 Brookline Avenue; 617–536–POOL; table $10–$16 per hour)—a far cry from the "trouble in River City" kind of place. In fact, this vast and classy hall was ranked tops in the United States by *Billiards Digest* and goes out of its way to encourage women as well as men. Shoot a few racks and quench your thirst before going back to the room to freshen up for dinner.

DAY ONE: evening

DINNER

At the corner of Massachusetts and Columbus Avenues you'll find **Bob the Chef's** (604 Columbus Avenue; 617–536–6204; moderate). Like the playing field at Fenway, several worlds converge here in common interests, as the restaurant stands on the borderland of the predominantly African-American neighborhood of Roxbury, the rather hip and traditionally gay neighborhood of the South End, and the upscale Back Bay. You'll want to dress with a bit of panache, as this soul-food restaurant attracts a stylish crowd. Most of the entrees are excellent and vary from their Southern roots chiefly by

A Lyric Little Bandbox

John Updike described this athletic shrine best in his classic essay on Ted Williams's last game, "Hub Fans Bid Kid Adieu":

"Fenway Park in Boston is a lyric little bandbox of a ballpark. Everything is painted green and seems in curiously sharp focus, like the inside of an old-fashioned peeping-type Easter egg. It was built in 1912 and rebuilt in 1934, and offers, as do most Boston artifacts, a compromise between Man's Euclidean determinations and Nature's beguiling irregularities."

being prepared in a more healthful fashion. The Soul Fish is always a good bet—catch of the day dredged in cornmeal and flour and fried light and crisp in canola oil. You could even learn to love collard greens here.

Stick around after dinner because the evening is just beginning. Owner Darryl Settles is a jazz buff, and the Berklee College of Music—known for its strong jazz program—is just a long block away. In fact, Settles features Berklee students and faculty on Wednesday evenings. There are intimate live performances on Wednesday through Saturday nights, as well as a lively Sunday jazz brunch.

DAY TWO: morning

After breakfast at the Gryphon House, walk up the sidewalk on Charlesgate West and cross at the light to the **Back Bay Fens,** one jewel in Frederick Law Olmsted's Emerald Necklace. As you walk around to the right, crossing H. H. Richardson's Boylston Street Bridge (a real beauty in the Romanesque style best appreciated from below), the **Fenway Victory Gardens** will begin on the left. Tremendous creativity goes into these plots, some of which look like spreads from *Garden Design* magazine. The hedged enclosure you see ahead of you is the **James P. Kelleher Rose Garden,** which is in bloom most of the baseball season.

BRUNCH

Watch for Jersey Street coming up on the right. Since you're already in the neighborhood, you can get a spicy, imaginative brunch from 11:00 A.M. at **Brown Sugar Cafe** (129 Jersey Street, The Fenway; 617–266–2928; inexpensive). This delicate and beautiful neighborhood restaurant serves Thai food that will confound any stereotypes you might have of this subtle cuisine. On weekends, they serve both breakfast and lunch menus. The "Thai breakfast menu" includes a creamy rice chowder filled with meat and vegetables and topped with an egg. Or opt for the Thai mango curry chicken. Be adventurous.

Continue down Jersey Street, which will become Yawkey Way, and you'll be back at Fenway Park. Again, the game begins at 1:05 P.M., though you'll want to be seated earlier for a last, longing look around. Admittedly, it seems as if tearing down Fenway Park would be tantamount to leveling St. Peter's in Rome, but when money talks, nostalgia walks. Catch it while you can.

FOR MORE ROMANCE

Since you're in the neighborhood, consider visiting **Mugar Library** at Boston University (771 Commonwealth Avenue) to see the celebrity memorabilia collection. The Special Collections Department collects papers and personal belongings of various celebrities and high achievers and shows samples in rotating exhibition.

If you're in the mood to move, plan on dropping in for dance night at **Avalon** (15 Lansdowne Street; 617–262–2424), Thursday through Sunday. (Sunday is primarily a gay and lesbian night.) The leading hard-rock club on a street known for dancing into the wee hours of the morn, Avalon has four lounges, a great balcony area, and some of the tightest security in the city to keep out the druggie crowd. With a strong history of supporting local bands, Avalon recently expanded its capacity to accommodate national touring acts.

Also see "Budget Boston: Biking Through the Parks."

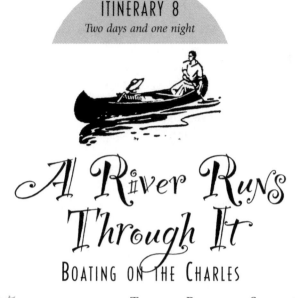

A River Runs Through It

BOATING ON THE CHARLES

L ONDON HAS THE THAMES, PARIS THE SEINE. Boston
has the Charles. Many of the world's great cities have
grown up along rivers, and their embankments evoke
the romance of great deeds and visions where land and water
meet. Because the Charles was not tamed by dams until the early
twentieth century, Boston always kept a step back from the river,
its buildings raised above the waterline. That strategy reserved a
glorious strip of land on each bank. The sedate broad basin of the
lower Charles that flows slowly past Back Bay and part of Beacon
Hill was girdled with parks and walkways to rival the great river
cities of Europe. It bustles with small sailboats and Olympic rowing shells that seem to skim along the surface like waterbugs. Yet
only a short distance upriver, the Charles shows a character barely
altered by human artifice. Great herons stalk the shallows, and a
water world rolls past a landscape where alder and swamp maple
have reclaimed the banks. Both are at your command—the proud
water at the edge of a city and the hidden coves and inlets that
remind you why the first European settlers called this a New
World.

PRACTICAL NOTES: Boating activities on the Charles are available from April Fools' Day to Halloween. The Sonesta's promotional package, however, runs only from Memorial Day to Labor
Day.

◆ Base yourselves at the luxurious and art-filled **Royal Sonesta Hotel** (5 Cambridge Parkway, Cambridge; 617–491–3600 or 800–SONESTA) on the Cambridge side of the Charles River Esplanade with wonderful views of the Boston skyline and the "pepperpot" bridge.

◆ Cruise the waters of the Charles River basin with the **Charles River Boat Company** (Cambridgeside Galleria, Cambridge; 617–621–3001), noting the small but elegant Arts and Crafts–era boathouses along the shore.

◆ Or, if you are experienced sailors, become visitor members of **Community Boating** (21 Embankment Road, Boston; 617–523–1038) and raise sail on a small sloop to enjoy the wind and waters of the wide Charles between Boston and Cambridge.

◆ Circumnavigate the green paths that make up the **Charles River Esplanade,** either with a casual, arm-in-arm saunter or on the bicycles you've borrowed from the Sonesta.

◆ Settle in for an evening of delightful dining on the imaginative, richly flavored cuisine of one of Boston's most celebrated small restaurants, **Salts** (798 Main Street, Cambridge; 617–876–8444).

◆ **Canoe and picnic** on the upper reaches of the Charles River, setting out from the historic boathouse in Newton.

DAY ONE: afternoon

Some hotels might as well be anywhere, but the **Royal Sonesta Hotel** (5 Cambridge Parkway, Cambridge; 617–491–3600 or 800–SONESTA; $199–$369; Summerfest promotion $169–$229) makes the most of its beautiful site on the Cambridge bank of the Charles River. Not only is the hotel on the river's edge (a yacht club lies just behind it), but it also overlooks the Boston skyline for a dramatic view of the city. To make it all the more inviting, the Sonesta's "Summerfest" package reduces room rates while boosting amenities—including use of bicycles and all the ice cream you can eat served every afternoon and evening in the lobby.

The Sonesta's spacious and soothing rooms are priced by view. We recommend the "deluxe" for a full river view ($209 in the Summerfest package). Whichever room you select, count on seeing some wonderful contemporary art in both public and private spaces—giving the hotel the feel of a discerning and adventurous art gallery. The Sonesta chain owns some 6,000 works of art distributed among its seventeen hotels.

LUNCH

Launch your river weekend by enjoying the light, bright menu of the Sonesta's **Gallery Café and Patio.** Try the Maine crab cakes (Maine crab is sweeter than any other) with a Caesar salad or grilled salmon with mango salsa as you sit on the patio and watch the sailboats glide past.

You can join the parade of sails if you can demonstrate your skill with line, sail, and rudder. (Either show certification from a boating course or be ready to give a quick sailing demonstration.) Cross the Longfellow bridge (a lovely walk, in any case) to **Community Boating** (21 Embankment Road, Boston; 617–523–1038). From April through October this enterprise is open weekdays from 1:00 P.M. to sunset and on weekends and holidays from 9:00 A.M. to sunset. One of you can obtain a visitor membership good for two consecutive days for $50. This entitles you to borrow any of the available boats, most of which are 15-foot centerboard sloops ideal for recreational sailing in the admittedly busy lower basin of the Charles. In the course of your maneuvers, have a good look at the "pepperpot" support structures of the Longfellow Bridge. Facing the water on each side are replicas of the prows of Viking ships. When the bridge was built in the late nineteenth century, some people thought that Boston was the site of Leif Eriksson's Vinland. Plan to be upriver from Community Boating as the sun sinks low in the sky so you can head back to shore from the west. This sounds counterintuitive, but the glint of sunset off Boston's buildings—especially some of the glass towers and the gilded dome of the State House—is nothing short of spectacular.

Of course, it's less strenuous to cruise the Charles River basin with the **Charles River Boat Company** ($8.00 for adults; 617–621–3001), and the Sonesta Summerfest package includes two passes for a one-hour sightseeing excursion. Boats leave on the hour beginning at noon from Cambridgeside Galleria, just next door to the Sonesta. The last trip is usually at 5:00 P.M. There are occasional sunset cruises on weekends.

You might also want to pick up bicycles from the hotel to pedal the bike path that rings the lower basin of the Charles—9 miles from dam to dam with paths on both sides. You can pedal along at your leisure with the river on one side and the built landscape of Boston or Cambridge on the other. Return early to enjoy some quality pool time at the Sonesta's exquisite indoor pool with sliding glass roof. It's roped off into lanes for some serious exercise with deep enough water to swim laps without scraping your knees at the shallow end.

DAY ONE: evening

DINNER

Make sure you have advance reservations for one of the small number of tables at Cambridge's intimate **Salts** (798 Main Street, Cambridge; 617–876–8444; moderate), as chef and co-owner Steven Rosen has risen to national prominence through several awards and magazine features. Unless you happen to have Russian/Polish roots, prepare for some startling culinary surprises. At a time when most American chefs are looking to the Mediterranean for inspiration, Rosen is reinvigorating beets, cabbage, sturgeon, horseradish, caraway, and, that *ne plus ultra* of Eastern European dining, caviar. The result is a New American cuisine unlike any other in Boston. For example, he smokes lamb with black tea and rosemary before roasting it and serves wild sturgeon fillets with golden horseradish sauce. There's great variety here— from a delicate potato and chanterelle mushroom soup to a hearty duck proscuitto with fresh figs and marsala syrup. Dinner at Salts (the name refers to the ancient custom of offering salt as a sign of hospitality) will be an experience you'll treasure for years.

After your luscious meal, you'll feel like walking. When you return to the hotel, walk around to the back side to get to the Riverwalk. Indulge in some leisurely strolling on this scenic walkway, enjoying the play of the moonlight on the Charles, the reflected lights of the city across the river, and the stars above. That *really* bright evening star isn't a star at all. It's probably Venus, the planet named for the goddess of love. (Of course, it could be Jupiter or Mars. If you really must know, check out the almanac in the *Boston Globe*. It's more fun to just assume that it's Venus.) In case you've forgotten, the formula for wishing on a star begins "Starlight, star bright, first star I see tonight. . . ."

If it happens to be a Friday night and you've finished your meal early, then continue along the river to the **Museum of Science,** where you can take advantage of free stargazing at the state-of-the-art facilities of the **Gilliland Observatory,** located on the roof. Summertime stargazing with a staff astronomer begins around 8:30, weather permitting, and continues into late evening. When the lights wink out at Gilliland, you're only steps from the Royal Sonesta.

DAY TWO: morning

BREAKFAST

Begin the day with a wake-up swim at the pool or a light workout on the exercise machines. Then, for a small fee, you can enjoy a continental breakfast buffet of fresh breads, croissants, juices, cereal, and fruit in the Gallery Café. You can take your choices back to the room or enjoy them on the patio.

Today you'll leave behind the busy waters of the urban river for a slow-paced, idyllic trip on a more rural segment of the Charles. Take the Massachusetts Turnpike west to the exit for I–95 North and follow the signs to Route 30 East. The canoe rental facility comes up immediately on the left, but continue down Route 30 for a mile to pick up bagel sandwiches, dessert bars, cookies, and beverages at **Bruegger's Bagel Bakery** (2050 Commonwealth Avenue, Auburndale) for a picnic lunch. Then return to **Charles River Canoe and Kayak** (2401 Commonwealth Avenue, Newton; 617–965–5110), which rents canoes for $10.00 per hour to a maximum charge of four hours. The fee includes paddles and life jackets. This concession is open from 10:00 A.M. to 8:00 P.M. on weekdays and from 9:00 A.M. to 8:00 P.M. on Saturday and Sunday.

The handsome turn-of-the-twentieth-century boathouse is a reminder of the heyday of canoeing on the Charles. In the early

1900s, this patch of river saw more canoes than any other stream in the world. The Marriott Hotel property, adjacent to the boathouse, was the site of Norumbega Amusement Park. Thousands of people would paddle to the park by canoe to dance at the Totem Pole Lounge and Nuttings on the Charles.

River life today is more quiescent. As the Charles River Watershed Association notes, "The silence of a canoe moving through the water reinforces the oneness of man with nature. It is without equal for the full enjoyment of the sights and sounds of a river environment." So dip your paddle and set off to the "Norumbega Lakes District," so called because the river broadens and the current slows. Stick to the shore if you want to see the wildlife, as this portion of the Charles is a regular *Wind in the Willows*. Mallard ducks and Canada geese are everywhere, and they may swim right up to the canoe to be fed. Somewhat more shy are the heron who fish in the shallows. This portion of the river supports great blues and the black-crowned night heron. On the more open patches, you may see ospreys diving for bass, shad, and pickerel. Listen for a "ker-plunk" as you come around an edge of shore to a hidden cove. If the sound is small, it's probably a painted or snapping turtle whose nap you've disturbed. If it's more of a splash, suspect muskrat.

LUNCH

Three downriver spots provide excellent sites for your picnic. **Auburndale Park** on Wares Cove offers picnic tables about a mile downriver. Farther along is the beautiful park-like cemetery of **Forest Grove** or, in midstream, the banks of **Fox Island,** both about 1.5 miles from the boathouse.

The trip down to **Moody Dam** in Waltham (just past the site of the legendary Waltham Watch factory) is about 3 miles of changing rural and town landscapes. But the towns have mostly forgotten about their river, so as you float by in your Old Town canoe, you can feel as if you are sneaking up on the community, observing it from a cloak of near invisibility. The river is tame, yet it is still the wild heart through a civilized world. When you reach the Moody Dam, you'll realize the wisdom of your downstream paddle. The current is too slight to impede your return, and you'll have the prevailing wind at your back.

FOR MORE ROMANCE

Just across the street from the Sonesta is the **Cambridgeside Galleria,** a rather posh shopping mall where you can select matching designer sunglasses to protect your eyes from glare on the river.

And if you happen to be in town on the right weekend in mid-June, be sure to catch the colorful competition of the **Dragon Boat Festival** (see Recommended Annual Events in Appendix).

Budget Boston
BIKING THROUGH THE PARKS

OMANCE WITHOUT FINANCE IS A NUISANCE"—or so says the old jazz tune. But you don't have to be rolling in dough to cook up something sweet in Boston, especially if you take advantage of the great outdoors. Imagine your own hideaway overlooking the classiest part of town combined with a leisurely bicycling tour through one of the greatest urban park systems ever created. You'll dine al fresco and be serenaded under the stars on the banks of the river. This is a trip to recapture the penurious days of young first love without all the discomforts—a filet mignon weekend on a hamburger budget.

PRACTICAL NOTES: Because this itinerary is designed for the peak tourism season (July and August), you'll need to make your room and bicycle reservations well in advance. Bring along your own knapsack for toting your picnic on the bicycle trip and maybe a blanket to spread on the grass at the Esplanade if you think you might be able to catch a concert. If you have your heart set on an outdoor Boston Pops concert, call (617) 266–1492 for a schedule.

DAY ONE: morning

Sign in and leave your bags at the **Newbury Guest House** (261 Newbury Street; 617-437-7666 or 800-437-7668; $125–$170). The main building of this group of linked town houses dates from 1882, but it has been delightfully modernized and expanded to create thirty-two rooms in one of the most pleasant B&B lodgings in the area. We suggest springing for the top of the line—room 12,

Romance AT A GLANCE

◆ Head to chic Newbury Street for a comfortable stay that won't break the bank at the **Newbury Guest House** (261 Newbury Street; 617–437–7666 or 800–437–7666).

◆ Spin your wheels together as you pedal through the **Emerald Necklace,** designed by that great landscape romantic, Frederick Law Olmsted.

◆ Feed each other nibbles from the tapas menu at **Tapeo** (267 Newbury Street; 617–267–4799).

◆ Stroll along the **Esplanade,** a riverside park with graceful plantings.

◆ Get high together at the Hancock Observatory (John Hancock Tower, Copley Square; 617–572–6429) for a sweeping impression of the multitude of green spaces in the urban surround of Boston.

◆ Stroll past Sunday painters and ride the corny but endearing **Swan Boats** in the lagoon of the Public Garden.

which has an ornamental mantel and fireplace, a queen-size bed, and overlooks tony Newbury Street. If you came to the inn by car, you'll appreciate that parking is available (for an additional fee) behind the building on the service alley. Run across the street to **The Secret Garden** (338 Newbury Street; 617–236–2294) to select some flowers to dress up your room.

Unburdened of your luggage, walk down a block to **DeLuca's Back Bay Market** (239 Newbury Street; 617–262–5990) for fresh fruit, sandwiches, juices—or even fresh bread and some wedges of cheese—for your luncheon picnic. While you're at it, get some cracked corn for feeding ducks and geese. You did remember a knapsack, didn't you?

Unless you brought your own bicycles, walk over to **Back Bay Bicycles** (336 Newbury Street; 617–247–2336) to pick up your transportation for the afternoon. Bikes rent for $20 per day; call far in advance to reserve the shop's tandem bicycle.

Helmets, locks, and maps are all part of the package. For this afternoon's tour, we suggest either a tandem bicycle (that is, a bicycle built for two) or two good hybrids. Honestly, the hybrids offer better maneuverability where Emerald Necklace paths are narrow. But there's something tremendously appealing about pedaling around while singing "Daisy, Daisy, give me your answer, do. . . ."

DAY ONE: afternoon

The jewels of the **Emerald Necklace** are the green parklands originally intended to surround the city of Boston. Landscape architect
Frederick Law Olmsted's intentions were thwarted by the cost of
purchasing land for the last link in the chain, but the 5-mile stretch
of linked parks remains one of the most impressive of Olmsted's
many accomplishments. (He is best remembered for New York's
Central Park, but he and his firm actually designed green areas for
hundreds of communities throughout North America.) Olmsted
himself chose to live at the edge of the Emerald Necklace, so you
can tell where his sympathies lay. The Emerald Necklace is the kind
of urban treasure almost impossible to build today, but to the wise
Victorians of Boston, green and rather wild places were amenities as
important as food and drink.

Cycling the Emerald Necklace is a joyous way to savor both the
natural beauties you encounter and the offhand artistry of its
designers. The only shortcoming is that getting from piece to piece
can be tricky.

Although the promenade of the Commonwealth Avenue Mall is
often considered part of the Emerald Necklace, connecting to the
rest of the Necklace means toting your bike across traffic, up a hill,
and over two barriers. So skip Commonwealth Mall and pedal out
Boylston Street, crossing Massachusetts Avenue, until you see green
lawn across a traffic light. Cross at the light and head around the
water to the right on the path. Welcome to Mr. Olmsted's world:
You're in the North Basin area of the **Back Bay Fens.**

Graceful freshwater grasses loom up to 15 feet tall around the
stream that flows out of the Fens here on the left. You'll be amazed
at the profusion of wildlife that call these grasses home. Some of the
braver mallard ducks and Canada geese may stride right up the
bank, as they're used to begging for tidbits. Songbirds (especially
redwinged blackbirds) will probably flush and flit to safety if you
stir the grass. On the other side of the path are the ornamental
Victory Gardens, individual private gardens, some planted in roses
and other perennials, many of them almost disappearing under the
thick foliage of a dozen different strains of sunflowers.

As you pedal over to the South Basin, the landscape takes on a
more planned appearance as you draw near the Veterans Memorial
Park, dominated by a huge angel with sheathed sword. Long before

Washington had the Wall, monuments like these spoke of the grief of a city over its children fallen in war. Right nearby, behind high hedges and trellises, stop to contemplate the voluptuous blooms in the **James P. Kelleher Rose Garden.**

Small footbridges across the South Basin lead to the Fenway highway, the high-speed version of the carriage road designed by Olmsted. Backing onto that road are the Museum of Fine Arts and the Isabella Stewart Gardner Museum (see "The Painters' Passion: A Fine Arts Weekend"). There's another tricky transit over the road at the end of the Fens (go up past the base-ball field and up the hill by the abandoned pumping station). But it's worth the wait to cross traffic in front of the former Sears building to get onto the paths of **The Riverway,** one of the least-touched portions of Olmsted's original park design.

This section along the Muddy River demonstrates Olmsted's wis-dom of advising that the best way to manage a landscape on limited funds is to leave it alone. As you pedal under the leafy canopy along the Muddy River—really more a big brook—it's almost impossible to believe that this entire landscape is manmade. It certainly looks natural unless you're a botanist and observe that all the trees on the far side of the water are native species and most of those on the near side come from Europe and Asia. The Muddy River is a border between Boston and the town of Brookline. Back in the 1880s, Olmsted chose what he thought were pretty trees for the Boston side; Brookline's park commis-

"Tranquility and Rest to the Mind"

Olmsted must have had something like this romantic sojourn in mind when he addressed the American Social Science Association in 1870, appraising the con-trasting virtues of cities and parks: "Let your buildings be as picturesque as your artists can make them. This is the beauty of a town. Consequently, the beauty of a park should be the other. It should be the beauty of the fields, the meadow, the prairies, of the green pastures, and the still waters. What we want to gain is tranquility and rest to the mind."

sioner picked native species. You be the judge: Which philosophy works better today?

Don't spend too much time gawking at the trees, at least not at the expense of looking out for pedestrians. Although few people outside of its neighbors use The Riverway paths, those neighbors walk them a lot. You might even encounter former governor and presidential candidate Michael Dukakis out for his daily constitutional. You'll almost certainly see young couples pushing strollers and not a few tykes on plastic tricycles. It's a real family park.

When The Riverway finally opens up, you'll have come to the 120-acre **Jamaica Pond,** a natural glacial pond that used to be part of Boston's water supply. It also used to supply ice to Jamaica via clipper ships in the 1840s! Now it's a handsome recreational area, with jogging and walking paths around its entire 1-mile circumference. Swimming isn't encouraged here, but there are some small beaches right along Perkins Street. Box turtles haul themselves out to sun on the rocks here, and geese and ducks flock greedily at the shore as soon as you toss some food. It's hard to tell which are more amusing—the birds or the toddlers who gleefully chase them.

LUNCH

Stay to the left of the pond until you get close to the boathouse at the end of Pond Street. Benches and picnic tables abound on either side, so this is a good spot for lunch—and a convenient place to deposit your trash and use the public rest rooms.

The next gem on the Emerald Necklace is the **Arnold Arboretum,** literally a living museum of trees operated by Harvard University but open to the public as a park from dawn to sunset. Here Olmsted's handiwork reached its apex in ample demonstration of his penchant for curving vistas on gentle slopes and use of near-far and vanishing point perspectives. As a result, it's probably the favorite spot in Boston for long strolls and slow bicycle rides (cars are banned).

It's fun to pedal around and see what strikes you. The 15,000 specimens on the 265-acre site include most species of trees and woody shrubs native to temperate zones around the planet. Because most specimens are tagged with scientific and common names (as well as date of planting), you can use the Arboretum to examine trees or shrubs you might want at home but have never seen outside of a catalog. Smack in the middle of the Arboretum is **Bussey Hill,** the highest spot. (Check the map posted on the entrance road.) Many people climb up here for the stunning view of trees with the Back Bay skyline in the distance. We like it for lying on our backs and looking up at the clouds.

The third Sunday in May is known as Lilac Sunday, when the world's most comprehensive lilac collection reaches its peak bloom and 20,000 or more visitors come to marvel and sniff. Actually, the lilacs bloom from early May into mid-June, when rhododendrons, azaleas, and mountain laurel succeed them as the main attractions, only to be followed by the roses.

The final bauble in Olmsted's chain, **Franklin Park,** is also the largest with its meadows and woods. Some of Olmsted's original pastoral idylls (meadows kept mown by sheep, for example) have given way to modern recreational uses (a golf course).

This is a good place to rest. Lock up your bicycle(s) and visit the **Franklin Park Zoo** (One Franklin Park Road; 617–442–2002), which has emerged as one of the country's most exciting zoos in recent years. The seven-acre **Bird's World** contains hundreds of species in naturalistic habitats, many within a free-flight cage. At the center is the **Oriental Bird House,** built in 1912 and one of the few remnants of the original zoo. Thrilling lion, cheetah, and snow leopard exhibits opened in 1997, but the zoo's longstanding centerpiece is **The African Tropical Forest.** Its exhibit pavilions reproduce African ecological zones of desert, tropical forest, veldt, and bush forest in which the animals move freely and humans are restricted. A similar **Australian Outback** exhibit opened in 1998. But not everything is about large animals: The magical **Butterfly Landing** features more than 1,000 butterflies in an enclosure filled with flowering plants and the strains of classical music. The zoo is open April through September, Monday through Friday from 10:00 A.M. to 5:00 P.M. and Saturday and Sunday from 10:00 A.M. to 6:00 P.M. From October through March it is open daily from 10:00 A.M. to 4:00 P.M. Adult admission is $7.00.

Follow the signs to the Forest Hill subway station, where you can pick up Boston's newest park, the **Southwest Corridor,** to pedal back almost to the doorstep of the bike rental shop. This string of connected green spaces parallels a former rail line until it reaches the South End, where it links together the small urban parks of this nineteenth-century neighborhood. It emerges at the Back Bay station of the MBTA.

DAY ONE: evening

You deserve a little break about now, so get settled in your room and enjoy it. You can sit in your chairs by the window and watch the young and the beautiful as they strut along Newbury Street.

DINNER

But don't linger too long. Continue to enjoy Boston's great outdoors by sharing delectable tapas dishes on the outdoor patio of **Tapeo** (267 Newbury Street; 617–267–4799; moderate), directly across the street from your B&B. If Spanish cuisine doesn't appeal to you, there are many other international patio choices within the block: Italian at **Davio's Cafe,** American at **Charley's Eating & Drinking Saloon,** Chinese at **Wisteria House,** or guess-what at **Thai Dish.** Dress casually and relax. Flaunt the healthy glow of your skin from the ride today.

Now it's time to stroll to the end of Newbury Street, then left on Arlington to cross the highways via the Arthur Fiedler Footbridge (named for the beloved longtime conductor of the Boston Pops Orchestra). You're on the **Esplanade,** which was created for exactly what you're doing—having an arm-in-arm stroll on the green banks of the Charles River. After the river was dammed in 1910, Boston's city planners slowly created riverside walks and islands on the models of the great capitals of Europe.

Check the *Boston Globe* "Calendar," published on Thursday, to see if any concerts are scheduled at the **Hatch Shell.** The **Boston Pops** plays almost nightly during the first week of July, and a variety of jazz, pop, classical, and folk groups also perform throughout the summer, or there might be a free outdoor movie on Friday evening. If your timing works out, settle down on the grass for an evening of free entertainment. If not, you could do worse than stroll along the banks of a quiescent river in the moonlight. As you walk up the Esplanade you can climb the stairs to Massachusetts Avenue. Turn left and walk to Newbury Street, then left again to get back to your room.

DAY TWO: morning

BREAKFAST

Breakfast at the Newbury Guest House is a casual affair. Head down to the front parlor for what your hosts call an "English-style continental breakfast." We think of it as "continental-plus" because it includes the essential fresh fruit (berries, melons) along with freshly baked muffins and breakfast pastry as well as juice, coffee, and tea. You can dine here or carry a tray to that nice windowside table in your room.

After breakfast, walk over to the John Hancock building on Copley Square—that mighty monolith of gleaming glass that recapitulates the beautiful older buildings of the square in its mirrored panels. Stop at the **Hancock Observatory** ticket office (open May through October daily 9:00 A.M. to 11:00 P.M., November through April daily 9:00 A.M. to 5:00 P.M.; corner of Trinity Place and St. James Avenue; $6.00, or $3.00 with CityPass; 617–572–6429). Then proceed inside for the lightning-fast elevator that swoops sixty floors skyward to the Observatory. Walk around to the western view to see the Back Bay Fens and you can follow the green route of the Emerald Necklace. You'll probably be surprised to see how much ground you covered on your bicycles yesterday. Keep walking around and you'll see the ocean; on the other side the distant hills of the Berkshires are visible on a clear day.

And now it's time to come down to earth for a glorious Sunday stroll up the Commonwealth Avenue mall into the **Public Garden,** America's oldest public botanic garden. (Its current design, modeled on English gardens, dates from 1859.) As you walk along the lagoon, you'll see the Sunday painters, some even attired in beret and smock, at work with paints and brushes *en plein air.*

Many are working away to capture the fancy and grace of one of the quintessential Boston experiences—the **Swan Boats** of the Public Garden. These fifteen-minute cruises have been a Boston tradition since 1877, when Roger Paget first put his foot-pedaled boats in the water. Their elaborate stylings were inspired by the scene in Wagner's opera *Lohengrin* where a Knight of the Grail is ferried across a river in a boat drawn by a swan. Since the knight was crossing the water to defend his lady's honor (and Paget had some spare bicycle parts and the concession for Garden lagoon boats), he thought the idea of swan-drawn boats was wonderfully inspirational. Thus was born the giddiest of Victoriana. His descendants still operate the concession. Swan Boat rides are $1.25.

LUNCH

Alas, each outing must come to an end. But before you part from Boston, there's still time to enjoy a casual and inexpensive French lunch right at the edge of the garden at **Café Paris** (19 Arlington Street; 617–247–7121).

FOR MORE ROMANCE

The Jamaica Pond boathouse rents rowboats and small sailboats.

Not far from Jamaica Pond, you can detour to visit Fairsted, the **Frederick Law Olmsted National Historic Site** at 99 Warren Street, Brookline. Tours of the home and grounds let you see Olmsted's design principles in miniature as he applied them to his personal domestic landscape.

See "Cozy in Back Bay: A Winter Idyll" for other Back Bay activities.

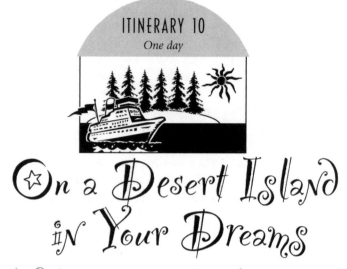

☆On a Desert Island in Your Dreams

W HILE THE ISLANDS IN BOSTON'S HARBOR are unin-
habited, they're not exactly deserted, thanks to daily
ferry service and water taxis. They offer the chance for
a swift getaway from urban life to a marine park where you can laze
on the grass and watch the ships go by, or even brave the cool currents for a refreshing swim. And if you choose one of the less developed islands, you'll find a little stretch of beach or a bluff where you
can imagine being stranded—but only as long as you like. As the
old skiffle tune goes, "Happiness could be ours, if for only three
hours . . . on a desert island in my dreams."

PRACTICAL NOTES: Bring a knapsack or satchel to tote your
lunch, a water bottle, sunscreen, windbreakers, and perhaps bathing
suits. Closed-toe, rubber-soled footwear is best for scampering on
rocks and walking on stony beaches and trails. The ferry to the
islands runs weekends and a limited weekday schedule from early
May until mid-June, then frequently every day until Labor Day,
when it resumes the limited schedule until Columbus Day.

DAY ONE: morning

Around 9:00 A.M. head down to Long Wharf (the foot of State
Street) and turn right to walk over to Rowes Wharf to **Rudi's** (30
Rowes Wharf; 617–330–7656) to purchase the fixings for a picnic.
Rudi's is a deli-bakery that offers excellent sandwiches on a choice
of breads baked on the premises as well as a delicious variety of

$\mathcal{R}$om**ance**
AT A GLANCE

♦ Catch a quick boat to one of the newest National Park areas, the fascinating dots of land known as the **Boston Harbor Islands.** Cruise along through Boston's busy inner harbor on your way to Georges Island.

♦ Explore the Civil War–era fortress of **Fort Warren,** a rather liberal internment camp for Confederate sympathizers and prisoners.

♦ Stroll among the beach roses, watch the ospreys diving for fish, and maybe take a brisk dip yourselves on the beach at **Lovells Island.**

baked goods. While you're about it, pick up some scones or croissants to nibble on the boat ride.

Then return to Long Wharf to buy your tickets for the **Boston Harbor Islands Ferry** from Boston Harbor Cruises (Long Wharf; 617–227–4321; adults $8.00). To make a full day of it, you'll want to catch the first boat to Georges Island at 10:00 A.M.

The ferry typically teems with naturalists, parks volunteers, and other day trippers. Don't be surprised if you're sharing a deck with a troop of exuberant Boy or Girl Scouts, as overnight camping is permitted on some of the islands. For optimum viewing on the outward passage, choose seats on the starboard (right) side, preferably on the less-crowded lower deck by a window where you can be shielded from the usually strong breeze. The ferry doubles as a harbor cruise, so the outbound leg is accompanied by narration explaining the shoreline landmarks. You'll notice immediately that Boston Harbor, especially the inner harbor, is a busy place. Large oil tankers going back and forth to the East Boston terminals share the channel with small sailcraft, whose gossamer spinnakers let them outrace the ungainly behemoths. Giant jets swoop overhead as they come in to land at Logan Airport, which buried a small group of islands under fill and asphalt to create the in-city runways. You'll pass the great fish wharves, where Boston's remaining fishing vessels unload (there's a 6:00 A.M. daily fish auction), and the container cargo terminal, a major port for bringing European and Japanese autos into New England.

That's the working port—the inner harbor. When you pass Castle Island (see "For More Romance"), you enter the outer harbor as the ferry threads its way through the channel into the archipelago of the **Boston Harbor Islands Park** (headquarters:

617-727-7676), an area that's a National Recreation Area administered by the National Park Service. Information booths (617-223-8666) at Long Wharf and Fan Pier are open daily in the summer from 9:00 A.M. to 4:45 P.M. Each of the islands of the park has a distinct topography, shoreline, and history. Most had farms at some point in their history—in fact, the first English explorers reported tall fields of corn covering the larger islands—and many had active forts from 1630 until the end of World War II.

The Lady in Black

However easy the confinement at Fort Warren, some prisoners tried to escape. The late Edward Rowe Snow, historian of the harbor islands, used to relate this ghost story. According to Snow, the new bride of Confederate naval officer Samuel Lanier dressed herself as a man and rowed out to Georges Island on a stormy night. She found her husband, but when she fired a pistol at a Union officer in making their escape, the gun exploded and killed Lanier instead. Sentenced to hang as a spy, she went to the gallows clad in a dress sewn of the black drapes from the mess hall. Legend has it that her ghost still stalks Fort Warren as an eerie, whistling wind.

Forty-five minutes after departing from Long Wharf, the ferry will swing up to the outer dock at **Georges Island,** one of the larger islands in the park and certainly the most strategically located. Georges lies at the "throat" of the harbor facing the shipping channel, making it an ideal outpost for keeping watch on the maritime traffic. It was first fortified in 1778 by the French Navy to help protect their American allies in Boston from British ships. In 1833, the American government began constructing **Fort Warren** from massive blocks of granite ferried across the harbor from Quincy. The task took two decades. Fort Warren saw "active" duty (if you can call it that) during the Civil War as one of the more genial prisoner of war camps. Beginning in 1861 some 600 Confederate soldiers and sympathizers were interned here. When the prisoners arrived, the people of Boston sent food, beds, and other supplies to them. Confederate officers and political prisoners were allowed to roam freely on the island, playing games of football and enjoying liquor and other gifts sent to them.

Georges Island is a tranquil place now, with time and dust slowly burying the external walls of the old fort—although Civil War reenactors do camp here each August. The interior of the fort is partially restored. Take an hour or so to walk the greensward of the picnic grounds and have a look at the fort. The view back to Boston, some 7 miles distant, is striking.

DAY ONE: afternoon

Besides serving as a popular destination in itself, Georges is the hub for free water-taxi service to as many as four other islands, all of them offering more secluded settings. Accessible islands vary by season, but one that is always serviced by the water taxi is **Lovells Island,** a sixty-two-acre complex ecosystem just across a narrow strait from Georges.

When you arrive at the Lovells Island dock, go straight across the island (a few hundred yards) to the pebble beach and turn right to walk down to the headland, where the relatively smooth beach begins to break up into chunks of rock. You'll probably be the only ones to see the advantages of this area, so you can enjoy your picnic in solitude as you look seaward to ships in the outer channel.

Lovells has its own fort, now nearly silted over with the deposition of time, on the seaward side. Much of the island is covered with dunes held down by low sumac bushes that turn a brilliant scarlet in the fall and begin attracting songbirds to their seed heads in July. The island is staffed in the summer by two resident park guides who can direct you to the trails and point out where you might see herons (the salt marshes) and plovers (the meadow and beaches near the fort). The side of the island facing inward toward Boston has sandy beaches but strong currents. If you'd like to take a swim, the beach of smooth pebbles on the ocean side has the best conditions, including a lifeguard. But you might prefer a secluded walk on the beach together, watching for seals and, if you're lucky, porpoises cavorting just offshore.

The last water taxi back to Georges to catch the last boat back to Boston leaves at 4:30 P.M.—sometimes earlier. Be sure to ask. The afternoon return voyage is even more spectacular than the morning outward sail. By mid-afternoon the heat of the sun on the land has created enough temperature differential to guarantee good sailing winds, so the harbor is filled with day sailors whipping canvas and lines about as they speed their sloops and yawls downwind and then tack in zigzag fashion back into the wind. As you enter the inner harbor, the towers of Boston's financial district gleam with the late sun, beckoning you back from your self-imposed island exile.

FOR MORE ROMANCE

Similar facilities—for instance, a fort with an extensive Civil War history and a good swimming beach—also exist in South Boston at **Castle Island** and the adjacent **Marine Park.** Castle Island has been attached to the mainland since the 1930s. From its tip there is a Victorian-era causeway that extends across Pleasure Bay to the South Boston mainland. At the beginning of the twentieth century, literally tens of thousands of Bostonians would dress up on weekends and make a fashionable promenade along the causeway, then around Pleasure Bay's shoreline back to Castle Island (then reached by bridge). It's still a popular walk; the neighborhood appears to be the largest single market in America for upscale European baby carriages, many of which you'll see on the Castle Island causeway. The connected beaches of South Boston are the best swimming beaches in the city but fill up quickly with local residents.

On weekends from mid-May through mid-October, you can also visit the windswept outpost of the last manned offshore lighthouse on the east coast of the U.S.—**Boston Light** on Little Brewster Island, one of the outermost Boston Harbor Islands. The first beacon on this island was raised in 1716, making Boston Light the country's oldest lighthouse, and the Coast Guard maintains a small museum at the base of the lighthouse. You might see seal nurseries and seabird rookeries on the nearby rocks, and you'll be able to climb the seventy-six steps to the top of the light. Tours run from Fallon State Pier, John F. Kennedy Library and Museum, on Friday at 10:00 A.M. and 2:00 P.M. ($29), and from Fan Pier in South Boston on Saturday and Sunday at 10:00 A.M. and 2:00 P.M. ($25). Advance reservations are required (617–223–8666).

Two days and one night

Brewpubs and Flashing Blades

HE TWO OF YOU CAN CREATE YOUR OWN Oktoberfest by combining the best of the brewer's (and quaffer's) art with the whoosh of skates on ice and the whir of in-line wheels on pavement. Great beers, great food, great hockey, and the great outdoors all conspire to make October a terrific time to get away in Boston. On this weekend trip you'll sample the "best beer in America" and several other serious pretenders to the throne, cheer for the Boston Bruins at a hockey game, and get a little workout of your own as you in-line skate together beneath a canopy of fall foliage on Cambridge's traffic-free Memorial Drive.

PRACTICAL NOTES: We suggest you plan this itinerary as a Saturday–Sunday trip, as traffic is banned from a portion of Memorial Drive only on Sundays, making it a skater's heaven. Be sure to get hockey tickets well in advance, as Bruins games usually sell out. For tickets, call Ticketmaster Sportscharge at (617) 931-2222. Reservations for brunch at the Brew Moon (617–499–BREW) are also recommended.

DAY ONE: afternoon

Plan to arrive at midday to check into the beautifully situated **Hyatt Regency Hotel** (575 Memorial Drive, Cambridge; 617–492–1234 or 800–233–1234; $219–$295; weekend specials $129–$199), where you have paid a $25 surcharge to reserve a river-view room. Built in the "Aztec" style of architecture, this hotel is better to look out from than to look at. Each floor is stepped, which creates a maximum

Romance AT A GLANCE

◆ Enjoy the convenience and spectacular views of the **Hyatt Regency Hotel** (575 Memorial Drive, Cambridge; 617–492–1234 or 800–233–1234) the "Aztec pyramid" located on a scenic bend in the Charles River.

◆ Tour the headquarters—and the tongue-in-cheek Beer Museum—at the **Boston Beer Company** (30 Germania Street, Boston; 617–522–9080), a pioneer in craft brewing.

◆ Savor inventive seafood cooking—like cornmeal-crusted halibut with smoked black beans and mango salsa—at **Commonwealth Fish and Beer Co.** (138 Portland Street, Boston; 617–523–8383).

◆ Watch the Boston Bruins carve up the ice (and maybe the visiting team) in the spacious arena at the **Fleet Center** (Causeway Street, Boston; 617–624–1000).

◆ Visit the ultra-stylish dining rooms of **Brew Moon** (50 Church Street, Cambridge; 617–499–BREW) for craft brews and a luscious Sunday brunch of beer-based cuisine.

◆ Strap on some blades to skate away all those extra carbs along the Charles River in Cambridge's premier de facto **skate park.**

◆ Wrap up a perfect weekend of active enjoyment with the fine ales and spicy cuisine of **John Harvard's Brew House** (33 Dunster Street, Cambridge; 617–868–3585).

number of rooms with unobstructed views of the Charles River and the Boston skyline. Not only does the Hyatt have an excellent pool and fitness center, but it also offers a free shuttle to Harvard Square every quarter hour.

Grab that shuttle no later than 1:00 P.M. and hop the subway inbound to Downtown Crossing, where you'll change to the Orange Line outbound toward Forest Hills. Get off at the Stoney Brook stop. Above ground, take a left onto Boylston Street and go straight. At the first set of lights, turn right onto Amory Street. Take the first left onto Porter Street and look for the SAMUEL ADAMS signs. Congratulate yourselves when you walk to the entrance of the **Boston Beer Company** (30 Germania Street, Boston; 617–522–9080); even Bostonians can't find their way by car.

You've allowed an hour of transit time so you arrive no later than 2:00 P.M. for one of the Saturday tours of the brewery. (Tours are given Thursday and Friday at 2:00 P.M.; Saturday at noon, 1:00, and 2:00

P.M.; and during July and August only on Wednesday at 2:00 P.M.) The tour is free, although a $1.00 donation is requested to help fund local youth programs. Don't fret about arriving early. The anteroom is the "Samuel Adams' Boston Beer Museum," a series of displays about the history and process of making beer in general and Boston Beer Company beer in particular. You can pore over copious fan mail (to keep it honest, one wall of letters is put up anew each week) and gawk at the slew of gold medals from The Great American Beer Festival. The original Samuel Adams Boston Lager started winning the consumer preference poll yearly in 1985, when it was introduced—hence the claim of "Best Beer in America."

The irony is that the recipe is Jim Koch's adaptation of his great-grandfather's lager beer from the 1930s and 1940s, brewed at the long-defunct Louis Koch Brewery. Louis unfortunately built a block from Adolphus Busch's brewery, which now uses the Koch site as a parking lot. Budweiser is hardly shaking in its boots, but Jim Koch did get some revenge by helping to launch the craft beer movement that now cuts slightly into Budweiser's market share. The tour covers all the basics of brewing inside this tiny (310-gallon) research and development facility. Most of

Beer As the Foundation of Domesticity

The earliest beer found by archaeologists dates from about 6000 B.C., but human beings didn't start making beer en masse until about 5000 B.C. in Mesopotamia. Having discovered that sprouted barley could accidentally ferment and produce a tasty and nourishing beverage, nomadic peoples began to stop wandering and stick around long enough to harvest the barley crop and make beer. It is possible that once they made enough beer, they lost the incentive to wander. Soon after beer domesticated the human animal, the role of brewing became a woman's art—through which she completed the domestication of her mate. Clearly beer is responsible for civilization as we know it and for the lifelong bond between mates.

the Samuel Adams beers are actually brewed elsewhere, but the Germania Street facility is where the brewmasters develop new seasonal beers and carefully repropagate the company yeast strains responsible for the flavor of Boston Beer Company products. Certainly the most popular part of the tour is the conclusion at the pub-style tasting room, where you'll each get a seven-ounce tasting glass to keep. Typically, three beers are offered—the original Samuel Adams Boston Lager and two others, depending on what they've brewed recently. "Recently" is a key word: Beer, like its first cousin bread, is best when fresh.

Following the tour, return on the Orange Line to the Haymarket stop, which will place you near Faneuil Hall Marketplace and the North End (see "The Snug North End"). You might want to do some looking around at the shops, but if you're serious about your beer, you'll make a pilgrimage to the **Green Dragon Tavern** (11 Marshall Street, Boston; 617–367–0055), not so much for what it is but for what it has been. This is the beer-drinker's obligatory history stop, for the Sons of Liberty (rabble-rousers such as John Hancock, Paul Revere, and Samuel Adams) were known to frequent this establishment to hatch plans to torment the British colonial government. Given their legendary thirsts, they probably frequented a number of such establishments, but this is the only one to survive. Have a pint in their honor before you move along to Boston's first brewpub since The Great Mistake (also known as Prohibition).

DAY ONE: evening

DINNER

The **Commonwealth Fish and Beer Co.** (138 Portland Street; 617–523–8383; inexpensive) opened in 1986 with the motto, "Let no man thirst for lack of real ale." Fortunately, they quickly came to realize that women also thirst for real ale and that their initial pub food couldn't compete with better dining nearby. With a French-trained chef who has done stints in some of Boston's leading fine dining destinations, Commonwealth now focuses on spicy seafood dining, with tasty delights such as corn-battered shrimp with a Cajun remoulade and charred tuna steak with pickled onions and fiery Japanese wasabi. Head brewer Jeff Charnick has crafted an ale called "Master Harry" to complement the cuisine.

You've purchased your **Boston Bruins** tickets ($29–$65 per person) several weeks ago, right? The Bruins, like the Boston Celtics of the National Basketball Association, play in the **Fleet Center** (Causeway Street, Boston; 617–624–1000). The Fleet Center is a modern, spacious, clean venue for sporting events, concerts, and family activities such as the circus. The Bruins (pronounced "broonz" by Boston sports fans) are the city's salvation; while they rarely win the Stanley Cup, they always seem to play well in a patented manly fashion. It's guaranteed that you'll leave breathless. By the time the game is over, it may be too late for the shuttle bus. The easiest way to get back to your hotel is to walk over to Faneuil Hall Marketplace and catch a cab—about $7.00. If you're up for another beer before you turn in, take the hotel's glass elevator up to the **Spinnaker Italia** restaurant and bar for a nightcap and gorgeous view of the city lights.

DAY TWO: morning/afternoon

After a good night's sleep to repair the damages from yesterday's carousing, you could work out the kinks by swimming synchronized laps together in the hotel pool before you return to Harvard Square via the shuttle van.

BRUNCH

This time your destination is the suave and hip **Brew Moon** (50 Church Street, Cambridge; 617–499–BREW; inexpensive), where you're headed for Sunday brunch. (If you didn't make reservations, you'll be handed a beeper and told when you can expect to be squeezed in. There's a moral here: Make a reservation.) This phenomenally successful brewpub is the third of a growing family of Brew Moons, all of which fuse a kind of hipster take on pub fare with a real flair for brewing elegant beers of great character and backbone. You needn't start with beer—the brunch menu is full of favorites such as French toast, waffles, and savory egg dishes. But when you do get around to malt, we suggest opting for the "lunar sampler," a rack of five four-ounce glasses of the different handcrafted Brew Moon brews on tap.

You saw some fancy skating by the Bruins last night, and now it's time for you to stretch a few muscles together. Walk over to **City Sports** (16 Dunster Street, Cambridge; 617–868–9232) to rent in-line skates ($15 per day, including helmet and pads, Friday-to-Monday weekend package $25). **Memorial Drive** is just a few blocks away. Normally a busy four-lane highway along the Charles River, Mem Drive is closed to motor traffic on Sunday afternoons from spring through late fall. The leafy canopy of maples along the sides of the road and the river make this mile-long, gently swerving road a Technicolor adventure on small wheels. Sure, you'll see some hotshots (this is a college town after all), but you'll find a lot of kindred spirits in couples of all ages out for a spin.

DAY TWO: evening

DINNER

City Sports closes at 7:00 P.M. on Sundays, so you'll need to get the skates back by then. But you have only to cross the street to visit the most pub-like of brewpubs in Boston, the charming and unfailingly cheery **John Harvard's Brew House** (33 Dunster Street; Cambridge; 617–868–3585; inexpensive). It's located a few steps from the site of Thomas Chesholm's 1636 tavern—the first licensed brewery in the Massachusetts Bay Colony (the Puritans may have been prudes, but they liked a pint). With that lineage, the brew house plays fast and loose with history (John Harvard was a preacher, not a brewer by trade)—but all in good fun. There's nothing funny about the beers, though, crafted in a very crisp and clean style by head brewer Brian Sanford. The dining is no laughing matter, either—and a consolation if one of you is abstaining as the designated driver for the trip home. Chef Frank L'Heureux is justly celebrated for his grilled homemade sausages with spaetzle, his mushroom fritters with Parmesan and cracked pepper dip, or the house specialty of grilled tuna steak salad with roasted potatoes, green beans, tomatoes, and artichokes over mixed greens.

FOR MORE ROMANCE

At this writing, Boston has two other excellent brewpubs where you might continue your explorations of the Hub's malt scene. **Boston**

Beer Works (61 Brookline Avenue, Boston; 617–536–BEER) near Fenway Park (see "Take Me Out to the Ball Game") is a cavernous hall with tables up front for restaurant service. The food is less the point here than BBW's broad selection of beers crafted on the premises. **Cambridge Brewing Company** (1 Kendall Square, Cambridge; 617–494–1994) stands out from other area brewpubs in that it makes beers in a San Francisco style—robust and hoppy. Best food bets here are the terrific brick-oven pizzas, either before or after catching a foreign or art film at the **Kendall Square Cinema** in the same complex of former industrial buildings.

Should you prefer roundball to brawn on skates, the **Boston Celtics** open their season at the Fleet Center in November, with pre-season games beginning in mid-October. Alas, Memorial Drive opens back up to Sunday traffic after Halloween, so the season for skating *and* basketball is brief.

The Muses

ITINERARY 12
Two days and two nights

The Painters' Passion
A FINE ARTS WEEKEND

URING THIS WEEKEND YOU'LL BOTH walk in beauty, to borrow Lord Byron's phrase. From your base in the city's most luxuriously gilded hotel, you will experience the fruits of Boston's artistic flowering in the Victorian and Edwardian eras. That confluence of money and taste brought many master-works of European art to Boston and simultaneously assembled the artistic geniuses of the age to create institutions to hold that beauty. Like all great love affairs, the Bostonian passion for art has not cooled over time. The flame waits only for your rapt attention to become a conflagration.

DAY ONE: afternoon

The **Fairmont Copley Plaza Hotel** (138 St. James Street; 617–267–5300; $279–$439; weekend rates $179–$229) anchors one end of Copley Square, Boston's most elegant public square. The hotel stands on the site of the first building for the Museum of Fine Arts, a flamboyant Victorian structure that opened in 1876. The rapid growth of the collections made a new location necessary, and the museum moved to its current site in the Fenway in 1909. You'll be going there as well.

But first, the hotel. Designed by the same architect who designed the Plaza Hotel in New York (look for the double P crest through-out), the Copley Plaza cost $5.5 million to build for its 1912 open-ing. Since then the Copley Plaza has hosted American presidents as well as royalty and cultural icons. Built with grand ballrooms and

85

Romance AT A GLANCE

♦ Stay at the **Fairmont Copley Plaza Hotel** (138 St. James Street; 617–267–5300), the gilt-and-marble Edwardian masterpiece of decorative arts in Copley Square. The sky's the limit when it comes to glamorous options, or you can choose to be resplendently (but frugally) cozy.

♦ Visit the **Museum of Fine Arts** (465 Huntington Avenue; 617–267–9300), where you'll share treasures of the ages from the riches of the pharaohs to the breathless brushstrokes of the Impressionists.

♦ Enjoy the rich, sensual flavors at **Anago** (Lenox Hotel, 710 Boylston Street; 617–266–6222), then catch some warm jazz at the Fairmont Copley Plaza's **Oak Bar** (617–267–5300), known for its extensive martini menu and history as a jazz spot since the Twenties.

♦ Tour the magnificent art and architecture of **Trinity Church** and **Boston Public Library,** two masterpiece buildings of Copley Square.

♦ Enjoy the collections (and the Venetian-style palazzo) of the **Isabella Stewart Gardner Museum** (280 The Fenway; 617–566–1401).

♦ Dine in baronial elegance in the soaring, paneled recesses of the Fairmont Copley Plaza's **Oak Room** (617–267–5300), the most over-the-top premium steak house in Boston.

triumphal corridors, the Copley Plaza has specialized in gala social events from the outset—a role it still plays. (It hosts more weddings every year than its Copley Square neighbor, Trinity Church.)

The hotel offers one of the more unusual amorous packages, "The Engaging Martini Weekend." It includes a Finlandia vodka dry martini garnished with an unusual rock: a one-carat Master Cut diamond in a classic platinum setting from Boston's most respected old-line jeweler, Shreve Crump & Low. The rest of the package includes dinner at the Oak Room and a one-bedroom suite fitted out with champagne, chocolates, and flowers. At last look, the weekend was priced a little under $13,000.

For a different kind of splurge, book the John Hancock Suite, where Richard Burton and Elizabeth Taylor stayed during their first honeymoon, when Burton was performing *Hamlet* in Boston. At the very least, one of you should carry the other over the Dartmouth Street threshold in imitation of Dick's theatrical gesture for Liz.

Actually, we prefer the ceremony of the grand front entrance, flanked by two three-ton lions embellished with gold leaf. The hotel reflects the "gilded age": Ornament everywhere glitters with gold. As you enter, you'll march down "Peacock Alley" (an arched passage of marble, faux marble, and gilt lit by gleaming chandeliers) until you emerge into the 5,000-square-foot lobby with 21-foot-high gilded ceiling. We suggest a room with a view of Copley Square, but whichever room you select, it will feel like a comfortable Boston pied-à-terre with excellent Edwardian reproduction furnishings.

Once you have settled in, survey Copley Square to get your bearings on the great buildings that grace this lively and lovely square. For this afternoon, however, you'll be heading out to the "second" home of the **Museum of Fine Arts** (465 Huntington Avenue; 617-267-9300) in the Fenway District. You can take the Green Line (E Train) from the outbound Copley Square T stop. It's a short ride. The museum is open Monday and Tuesday from 10:00 A.M. to 4:45 P.M., Wednesday from 10:00 A.M. to 9:45 P.M., Thursday and Friday from 10:00 A.M. to 9:45 P.M. (West Wing only after 5:00 P.M.), and Saturday and Sunday from 10:00 A.M. to 5:45 P.M. Admission is $12 for adults, but is by voluntary contribution on Wednesday after 4:00 P.M.

In its "new" location, the MFA continued growing to become the largest museum in New England and one of the five largest in the country, with more than one million objects in its permanent collection. The granite Classical Revival main building holds the permanent collection. The soaring West Wing, designed by I. M. Pei and inaugurated in 1981, houses temporary exhibitions, the gift shop, restaurant, and cafe.

The MFA's holdings reflect the wealth and interests of the city's nineteenth-century collectors. You can head for the galleries that most match your interests or seem the most intriguing. In truth, daily visits for a week would only begin to scratch the surface of the MFA's treasure trove, but here are some highlights for an overview, beginning in the main building.

The museum has more than sixty portraits by John Singleton Copley, perhaps America's most talented eighteenth-century painter. (Your hotel is named for him.) Look for the visages of John Hancock, Paul Revere, and Samuel Adams; you'll recognize other personages from the Boston streets that bear their names. Two cases of Revere silver are here, as is Revere's Liberty Bowl.

The Asiatic art collection—representing China, Japan, Korea, the Indian subcontinent, and Islamic culture—is said to be the

The Court Painter Down the Hall

John Singer Sargent has been described as the "court painter" of the Back Bay. Born in Florence of a respected Philadelphia family that had retired to Italy, Sargent enjoyed the world of cultivated leisure. So it is not surprising that he turned his artistic talents to painting the portraits of the fashionable international set, becoming the most popular and expensive portraitist of his day. Isabella Stewart Gardner met Sargent in his London studio and became his sponsor. (Speculation at the time suggested more.) In addition to his portraits, Sargent's murals for the Boston Public Library and the Museum of Fine Arts are considered among the best painted in America in the early twentieth century.

largest under one roof in the world. We always like to pause in the Japanese gallery to look at the fourteenth-century wooden sculpture of *Aizen, King of Passion.* He has six arms, three eyes, and wears a lion-headed crown. A deity in the Esoteric Buddhist pantheon, he transforms the desire for worldly gain into the desire for enlightenment.

As you pass from distant to not-so-distant past in the main building, you'll go through a high, dimly lit hall. Pause and look carefully, for the immense coverings on the walls are medieval tapestries, some of them narrating complex tales of love.

By far, the most popular galleries hold the works of the Impressionists and Postimpressionists. The MFA's collection of work by Monet is surpassed only in Paris. Be sure to look for the two portraits that Monet painted of his wife Camille—two different loving views of the same woman. In the first, *Camille Monet and a Child in the Artist's Garden in Argenteuil* (painted in 1875), she sits in a long blue dress with needlework on her lap and a child at her feet. Her brown hair is pulled up on her head. In *La Japonaise* (1876), Camille wears a blonde wig, poses in a Japanese theatrical costume, and is surrounded by fans. More than a century later, Monet's sensual brushstrokes convey her flirtatious stare.

Don't miss the murals for the central rotunda and stairway painted by John Singer Sargent from 1916 to 1925. (From 1919 until his death in 1925, Sargent kept a suite of rooms at the Copley Plaza.) The last decorative works Sargent completed, the murals depict characters from Greek myth, glorify the seven arts, and pay tribute to the power of knowledge and imagination. Sargent was also a master portraitist. The MFA owns his *Mrs. Fiske Warren and her Daughter,* posed at Fenway Court, where you will be returning tomorrow.

When you need to take a break, have coffee and a pastry or a cheese and fruit plate and a glass of wine in the **Museum Café** on the first floor of the West Wing. For a private moment together (and a breather from the intensity of so much art), step through the door from the main rotunda to the Fraser Court, which reopened in 1996 after more than a decade. Museum director Malcolm Rogers calls it "a classic sleeping beauty" and "one of the museum's greatest treasures." The courtyard is filled with fountains and bronze and stone statuary with American, European, and Asiatic motifs.

DAY ONE: evening

DINNER

After freshening up in your room, you'll be dining tonight in one of the most sumptuous restaurants in Boston, **Anago** (65 Exeter Street; 617–266–6222; moderate). Since moving from a small neighborhood restaurant in Cambridge to this elegant, spacious room in the Lenox Hotel, chef Bob Calderone has only furthered his deserved reputation as a master of sensual food. The portions are generous, but be sure to leave room for pastry chef Ryan Binney's desserts—among the best in the city. His inventive "chocolate bag for two" is a wrapped presentation of all sorts of delights for chocolate lovers. The bag includes slices of fresh fruit for dipping, a selection of delightful small cookies, and an assortment of miniature chocolates (made on the premises, of course) that is likely to vary from day to day. The dessert is good to the last bite—you're meant to eat the bag as well! If you're loathe to split this veritable chocolate buffet, one of you can order the trio of chocolate profiteroles while the other digs into a champagne sorbet.

After dinner, walk back to the Fairmont Copley Plaza and head to **The Oak Bar.** This is no "set-'em-up-Joe" place, as the ornately gilded ceiling, marble, mirrors, and rich dark wood paneling signal immediately. The house specialty is the martini, perfectly presented in traditional Deco-style martini glasses with the back-up caddy on ice in a miniature cut-glass ice bucket. One of the Oak Bar's great traditions is the live jazz combo several nights a week—one of many reasons that *Boston Magazine* designated it the best "Trysting Place" in the city. After trying out the dance floor, you can confirm the magazine's speculation that many an evening begun in the bar concludes in a room upstairs.

DAY TWO: morning

Following a sunlit breakfast of freshly squeezed orange juice and berry crepes in **Copley's Grand Cafe** in your hotel, walk over to visit **Trinity Church** (Copley Square), considered by most architects to be one of the ten best buildings in the United States. Architect Henry Hobson Richardson freely adapted the French Romanesque style for the main body of the church, which demonstrates an unusual balance of grace and solidity. The powerful tower recalls one that graces the Old Cathedral in the medieval university city of Salamanca, Spain. Completed in 1877, Trinity benefited from one of the greatest concentrations of artistic talent lavished on a church anytime in the nineteenth century. Artist John LaFarge and his assistants virtually covered the tower walls with paintings that still stand as the pinnacle of the American Arts and Crafts style. The high, stained-glass windows rain down heavenly colors on the walls of dull terra cotta and gold, a luminescence that glistens off the black walnut woodwork.

The riches of early twentieth century decorative arts continue with an 11:00 A.M. **Boston Public Library Art & Architecture Tour** (free; 617–536–5400, ext. 216), which departs promptly from just inside the Dartmouth Street entrance on Copley Square. The massive bronze doors representing Music and Poetry, Knowledge and Wisdom, and Truth and Romance hint at the grand ornamentation inside this original palace of the people, designed by Charles Follen McKim and built between 1887 and 1895—a high point in American decorative art. (Tours are offered Monday at 2:30 P.M., Tuesday and Thursday at 6:00 P.M., and Friday and Saturday at 11:00 A.M.)

McKim modeled his library on an Italian Renaissance palazzo, believing that it was appropriate to surround Knowledge with

Beauty. Thanks to massive fund-raising efforts, the early twentieth century murals on the library walls were restored to their original opulence in 1995. The murals by Puvis de Chavannes, a leading French painter of the time, that wind up the marble staircase past the lions and along the second-floor corridor depict the Muses of Inspiration. Edward Abbey's pre-Raphaelite masterpieces representing the Quest for the Holy Grail grace the book request room on the second floor. Pick up the handout of Henry James's summary of the story and commentary to learn the elaborate, highly symbolic tale of Sir Galahad's trials and triumph. The third floor is called the Sargent Gallery in honor of John Singer Sargent's murals of the history of Judaism and Christianity.

DAY TWO: afternoon

LUNCH

Papa Razzi (271 Dartmouth Street; 617–536–9200; moderate) is a hip little underground (literally) restaurant with some scrumptious pastas at lunchtime and an unusually well-chosen wine list. Seating choices depend on your mood. Select one of the raised window tables if you're in the frame of mind to be on display (people on the street will smile when they see you holding hands) or one of the small tables all the way in the back for quiet seclusion.

After lunch, take the Green Line back to the MFA stop and walk around the outside of the MFA's West Wing, following signs to the **Isabella Stewart Gardner Museum** (280 The Fenway; 617–566–1401), which is open Tuesday through Sunday from 11:00 A.M. to 5:00 P.M. Few places in the world can boast such quirky treasures as this museum, which speaks not only of a time but of an infinitely engaging personality.

Isabella Stewart Gardner, a New Yorker who married into a Brahmin family, was one of the most colorful characters ever to grace Boston. After the death of her husband, John Lowell Gardner, she became a pioneer in moving to the marshy and unpopulated Fenway area of the city, where she collaborated with architect Willard T. Sears to create a Venetian-style palazzo to house her art collection. Called Fenway Court, it was finished in 1901 and officially opened in a gala party on New Year's Night 1903.

The portrait of Gardner by John Singer Sargent, her friend and one of her artistic advisers, will give you a good sense of her character. (It was judged so scandalous when it was first shown in 1888 that it was withdrawn from public view until after her death.) Another of her advisers, art historian Bernard Berenson, described her as "the one and only real potentate I have ever known."

Fenway Court became a museum in 1925, following Gardner's death the previous year, but her psyche continues to rule the palace. Under the terms of her will, the museum remains as she created it: an environment of rooms arrayed around a showpiece central garden courtyard. There's really no set pattern for seeing it, so wander from room to room, imagining yourselves the guests of "Mrs. Jack," as she was known, invited over to admire her taste. The art, collected in large part with Berenson's assistance, represents an impressive collection of Italian Renaissance paintings as well as French, German, and Dutch masters. One of her well-represented favorites was Degas, and the museum owns the first Matisse to enter an American collection. Adult admission is $10, $11 on Saturday and Sunday.

DAY TWO: evening

DINNER

If your schedule allows, plan to spend another evening and conclude your weekend with dinner at the **Oak Room** (Fairmont Copley Plaza; expensive). This is sumptuous Edwardian splendor at its best: walls of dark wood panels inset with mirrors that reflect the lavish gold, red, and green fabrics and draperies and the two Waterford crystal chandeliers hanging from a 30-foot ceiling. The menu reflects an era when "continental" meant rich flavors and culinary finesse, featuring such plates as a grilled veal chop, parsley-sage roasted rack of lamb, and grilled swordfish. The deep wine list reflects a concentration on Burgundies and Bordeaux to match the cuisine. In 1995, the ever-fussy *Condé Nast Traveler* gave the setting of the Oak Room a perfect 100 percent rating.

 FOR MORE ROMANCE

The Museum of Fine Arts offers **Concerts in the Courtyard** on Wednesday evenings mid-June through early September ($19 non-members). For information, call (617) 369–3300. To charge tickets by phone, call (617) 369–3306. The Courtyard opens at 6:00 P.M.; the concerts begin at 7:30 P.M. Bring a picnic or select from the museum's menu of barbecue, grilled fish, salads, desserts, and drinks and settle in for an evening of light jazz, singer-songwriter pop, regional dance music, or occasional solo instrumental recitals. If you want to take advantage of one of the nicest ways to spend a summer evening in the city, this itinerary works as well on Wednesday and Thursday as it does on Friday and Saturday.

For information about the music series at the Gardner Museum, see "Ode to Joy: Classical Weekend."

⍟de to Joy
Classical Weekend

ELESTIAL HARMONIES RING OUT. A flourish of trumpets announces your arrival. And zing go the strings of your heart. Boston is a city of music, especially classical music. One of the great symphony orchestras of the world is based here, and classical music is a deep and enduring tradition. A crescendo of tympani, please, maestro, as our lovers embark on a weekend ode to joy. They will be making music of their own. . . .

PRACTICAL NOTES: The Boston Symphony Orchestra performs from late September to early May. Call (617) 266-2378 for recorded concert listings, to request a full season brochure, or to order tickets. The Saturday and Sunday concert series at the Gardner Museum runs September through April. Call (617) 734-1359 for recorded concert information. (Only museum members may reserve tickets.)

DAY ONE: afternoon

Situated only a couple of blocks from Symphony Hall, **The Eliot Suite Hotel** (370 Commonwealth Avenue; 617-267-1607 or 800-443-5468; double rooms $205-$345; one-bedroom suites $255-$395) surprises guests more accustomed to American hotels with grand lobbies. The Eliot devotes its space to the rooms instead, giving you the luxury of spreading out. Opt for either a guest room or a one-bedroom suite, which includes a sitting room and pantry. Check in early to get settled.

Romance AT A GLANCE

♦ Spread out in the large and comfortable quarters at the **Eliot Suite Hotel** (370 Commonwealth Avenue; 617–424–7000 or 800–962–3030), just a short walk from Symphony Hall.

♦ Tour the world headquarters of Christian Science—**First Church of Christ, Scientist** (visitor entrance at 175 Huntington Avenue; 617–450–3790)—to see one of the world's largest liturgical organs.

♦ Sample the subtle and exciting inventions of celebrity chef Anthony Ambrose at **Ambrosia on Huntington** (116 Huntington Avenue; 617–247–2400).

♦ Sit in the historic seats of **Symphony Hall** (301 Massachusetts Avenue; 617–266–2378) to listen to a performance of the world-acclaimed Boston Symphony Orchestra. Then drop by a hot local jazz spot for a syncopated rejoinder to classicism before heading home to your room.

♦ Listen in awe to one of the beautiful **Bach cantatas** as part of the Sunday liturgy at **Emmanuel Church** (15 Newbury Street; 617–536–3355).

♦ Enjoy a sprightly lunch at the **Gardner Café**—outdoors, if weather permits—and listen to a measured concert of chamber music at the **Isabella Stewart Gardner Museum** (280 The Fenway; 617–566–1401).

LUNCH

Enjoy a light French lunch at **Brasserie Jo** in the Colonnade Hotel (120 Huntington Avenue; 617–425–3240). This is a true brasserie in the Parisian style, which is modeled in turn on the casual brewery restaurants of Alsace. Too big to be a bistro and too casual to be a restaurant, it's the ideal spot for a quick, light meal—maybe a real quiche. The sidewalk patio is great for people-watching in warm weather, but even if you're seated inside, the large windows afford a good view of the Prudential Plaza and the Christian Science complex, where you will be heading next.

The fourteen-acre complex on the corner of Huntington and Massachusetts Avenues is the **World Headquarters of The First**

Church of Christ, Scientist—the church established in 1879 by Mary Baker Eddy. While **The Mother Church** (visitor entrance at 175 Huntington Avenue; 617-450-3790) dates from 1894, the entire complex achieved its orderly monumentality during a 1968–73 makeover by the legendary design firms of I. M. Pei & Partners and Cossuta & Ponte. The Mother Church was built of New Hampshire granite in the Romanesque style popularized a generation earlier in Boston by H. H. Richardson. It only seats 1,000 worshippers, so it was augmented by the large domed Extension in a blend of Renaissance and Byzantine styles in 1906. Free tours are offered Monday through Friday from 10:00 A.M. to 3:00 P.M., Sunday at 11:30 A.M. One of the world's largest organs is housed here; it is played at all services (10:00 A.M. Sundays year-round or 7:00 P.M. September through June). This magnificent organ is also part of the guided tour. Built by the Aeolian-Skinner Company of Boston, its 13,595 pipes cover nine octaves.

Following your tour of the church, walk along the beautiful reflecting pool that parallels Huntington Avenue. You'll almost certainly notice couples of all ages lingering on the benches. The vistas here combine aspects of the great piazzas of Italy with the soaring modern architecture of the newer Christian Science buildings.

On the Massachusetts Avenue side, **The Christian Science Publishing Society** is closed for major renovations. The building

Love on the Wing

Although the Christian Science complex looks like a triumph of manmade space in the middle of an urban center, some wild denizens have stamped their imprimatur of approval on the design. In 1996 the modern tower building that rises on one side of the reflecting pool became the home of Boston's second nesting pair of peregrine falcons, an endangered species. (The first pair inhabits the Custom House tower near the waterfront.) These magisterial raptors—the female from the banded colony on Maine's Mount Desert Island, the male from previously unobserved wild stock—set up housekeeping in a window niche near the top to raise their first brood of four chicks, the maximum nest for peregrines. What better place than a church building to promote ornithological family values?

is home to *The Christian Science Monitor* newspaper and one of Boston's most unusual attractions, the **Mapparium.** This 30-foot stained-glass globe, constructed 1932–34, represents the worldwide activities of Christian Science. The only map of its kind in the world, the Mapparium's colored land areas show the political boundaries of the world in the early 1930s—which were left unchanged rather than revise an original work of art. When the building is open to visitors, you can step inside the globe via a glass bridge that cuts through the sphere, and, for a moment, the two of you are together, surrounded by the whole wide world. Prior to renovations, the Mapparium was open Monday through Saturday from 10:00 A.M. to 4:00 P.M. Call (617) 450–3790 to inquire about when the building will reopen to visitors.

DAY ONE: evening

DINNER

You'll dine early before the concert on a symphony of flavors at **Ambrosia on Huntington** (116 Huntington Avenue; 617–247–2400; expensive), another triumph of dramatic interior design. Chef Anthony Ambrose's cuisine features the heartiness of provincial French dining brightened with Asian accents—such as the simple salad of arugula and frisée with prosciutto, honey, soy, and lime; or the smoked "pig chop" with Chinese five spices and a Japanese rice cake. Save room for Ambrose's opulently rich desserts such as a warm blueberry cobbler with lemon verbena and blueberry lemon ice.

After dinner, it's a leisurely walk to the evening concert at **Symphony Hall** (301 Massachusetts Avenue), almost directly across the street from the Christian Science complex. Often called "the Stradivarius of concert halls," Symphony Hall is rich and sonorous, entirely devoid of acoustic dead spots. The Boston Symphony Orchestra, one of the world's great orchestras, is equal to its venue. Center orchestra and balcony seats will be sold out (season subscribers snap them up), but of the remainder no seats are obstructed either visually or aurally. Isabella Stewart Gardner and her husband used to sit in seats A-15 and A-16 in the balcony.

You will be filled with music as you leave Symphony Hall, but take a walk up the street to 427 Massachusetts Avenue, which happens to be home to **Wally's Cafe** (617-424-1408), an intimate little neighborhood spot where the local jazz musicians won't even start tuning up until the BSO concert is over. The crowd will vary from jeans-clad college students to fellow symphony-goers, and the Latin jazz is almost always good. Don't fret that you've never heard of the musicians—they're just starting out, and years from now you can score big points in conversation saying, "I remember when we heard Ishmael blowing his horn in this tiny little Boston dive. . . ." Who knows? You might even find space in the crowd to dance in place.

DAY TWO: morning

The Eliot rooms are so pleasant that you should indulge yourself with room service at breakfast (although you can go downstairs to the restaurant, **Clio,** for the same menu). We're particularly fond of the "Breakfast Bake Shop Buffet" of all sorts of goodies from the Clio ovens, including a variety of freshly baked sour cream and fruit muffins, scones, raisin pecan bread, bagels, and crisp croissants with assorted berry preserves. This breakfast also includes a choice of dry cereal or Iggy's natural granola; yogurt and fresh fruit salad are served with freshly squeezed juice, and coffee or tea.

On a Sunday morning the Back Bay streets will be quiet as you stroll to the **Emmanuel Church** (15 Newbury Street; 617-536-3355), which is famous for its music program. Part of the liturgy every Sunday at 10:00 A.M. is a Bach cantata with chorus and orchestra under the baton of Craig Smith; as a result, the Emmanuel is the only church in North America to have performed the entire cycle of all 178 Bach cantatas.

By now you'll have realized that music permeates Boston. On Sunday afternoons you can enjoy a chamber music concert and a delicious lunch at the **Isabella Stewart Gardner Museum** (280 The Fenway; 617-566-1401). The **Gardner Café** offers soups, salads, sandwiches, pasta, fish, and desserts in a pleasant dining spot tucked away beside the Gardner's famous courtyard and near the gift shop. You should have a little time to enjoy the beautiful courtyard plantings and some of the galleries as you make your way to the 1:30 P.M. concert. (The concerts are offered on Sunday, September through

April. A $17 fee includes admission to the museum, which is open Tuesday through Sunday 11:00 A.M. to 5:00 P.M.)

Gardner is best remembered for her fabulous art collection, but she was also a great lover of music. When she first opened her private palace to guests on New Year's Night in 1903, they were entertained by a concert of Bach, Mozart, Chausson, and Schumann played by fifty members of the Boston Symphony Orchestra in the two-story concert hall, the upper half of which is now the Tapestry Room, where the Sunday concerts are held. Fenway Court continued to be a meeting place for local musicians and European visitors, and Isabella Stewart Gardner supported and encouraged Boston's aspiring musicians and artists.

That tradition continues with the concert series. Some programs feature the Gardner Chamber Orchestra under the direction of co-conductors Leon Kirchner, a preeminent composer, and Paula Robison, a world-renowned flutist. Perhaps a little Bach will make the hall ring to send you home with a sense of sonorous clarity and bliss.

FOR MORE ROMANCE

The Gardner Museum also offers **Young Artists Showcase** concerts on Saturday afternoons at 1:30 P.M.

Also located in the Fenway, the **New England Conservatory of Music,** one of the most prestigious music schools in the country, presents more than 450 free classical and jazz concerts each year featuring faculty members and professional-level student ensembles. For information, call NEC's Concert Line at (617) 585–1122. Some concerts take place in **Jordan Hall** (30 Gainsborough Street), a National Historic Landmark known for its acoustics, intimacy, and beauty. When the 1,013-seat hall reopened in 1995 after an $8.2-million restoration, the *Boston Globe* observed, "The warm, dark wood-lined, acoustically perfect space, nestled inside the walls of the New England Conservatory of Music, is considered an instrument in itself, loved the way a violinist reveres a Stradivarius."

The **Museum of Fine Arts** (465 Huntington Avenue; 617-267-9300), just a block from the Gardner Museum, also presents classical music concerts on selected Sunday afternoons. Call (617) 267-9300 for information on concerts and other programs. The Museum's **Musical Instruments Collection** (open Monday through Friday from 2:00 to 4:00 P.M. and Saturday and Sunday from 1:00 to 4:45 P.M.) chronicles the development of many orchestral instruments, particularly various horns, over the last several centuries.

For another elegant dinner spot, try the independent restaurant right in your hotel, **Clio** (617–536–7200; expensive). With its chic leopard-skin and beige decor and Ken Oringer's New American culinary finesse, Clio is one of the stars in the firmament of Boston fine dining. You'll have to reserve far ahead, as visitors from far away flock here for elegant touches like the caviar on scallops or the white truffle shavings on the vegetables.

A Stage for Romance

PART OF ROMANCE IS THE ART of make-believe—"All the world's a stage and all the men and women in it merely players," as the Bard said. Not only is Boston a grand set for love's labors but it's a good place to partake of the thespians' art. Not even Broadway can boast Boston's concentration of architecturally eminent theaters from the early days of the American stage. Nestled together off one corner of the Boston Common, these stages feature major touring shows, local productions, and plays undergoing tryouts. Take your seats together in one of these historic playhouses as the lights dim and the velvet curtain lifts. What follows is a special kind of magic that only live theater can conjure.

PRACTICAL NOTES: For advance information about commercial and nonprofit theater productions, call (617) 423–0372 for ArtsMail's monthly catalog of discount tickets—which includes many, but not all, productions. If you're adventurous enough to go without plans, the Bostix ticket booths at Faneuil Hall and Copley Square sell half-price, day-of-show tickets (cash only). Or you can call the box offices in advance: Charles Playhouse: (617) 426–6912; Colonial Theatre: (617) 426–9366; Wang Center for the Performing Arts and Shubert Theatre: (617) 482–9393; Wilbur Theatre: (617) 423–4008. Boston's traditional theater season is Labor Day to Memorial Day, but in recent years several stages have been lit across the summer. If you opt to have theatrical head shots taken, make an advance appointment.

DAY ONE: morning

Check in at the **Swissôtel Boston** (1 Avenue de Lafayette; 617–451–2600 or 800–621–9200; $219–$360). Because other development near this

Romance AT A GLANCE

♦ The Swiss are renowned as the world's greatest hoteliers. You'll learn why when you slumber in splendor at the luxurious **Swissôtel** (1 Avenue de Lafayette; 617–451–2600 or 800–621–9200), literally steps from the historic Theater District.

♦ Have your own flattering theatrical head shots taken at **Thomas Neforas Photography** (617–266–4466) and tour the historic Theater District, paying special attention to the extraordinary facades from the era when Broadway stretched all the way to Boston.

♦ Relish the panoply of flavors as you dine on classic Abruzzese Italian dishes complemented by wines from the boutique Italian vineyards at **Galleria Italiana** (617–423–2092).

♦ You're out on the town in a big way—so see both **matinee and evening performances** in Boston's finest classic theaters.

♦ Even if the play was tragic, you can delight in the sweetest of endings with dessert together at **Finale** (1 Columbus Avenue; 617–338–3095).

♦ If variety is the spice of life, then dim sum is as zesty as it gets. Select from dozens of tiny plates at the **Golden Palace** in Chinatown (14 Tyler Street; 617–423–4565).

498–room luxury hotel stalled shortly after the hotel was built, surprisingly few people even know it's here. The large number of rooms is also deceiving. Four service floors with comfortable indoor lounge seating and outdoor terraces effectively divide the property into four boutique hotels with classically elegant and efficient Swiss service (it's owned by Swissair). During the week, the main clients are businesspeople, especially European businesspeople. On weekends, Swissôtel offers remarkable packages beginning at $139 per night.

It's worth an extra $90 or so for the "Swiss Butler Executive Level" rooms on the top four floors, with slightly finer detail in the furnishings and extra amenities such as evening hors d'oeuvres, fruit baskets, mineral water, and a continental breakfast. For a private terrace, lots of room to spread out, and great views of Boston Common and the State House, consider suites 2137 or 2139.

This elegant European hotel is situated in the neighborhood where vaudeville, one of the most American forms of the stage, was born. In the heady days before talkies, this end of Washington Street was lined with theaters. Benjamin Franklin Keith began putting on variety shows of wholesome entertainment in this area in the 1880s and had expanded to more than 400 "vaudeville" (as he christened the form) venues around the country by 1914. The wonderfully baroque Opera House was built in his memory. Alas, it stands empty, along with the adjacent Paramount and Modern theaters, all three on the National Trust for Historic Preservation's list of "America's Most Endangered Places."

Times and tastes change in every city. About a block of this once glittering end of Washington Street is currently a frayed "adult entertainment" district, safe enough during the day but unsavory. We suggest walking up West Street to Tremont for a more pleasant stroll between the hotel and the Theater District.

DAY ONE: afternoon

LUNCH

Grab a quick bite to eat at the hotel's **Café Suisse,** just off the reception lobby. The evening specialties here are Swiss, French, German, and Austrian, but lunch is a buffet affair with a selection of hot and cold meats, salads, and—of course—a cheese station. Alternately, you might order a salade niçoise or sandwiches.

Since the two of you are headlining your own romantic comedy, you really ought to have publicity photos. Besides, have you ever noticed how actors' head shots make them look younger and thinner? Those are effects that entertainment photographers know how to duplicate time after time on black and white film with special lighting setups and lenses. You can have this kind of photo session yourselves if you make an advance appointment. One of the closest studios is **Thomas Neforas Photography** (207 Newbury Street; 617–266–4466). You could walk, but it's a busy afternoon, so we suggest you take a cab to his studio in the Back Bay. For theatrical head shots, Neforas charges $150 for the first roll plus $15 for each 8 by 10.

After the photo session, return to the **Theater District** on Boylston Street at the Common to do a walk-through tour of some of Boston's surviving theaters. Their facades are all striking, and you can usually enter the vestibules for a glimpse at their interior glories. And if you ordered tickets by phone, now is the time to pick them up to avoid the evening crowd at the window.

The oldest of Boston theaters is the 1,700–seat **Colonial Theatre** (106 Boylston Street). Built in 1900, its lavish gilt and fresco interior was completely restored in 1995. The Colonial has always favored spectacle, debuting with *Ben-Hur*, complete with chariots drawn by horses on treadmills. Florenz Ziegfeld launched his Follies here in 1927 and returned yearly to polish each edition.

Around the corner is the **Emerson Majestic Theatre** (221 Tremont Street), which reached its apex with performances of Lena Horne, Ethel Merman, Harry Houdini, and the Marx Brothers—and its nadir in the 1970s as a movie theater showing horror films. Emerson College recently restored the Majestic and now books it mostly for major nonprofit dance, opera, and theatrical events as well as Emerson student productions.

Banned in Boston

Until official censorship finally faded away in 1975, a surefire way to boost the commercial success of a play was to get it "Banned in Boston." Perhaps the most infamous brouhaha came with the presentation in 1929 of Eugene O'Neill's Strange Interlude, a Pulitzer Prize–winning drama about a woman's quest for fulfillment that was deemed by Boston clerics to be "drenched with sex and written to point out the futility of religion." So the backers mounted it in neighboring Quincy, where it played to packed houses every night.

The 1914 **Wilbur Theatre** (246 Tremont Street) is one of the more intimate commercial theaters, seating about 1,200 in its most economical configuration. A deep balcony makes it seem even smaller; the steep rake of the upper-balcony seats may also account for the oft-repeated description of the Wilbur as "Beacon Hill in theater dress." Both Thornton Wilder's *Our Town* and Tennessee Williams's *A Streetcar Named Desire* made their debuts here. (*Streetcar* also received some heavy doctoring, based on the response of Boston audiences.)

The Renaissance Revival palace, next door at 268 Tremont Street, was called the Metropolitan when it was built in 1925 as a variety show and movie theater then seating more than 4,000 people (now reduced to about 3,700). Initial construction cost $8 million, and the restoration, completed in 1992, cost $10 million. Now called **The Wang Center for the Performing Arts** in honor of patron An Wang, this is where you'll see the Broadway megashows (Andrew Lloyd-Webber musicals, for example) as well as the Boston Ballet. The theater was modeled on the Paris Opera House, whereas the Grand Lobby (a set in the film *The Witches of Eastwick*) was based on the design of Versailles.

The prestigious **Shubert Theatre** (265 Tremont Street), across from the Wang Center, was the last property of seven in Boston owned by the New York–based Shubert family. Built in 1910, this 1,600-seat theater was the pre-Broadway home of *South Pacific, Camelot,* and Richard Burton's *Hamlet.*

On the way back to the hotel, you'll pass the **Brattle Book Shop** (9 West Street; 617–542–0210). This Boston institution is known around the Northeast as a great center of antiquarian and used books. Now headed by Ken Gloss, son of the founder, the Brattle has an excellent (if ever-changing) section of books devoted to the entertainment industry, including the "legitimate theater."

DAY ONE: evening

DINNER

Dinner tonight is at **Galleria Italiana** (177 Tremont Street; 617–423–2092; expensive; reservations essential), and you'll want to go early, around 5:30, to have the time to savor your meal. Since it opened, Galleria Italiana has been the home kitchen of several exciting and talented chefs, but with chef and co-owner Marissa Iocca keeping a sharp eye on the kitchen and co-owner Rita D'Angelo making sure the service flows smoothly, you're assured of a fabulous meal no matter who the chef de cuisine may be. The cooking is Abruzzese—a hearty Italian style where pasta takes a back seat as an interim course, salads are inventive, and main dishes are usually rather simple. The menu changes almost daily. With striking photographs and paintings every few inches on the walls, Galleria Italiana functions as a fabulous trattoria steps from the theaters.

And now for the main event: the play. Although you'll encounter some casually dressed folks, Bostonians as a general rule dress up to go to the theater on the theory that it's a major event and you should look the part. Business or evening dress also prepares you for the evening finale.

After the curtain calls, you have a couple of interesting options. In the basement of the Wilbur Theatre is **Aria** (617–338–7080), an after-theater lounge where clusters of animal-print sofas, lots of mirrors, and blood-red walls create an atmosphere that has been described as looking like the living room in *Phantom of the Opera*. One small room features seating on a miniature canopy bed.

Or, for a quieter scene more oriented to dessert than drinks, pop over to **Finale** (1 Columbus Avenue; 617–338–3095), which keeps hours designed specifically for the theater-going crowd. If you have the appetite for it, go for the sinful "Chocolate Plate for Two." The six small desserts, featuring Valrhona and Callebaut chocolate, include a dark chocolate tower of orange chocolate mousse, bittersweet chocolate decadence cake, and a white chocolate gelato.

DAY TWO: morning

In the 1940s and 1950s, when Broadway tryouts kept the Theater District lit almost every night, Chinatown restaurants flourished for both pre- and post-theater dining, and they're enjoying a renaissance, thanks to innovative chefs whose skills attract Boston foodies and chefs from more mainstream restaurants. Beginning around 10:00 A.M., especially on Sunday mornings, the region bustles with folks descending on the neighborhood for *dim sum* (literally, "touch of heart")—lots of small dishes that keep coming around the individual restaurants on carts. This now-traditional form of dining on snack-sized morsels originated a century ago in South China during the Ching dynasty, when it was customary for invited guests to bring little dishes to the host.

Before you eat, walk around a while. From the street-level exit of the hotel, turn left and walk a half block to Chauncy Street; then turn right and continue into **Chinatown**. Boston's Chinatown is a small district between Washington and Hudson Streets along Essex, Beach, and Kneeland Streets. Its Chinese flavor dates back to the

1870s, when Chinese workers came here to lay the first telephone lines (Alexander Graham Bell's company headquarters was nearby). The major streets support many gift shops and even more restaurants. Perhaps you should have someone snap your picture as you crowd together into one of the red pagoda phone booths.

LUNCH

When you've worked up an appetite, head to the **Golden Palace** (14 Tyler Street between Beach and Kneeland; 617-423-4565). Consistently voted the best *dim sum* in the city, Golden Palace tends to attract a lot of hungry diners to share the round tables covered with pink tablecloths. Among the specialties are pan-seared ravioli with shrimp, pork, and fresh coriander; dumplings with shrimp and scallops; and *char shui* buns with bright red pork pieces and hoisin sauce. Golden Palace is huge, so even if you're in line, you'll be seated soon. Depending on your appetite, brunch for two will set you back about $35.

DAY TWO: afternoon

Last night's production should have whetted your appetite for more. Before you leave, go to a matinee at another theater. *Exeunt.*

FOR MORE ROMANCE

In addition to the commercial theaters, you might also try to attend a production of one of Boston's two excellent regional nonprofit companies: the **Huntington Theatre** (264 Huntington Avenue; 617-266-0800), which is known for its role in developing the plays of Pulitzer Prize winner August Wilson; and the **American Repertory Theatre** or ART (Loeb Drama Center, 64 Brattle Street, Cambridge; 617-547-8300), known for its cerebral and avant-garde productions. (See "In the Groves of Academe.")

Poetry and All That Jazz

CAMBRIDGE COOLEST

OW DO I LOVE THEE?" asked Elizabeth Barrett Browning while thinking of her husband, Robert. You can ask it, too. Poetry is a living art in Cambridge, linked closely to the jazz of the streets. What they share is a meter based on the heartbeat (buh-BOOM, buh-BOOM). Sure, Cambridge is something of a hipster's town, but beneath every beret stands a romantic. Cantabrigians, as they so like to call themselves, respond in full, melodic voice to an ancient Greek poet's rhetorical question, "What good is it to toil in the fields all day if we have no song?" You'll have songs aplenty on this journey through a lyrical world—and maybe the inspiration to pen a line or two each to answer Elizabeth's question for yourselves.

PRACTICAL NOTES: This visit to the lyric side of Cambridge works in almost every season, although in winter Harvard Square has few, if any, street musicians and Mount Auburn Cemetery becomes a bit austere.

Seating is limited for the House of Blues Gospel Brunch, so reserve as far in advance as possible by calling (617) 497–2229. And note that the Longfellow National Historic Site will be closed for restoration work until early 2002. Be sure to double-check hours once it reopens.

◆ Slip into your comfortable and ideally located room at the **Harvard Square Hotel** (110 Mount Auburn Street, Cambridge; 617–864–5200).

◆ Shop for music and books. Your search will take you to the **Grolier Poetry Book Shop** (6 Plympton Street, Cambridge; 617–547–4648), which has the most extensive poetry selection in the world.

◆ Stop for drinks where you can act as cool as Bogart and Bergman beneath the film-inspired murals at **Casablanca** (40 Brattle Street, Cambridge; 617–876–0999).

◆ Enjoy parsing the delectable Mediterranean cuisine at **Rialto** at the Charles Hotel (1 Bennett Street, Cambridge; 617–661–5050) where chef Jody Adams elevates the culinary arts to a par with poetry.

◆ Snap your fingers and tap your feet as you catch the late show at Boston's best jazz room, the **Regattabar** (617–876–7777) in the Charles Hotel.

◆ Shout to the rhymes and rhythms of the **House of Blues Gospel Brunch** (96 Winthrop Street, Cambridge; 617–497–2229).

◆ Pay your respects to great lovers past on the beautiful garden grounds of **Mount Auburn Cemetery.**

DAY ONE: morning

Harvard Square is a unique synthesis of high and pop culture—one of the greatest places in the world for the life of the mind. Sure, it's a little zany at times, but nowhere else in Boston is there so much poetry on the street—and in the bookstores. The Square also manages to embody jazz with a syncopation of the serious and the comic, the weighty and the frivolous. This visit takes advantage of the Square's deserved reputation as Boston's center of all that is sublime.

Check into the **Harvard Square Hotel** (110 Mount Auburn Street, Cambridge; 617–864–5200; double rooms $159 with AAA or AARP discount, otherwise $199). Formerly a motor inn, it has been redone to make the rooms stylish and comfortable. The location in the heart of Harvard Square is hard to beat, yet excellent sound-proofing and black-out shades make sure that you'll dream away without being disturbed. If you're feeling anxious about being so far from your e-mail, you can use the lobby computer to check in from time to time. (Bring your own floppy disk and you could even tap out a few love poems.)

You can pick up a map and directory of Cambridge bookstores at the **Cambridge Information Kiosk** next to Out of Town News at the entrance to the Red Line subway. With more than twenty shops, you could say that Harvard Square has bookstores the way a flower garden has bees. As one of the most literate cities in the world, Cambridge has a resident audience for every type of book and draws bibliophiles from around the world. **The Grolier Poetry Book Shop** (6 Plympton Street; 617-547-4648) is legendary. Somehow owner Louisa Solano has managed to cram 15,000 titles into her tiny store located just off Massachusetts Avenue. And if you can't lay your hands on a particular volume on those densely packed shelves, she can. The Grolier is also a likely spot to encounter poets, since almost everyone who shops here or works here also writes verse. Check the notices in the front window for poetry readings and contests.

The venerable **Harvard Bookstore** (1256 Massachusetts Avenue; 617-661-1515)—which, despite the name, is not connected to the university across the street—remains the choice of the literati of Greater Boston for its range of intriguing titles on many subjects. The store also carries so-called "quality" remainders— including many luscious art books reduced to a fraction of list price because they have been discontinued. Harvard Bookstore frequently sponsors readings by visiting writers, so check for a schedule at the front desk. The blockbuster bookstore of the Square is **Wordsworth** (30 Brattle Street; 617-354-5201), which carries 100,000 titles and discounts everything except textbooks. Because Wordsworth keeps long hours seven days a week, it's the favorite spot for late-night browsing. **The Globe Corner Bookstore** (28 Church Street; 617-497-6277), like its sibling in Back Bay, specializes in travel books, maps, and the like. No poetry, but a good place to plan the next getaway together.

With its plethora of street musicians (some of them *very* good) it's probably no surprise that Harvard Square is a good place to hear and buy music. **Tower Records** (95 Mount Auburn Street; 617-876-3377) takes the prize for show tunes and sound tracks, whereas **HMV** (1 Brattle Square; 617-868-9696) gets the laurels for jazz. (For pop, classical, and rock it's a dead heat.) HMV often runs promotions on the recordings of the artists playing that week at Regattabar, whereas Tower's specials feature the artists appearing at the House of Blues. Consider acquiring an album by Cambridge singer-songwriter Chris Smither, whose best known tune "Love You Like a Man" became a Bonnie Raitt anthem after she gave it some slight tweaks for gender.

DAY ONE: afternoon

LUNCH

You're probably loaded down with bags, but try to squeeze into **Iruña** (56 John F. Kennedy Street; 617–868–5633), which is tucked in behind the street-front stores. This Basque-Spanish restaurant has been a favorite of poets and musicians for years. The squid dishes and the roast chicken are delectable. After all these years as a Cantabrigian restaurant, Iruña still feels like an authentic Cantabrican taberna. (Cambridge residents, who call themselves Cantabrigians, are fond of this sort of obscure, bilingual pun. Iruña serves a cuisine found in the Cantabrica area of Spain.)

You might swing by your room to drop off those bags before spending a good portion of the afternoon at the **Longfellow National Historic Site** (105 Brattle Street; 617–876–4491). The bright yellow mansion is just a short distance from the Square past the colonial mansions known as Tory Row. The National Park Service interprets the home as it was when Henry Wadsworth Longfellow lived here with his wife Fanny. With their six children, it's no wonder that he wrote "The Children's Hour." In recent years, the Longfellow Site has been open mid-June through October, Wednesday through Sunday from 10:00 A.M. to 4:30 P.M. From November through mid-June, it has been open Wednesday through Friday from noon to 4:30 P.M., and on Saturday and Sunday from 10:00 A.M. to 4:30 P.M. Adult admission has been $2.00. The site is closed for restoration work until early 2002 and may change its schedule and fees when it reopens.

Already a widower, Longfellow was boarding at 105 Brattle Street when he courted Frances Elizabeth "Fanny" Appleton by walking through Cambridge, across the bridge to Boston, and up Beacon Hill to see her several times a week. Although the family initially disapproved of the church-mouse scholar, his devotion won them over, and the Appletons purchased the boardinghouse as a wedding gift.

After eighteen devoted years together, tragedy struck the Longfellows. In 1861, Fanny was sealing locks of the children's hair when she accidentally lit the sealing wax. In a matter of moments, her own garments caught fire. Henry rushed to her aid, trying to crush out the fire. She died of her injuries and he was so scarred that he wore a full beard for the rest of his life.

Although he's best known for his epics (*Hiawatha, Evangeline*) Professor Longfellow spent much of his remaining life creating what still stands as one of the definitive English translations of Dante's *Divine Comedy*. Dante's narrator spends eternity seeking his beloved Beatrice in the afterlife because he is bereft without her. Henry's grief mingles with Dante's verse.

Back in the Square, reflect on that kind of loving devotion over a drink at **Casablanca** (40 Brattle Street; 617–876–0999). This popular restaurant and bar is located in the basement of the **Brattle Theatre** (40 Brattle Street; 617–876–6837), the repertory movie house that revived the now-classic film. Gaze up from your drinks to the mural of Bogart in trenchcoat, looking doggedly heroic as ever. The burgers and other light fare here are pretty good, but save your appetite. You might try your hands at penning short love verses on the napkins. Then fold them up to read later in the evening.

DAY ONE: evening

DINNER

It's no overstatement to say that **Rialto** (1 Bennett Street; 617–661–5050; formal; expensive; reservations essential), located in the Charles Hotel, is one of the great restaurants of the region. Everything comes together here like a complex poem: lyrically conceived and executed food, decor that offers every comfort without being self-consciously posh, and attentive but unobtrusive service. Chef-partner Jody Adams is a poet of the kitchen, and her plates are both a delight to behold and a deep pleasure to devour. One of you should have the signature Provençal soup with basil oil as a starter, if only to marvel at its simple appearance and complex flavors. Fishes and meats are inevitably spectacular, but Jody lavishes equal care on the vegetarian entrees—every bit as filling and stunningly beautiful to boot. The wine list can be intimidating, but it runs from reasonable and good to expensive and superb. We prefer a window table in warm weather for the view of Charles Square, one of the little banquettes in the winter to avoid the inevitable draft.

After dinner plan to catch the late show upstairs in the hotel at the **Regattabar** (1 Bennett Street; 617–876–7777 for tickets; reservations recommended; semicasual to semiformal). One of the finest jazz rooms in the country, the Regattabar books everyone from national headliners such as the Marsalis brothers and McCoy Tyner to local favorites like legendary pianist-singer Charles Brown and hot saxophonist Stan Strickland. Sightlines and sound system are both excellent; the only shortcoming is that there's rarely room to dance. (Sigh.)

Poetry for Lovers

Asked to recommend poetry for lovers, Grolier owner Louisa Solano jokingly suggests Tigers of Wrath, *an anthology of "poems of hate, anger and invective" edited by X. J. Kennedy. More seriously, she offers these five:*

1. The Governor of Desire *by Elizabeth Morgan*

2. The Country of Marriage *by Wendell Berry*

3. Lust: An Anthology, *edited by Sam Hamill*

4. Available Light *by Marge Piercy*

5. A Shropshire Lad *by A. E. Housman*

DAY TWO: morning

BRUNCH

You'll stretch and wander downstairs to the tiny bakery **C'Est Bon** (110 Mount Auburn Street; 617–492–6465) at street level below the hotel. You could be good and just order some coffee and juice to go, then head back upstairs to read the paper. Or you could add some melt-in-your-mouth butter cookies to that order. Keep in mind that you'll be enjoying some hearty Southern-style fixings at the **House of Blues Gospel Brunch** (96 Winthrop Street; 617–497–2229; $26). This Harvard Square spot is the original of the successful chain created by the founder of the Hard Rock Cafe. The live gospel music with buffet brunch (ribs and biscuits, chicken and dumplings) may have the two of you speaking in tongues by the time you get to the pie. *Halleluia! Say amen. Amen.*

DAY TWO: afternoon

It may seem peculiar to spend a glorious afternoon in a cemetery, but **Mount Auburn Cemetery** (580 Mount Auburn Street; 617-864-9646) is no ordinary graveyard. As America's first garden cemetery, consecrated in 1831, its extraordinary beauty fueled national movements to establish other garden cemeteries as well as public parks. Mount Auburn remains a horticultural landmark for the quality and quantity of its plantings, which provide sanctuary for urban wildlife. Maps are also available to help you locate famous Bostonians, including Henry Wadsworth Longfellow, who was reunited with his departed wife Fanny in 1882. The cemetery is open daily from 8:00 A.M. to 7:00 P.M.

FOR MORE ROMANCE

When the dogwoods, apples, and cherries bloom, and the war-blers, vireos, orioles, and scarlet tanagers arrive, birding becomes a rite of spring at Mount Auburn Cemetery. During peak migration (about May 10), you could spot as many as one hundred species in a single day. Even if you miss the migrations (there's another, less-concentrated one in the fall) you'll see many of the thirty or so species of birds that make Mount Auburn their home for at least part of the year. The Brattle Street gatehouse has a "Bird Sightings" bulletin board. For birding information, call (617) 547-7105, extension 824.

See "In the Groves of Academe" for other activities.

If you want to walk back to your room after dining at Rialto and listening to jazz at the Regattabar, make reservations at **The Charles Hotel** (1 Bennett Street; 617-864-1200 or 800-882-1818; $215-$390). The Charles often offers weekend promotions for $185 per night.

The weekly **Tango Rialto** ($10) is held on Thursday nights after dinner hours at Rialto in the Charles Hotel (1 Bennett Street, 617–661–5050). During the summer months, the Tango Society of Boston also sponsors a free outdoor Tango by Moonlight series on nights with a full moon. Step to the beat on the Weeks Footbridge over the Charles River. Call the Tangoline at 617–699–OCHO for details.

The Artist's Touch

TWO AUTUMN WEEKENDS

AYBE IT'S THE BELL-LIKE AUTUMN LIGHT shining through the trees in the Public Garden. Or maybe it's the soft glow on Arlington street at twilight. Or the jigsaw mosaic of Beacon Hill rooftops visible from the Longfellow Bridge. Or any of a number of other scenes, points of view, times of day. Strolling through Boston in fall is like strolling through the palpable light of a Monet painting. Substitute Trinity Church for Nôtre Dame and Commonwealth Avenue for the Champs Élysée and you'd swear you were in Paris more than a century ago. Wander into the bohemian quarters of the South End or Fort Point, and you half expect to encounter a man with paint-stained smock and only one ear.

These two weekend variations offer the serene beauty of upscale artistic Boston with the chic galleries of Newbury Street as well as peeks into the lives and art of Boston's cadre of working artists. It has become a tradition for each area to host an annual "open studios" weekend. Participating artists fill up their studios with recent work and lay out food and drink for visitors. Many of those visitors are other artists, and some lively discussions ensue. This weekend comes with two options—one for September, the other for October. Both begin on Newbury Street in the Back Bay. September then embraces the open studios of the South End, October the up-and-coming bohemian district of Fort Point. With so much art offered at every price range, you may find yourselves heading home with something more tangible than vivid memories.

PRACTICAL NOTES: This itinerary should be done on Friday and Saturday to best coordinate open studios with the broadest

Romance AT A GLANCE

◆ Check into the landmark **Copley Square Hotel** (47 Huntington Avenue; 617–536–9000 or 800–225–7062), a late-Victorian hotel in one of the area's most convenient locations.

◆ Browse the galleries (and the boutiques, for that matter) of **Newbury Street,** where the city's most-established art dealers are firmly ensconced.

◆ Advance together into the unknown—or at least the cutting edge—in the galleries of the **Institute of Contemporary Art** (955 Boylston Street; 617–266–5152).

◆ Dine on chef Chris Parsons' lean and vibrant grill cuisine and then dance away the night inside the ultra-hip decor of **Pravda 116** (116 Boylston Street; 617–482–7799).

◆ Get in touch with your own sense of creativity by visiting Boston's **artists in their studios**—many of them live/work spaces—in the South End or along Fort Point Channel.

choices for meals and evening entertainment. The South End Open Studios are usually held the third full weekend in September; to confirm dates call (617) 267–8862. The Fort Point Arts Community usually holds its open studios on the third weekend in October; to confirm dates call (617) 423–4299.

DAY ONE: morning

Check in at the **Copley Square Hotel** (47 Huntington Avenue; 617–536–9000 or 800–225–7062; $195–285; weekend specials often available). Built in 1893, the Copley Square Hotel has stood its ground to command one of the most convenient locations at the edge of Back Bay—sandwiched among the Hynes Convention Center, the Prudential Center, and Copley Place. Furnishings and public spaces have been brought up to comfortable contemporary standards, though some of the rooms remain small or oddly shaped. But we'll settle for charm and value over uniformity any day. And the friendly staff more than compensates for any architectural idiosyncrasies. We advise a room near the top of the seven stories for light and quiet. Rooms 714 and 716, for example, each have a deep tub, a queen-size bed, and a sitting area with a round table and two chairs. There's also a coffeepot in the room, a convenience if you're early risers.

Begin your foray into Boston's art scene on **Newbury Street,** where the city's most-established art galleries are found. These upscale galleries, roughly analogous to New York's midtown scene, represent the city's best-known artists as well as others from around the world. It truly takes the better part of a day to browse in the galleries situated in Newbury's marvelous Victorian town houses. You'll climb a short flight of stairs to reach many of those at "street level." Others are tucked below street grade, whereas still others occupy upper levels, so keep your eyes peeled. Exhibitions change constantly, so it's hard to predict exactly what you'll see, but many galleries will gladly bring out other work in storage if you have a particular interest. Start up by the Public Garden and work your way down the street.

L U N C H

Along the way you'll want to stop for lunch. Newbury has no shortage of restaurants, but one you might consider—you could even just pop in to look around—is **29 Newbury Street** (617–536–0290). Not only does this place serve New American cuisine in a casually elegant setting, it also features a changing gallery display on its walls.

Sharing the block with some very upscale designer boutiques, the **Barbara Krakow Gallery** (10 Newbury Street, 5th floor; 617–262–4490) specializes in contemporary painting, drawing, prints, and sculpture by emerging and established artists. The **Robert Klein Gallery** (38 Newbury Street, 4th floor; 617–267–7997) specializes in vintage and contemporary works by renowned photographers. **Gallery NAGA** (67 Newbury Street; 617–267–9060) focuses on Boston and New England artists. In addition to works on paper, the gallery often displays studio furniture and supplies a rotating collection of paintings and graphics to Rialto, the upmarket Harvard Square restaurant.

The **Judi Rotenberg Gallery** (130 Newbury Street; 617–437–1518) is curated by a well-known Boston artist with a good eye for the work of her peers. The **Copley Society** (158

Newbury Street; 617–536–5049), the oldest art association in America, displays the work of its members. Look for Boston cityscapes from all views and in all weather and seasons.

As you approach the corner of Newbury and Dartmouth Streets, you can't miss the **Newbury Street Mural,** a 1991 architectural fantasy with famous historical figures and great works of art painted as a backdrop to a parking lot. You might see which of you can identify more of the seventy-two figures depicted. A hint to get you started: Among them are John F. Kennedy, John Hancock, Mary Baker Eddy, Isabella Stewart Gardner, Charles Bulfinch, Frederick Law Olmsted, Arthur Fiedler, Louisa May Alcott, Henry Wadsworth Longfellow, and the inventor of the safety razor, King Gillette.

Just before you reach the Society of Arts and Crafts (a hard-to-miss landmark at 175 Newbury Street), you'll encounter two galleries that share a below-grade landing. The **Pucker Gallery** (171 Newbury Street; 617–267–9473) has four stories of very eclectic displays, including changing exhibitions, art porcelain, and works by Inuit artists. Pucker also has a broad selection of art calendars and agendas, including some with the intricate scenes of Hundertwasser. Just next door, the **Chase Gallery** (129 Newbury Street; 617–859–7222) offers rotating exhibitions of bright paintings and prints. In the same block, the **Nielsen Gallery** (179 Newbury Street; 617–266–4835) deals in contemporary painting, drawing, prints, and sculpture by both emerging and established artists. The matrix of several small rooms allows Nielsen to display work very well.

Not all Newbury galleries are devoted to the Big Art Scene. **International Poster Gallery** (205 Newbury Street; 617–375–0076) has one of the largest and most international inventories in the world, according to president Jim Lapides. On the lighter side, **American Animated Classics** (259 Newbury Street; 617–424–0640) specializes in fine animation art from all the major studios.

When you've finished gallery browsing, visit the **Institute of Contemporary Art** (955 Boylston Street; 617–266–5152). Housed in an early twentieth century former fire station, the ICA mounts rotating avant-garde exhibitions of national and international art, often with provocative themes. It is open Wednesday, Saturday, and Sunday from noon to 5:00 P.M., Thursday from noon to 9:00 P.M., and Friday from noon to 7:00 P.M. Admission is $6.00. Admission is free on Thursday from 5:00 to 9:00 P.M.

As you return to the hotel, you might want to stop in at the **Wiggin Gallery of the Boston Public Library** in Copley Square. Exhibitions are drawn from the BPL's extensive collection of historic and contemporary prints, drawings, and photographs. Curator Sinclair Hitchings is known for his astute eye in spotting new talent.

Before you go out for dinner, you *must* descend to the lower level of your hotel to have a drink at the bar of the **Café Budapest** (617-266-1979). This landmark Boston restaurant preserves the ambience of an emigré demimonde between the world wars. Order up a pair of Black Russians or a silvery martini and quietly hum a stanza of "Those were the days, my friend. . . ." If you can't remember the song, this vaguely Eastern European bar and expensive restaurant may seem simply a little seedy for the prices, and you're permitted to move on to brighter, livelier surroundings.

DAY ONE: evening

DINNER

The bright lights of the contemporary big city beckon in the form of the stylized Moscow-hip decor of **Pravda 116** (116 Boylston Street; 617-482-7799; moderate). The chef finds a way to coax intense flavor from lean dishes, making Pravda a great choice for the figure-conscious. The secret lies in the wood-fired grill, and if you look carefully, you'll find you can order your whole meal, from appetizer to dessert, off the grill.

You won't need to rush your meal, as further entertainment doesn't begin to roll (let alone rock) until well after 10:00 P.M. So linger a while over drinks before wandering around through the back of the Pravda 116 into a really hot dance club where muscular young things carry on until all hours of the morn. If you'd prefer sitting for entertainment, the second show begins at 10:30 P.M. at **Nick's Comedy Stop** (cover varies; 100 Warrenton Street; 617-482-0930), just a few blocks away in the Theater District. Nick's is known for nurturing local talent as well as occasionally giving the stage over to performers that some critics consider to be avant-garde monologists. Love and laughter mix well. (Or, as the comedian said, "smile when you do that. . . .")

SEPTEMBER DAY TWO: morning

BREAKFAST

Your hotel sits in the midst of a business district, which means a shortage of places to enjoy a good weekend breakfast. Fortunately, the first-floor cafe offers a full, if conventional, selection of morning meals. Eating light is a pretty good idea, as most of the artists you visit will be setting out snacks.

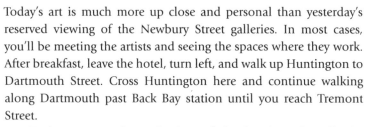

Today's art is much more up close and personal than yesterday's reserved viewing of the Newbury Street galleries. In most cases, you'll be meeting the artists and seeing the spaces where they work. After breakfast, leave the hotel, turn left, and walk up Huntington to Dartmouth Street. Cross Huntington here and continue walking along Dartmouth past Back Bay station until you reach Tremont Street.

You're now on the main drag of the **South End,** a district built for trendy Victorians that slid into disrepute and disrepair, only to enjoy substantial gentrification in recent years. As Ed Koch, one-time mayor of New York, observed, "The role of the artist . . . is to make a neighborhood so desirable that artists can't afford to live there anymore." That hasn't quite happened yet in the South End, but the area is brightening almost daily. It's a great area for dining and has an eclectic and interesting street life as well as the largest concentration of the city's gay and lesbian communities. As you visit the studios, you also get to see the neighborhood.

A good place to begin your South End Open Studios tour is at the **Boston Center for the Arts** (539 Tremont Street; 617–426–5000), an institution that claims the largest concentration of artists in New England. The BCA, which includes three theaters, a gallery, and a restaurant beneath its roof, also provides studio space for visual artists in a former organ-factory building. You'll see prints of all types, paintings, photography, and sculpture in this haven of small and (occasionally) large studio spaces. While you're at the BCA, stop in at the **Mills Gallery,** which has built a well-deserved reputation for high-quality exhibitions. You can also pick up a map to lead you to other studios in the neighborhood.

SEPTEMBER DAY TWO: afternoon

LUNCH

As you wander from studio to studio, take advantage of the South End's affinity for weekend brunch and have a midday meal at **On the Park** (315 Shawmut Avenue; 617–426–0862). Many neighborhood residents consider this very cozy little spot at the corner of Union Park Street to be *the* place for brunch. Perhaps you'd like to try a roasted vegetable and feta omelet along with some butterscotch scones, sesame bagels, or raspberry walnut muffins.

You reach On the Park by following Union Park Street. The green oval for which the street is named is typical of the South End—a collection of town houses centered on a small green. It's an English approach to building a neighborhood, a form you see over and over in the United Kingdom but rarely in the United States. Consider how different the feeling is from the boulevards of Back Bay where you were walking yesterday. (*That* street plan was borrowed from the French.) You may wish to explore some of these side streets just to look at the architecture and the colorful pocket gardens that enliven the urban environment. The organization of dwellings around a common space helps create a real sense of community.

Before you call it a day, stop for a café au lait and a pastry at the wonderfully named **Garden of Eden** (571 Tremont Street; 617–247–8377), one of several good cafes along Tremont Street near the BCA.

FOR MORE ROMANCE IN SEPTEMBER

If your schedule allows you to spend another night in town, plan to have dinner in the South End at **Icarus** (3 Appleton Street; 617–426–1790; moderate to expensive), a dynamic New American spot voted the most romantic restaurant in the neighborhood by readers of the *South End News*. Or try **Hamersley's Bistro** (533 Tremont Street; 617–423–2700; expensive) within the BCA complex. The restaurant's rent payments help to upgrade the studios at the BCA. Between the teal carpet and wainscoting and walls the rich color of egg-lemon soup, Hamersley's looks good enough to eat—and it is, with distinctive American takes on French provincial bistro dining. Consider this exercise in culinary artistry: a brace of quail served with polenta, grilled corn, asparagus, and white truffle oil. . . .

Did something catch your eye at one of the BCA theaters? Ranging from about forty to about 140 seats, the three intimate spaces are among the best places in the city to see theater, dance, and performance art by fresh faces. They are also tops for work that pushes the limits of form and subject matter. Call the box office at (617) 426-2787.

Take a break for Latin dancing on Friday nights (only) at **El Bembé** at the Jorge Hernandez Cultural Center (85 West Newton Street; 877-302-1707). Salsa dance lessons begin at 9:00 P.M. and live music follows for dancing into the small hours. Sneakers and jeans are not permitted. The $14 admission includes valet parking (useful in the South End), dance lessons, Hispano-Caribbean appetizers, and a night of dancing to Caribbean beats.

OCTOBER DAY TWO: morning

Following a light breakfast in the first-floor cafe, walk over to the Green Line T station right in front of the Boston Public Library on Boylston Street. Take any inbound train to Park Street, then change to the Red Line (either Ashmont or Braintree) for two stops to **South Station,** itself a work of art.

Dedicated on New Year's Eve 1898, South Station was the busiest passenger station in America during the heyday of rail transport. At present it still bustles with passengers on commuter trains from the south, Amtrak's Northeast Corridor trains, and the T's Red Line. A 1989 renovation recaptured the building's Neoclassical Revival splendor so successfully that area office workers join travelers here to shop and grab a bite to eat from a variety of food vendors in the large, bright waiting area. If you didn't eat earlier, this is as good a place as any in the city to have a casual breakfast at one of the round cafe tables.

Your chief destination is the **Fort Point Arts Community,** but a few blocks away. Exit South Station on the Summer Street side and head toward the bridge, taking the stairs on the left once you've crossed the Fort Point Channel. Walk up Congress Street to A Street. This warehouse district along the Fort Point Channel has been colonized by artists seeking large working spaces, freight elevators, and cheap rents. Even so, Fort Point remains much more an industrial district than the South End. But during the third weekend in October, more than one hundred artists in twenty-three buildings open their studios to visitors.

This area is a classic example of artists making a neighborhood desirable. Barred by zoning regulations from living in their warehouse studios, a group of artists banded together in the 1980s and, in a show of strength, managed to purchase, rehabilitate, and rezone the building at **249 A Street** and, more recently, 300 Summer Street. We suggest starting at 249 A Street, the original artist-owned live-and-work space, where you can pick up a guide to other studios on the tour. With a limited number of elevators, we find it easiest to take one to the top floor and work our way down. Though you've come to see the art, we have to admit that much of the attraction is to see how artists have chosen to design and decorate their living spaces.

You'll also find a large concentration of artists at **300 Summer Street**. You reach the front door by climbing the iron stairs beneath the overpass. This building also houses a gallery featuring the work of Fort Point Artists and an adjacent lunch spot, **Café 300** (300 Summer Street; 617–426–0695; no credit cards). This smart, innovative cafe is dedicated to the proposition that even poor artists should eat well, with entrees in the $5.00–$8.00 range. Look for such savories as a roast pork sandwich with eggplant and vinegar peppers or a mussel stew with red potatoes, cream, and saffron.

When you've finished touring the studios, stop by at the exhibition and performance space of 288–300 A Street, a delightfully bizarre spot known as **The Revolving Museum** (617–439–8617). This gallery is open Tuesday through Friday from noon to 6:00 P.M. and is known for being unpredictable. There's always a somewhat funky, impromptu quality about exhibitions, but they're guaranteed to amuse, outrage, and stimulate. There's also a small gallery of rotating exhibitions by Fort Point artists in the basement of 300 Summer Street, across from Café 300.

When you're done on this side of Fort Point Channel, brave the far shore by walking back to South Station and crossing Atlantic Avenue at the Essex Avenue light. This small area, orphaned by the highway interchanges that surround it, is known as the **Leather District** and is attracting a growing number of artists and galleries to its handsome industrial buildings. You can wrap up your art-viewing day at **Les Zygomates Bistro & Wine Bar** (129 South Street; 617-542-5108; moderate). More akin to Paris's bourgeois Marais district than to the bohemian Left Bank, Les Zyg (as its habitues call it) nonetheless conjures up the image of intense men and women with pigment embedded beneath their fingernails having a glass of *vin ordinaire* after a grueling day wrestling with muse and canvas. The wine bar side offers more than thirty wines by the glass. The "zygomates," by the way, are the muscles involved in the act of smiling—and they get a workout here.

The best wine choices from the truly select list are, alas, only by the bottle. They change all the time, depending on what the owners encounter on their frequent trips to France. So settle in for a hearty French bistro meal at American prices. Since you're spending a romantic weekend, start with cold oysters on the half shell. Then try the roasted rabbit marinated with white wine and whole grain mustard. Before you're seated, let them know you plan to stay for the jazz combo that plays later in the evening. Diners get the prime seats, and you'll get the chance to investigate some more of the extended wine list.

FOR MORE ROMANCE IN OCTOBER

One of the city's most avant-garde performance arts groups also makes its home in the Fort Point neighborhood. Call **Mobius Art Space** (354 Congress Street; 617-542-7416) to see what they might be presenting.

FOR EVEN MORE ROMANCE

Greater Boston's other major studio building—**Brickbottom Artists Studios** in Somerville—holds its open studios the weekend before Thanksgiving. You could start planning a return trip by calling (617) 776-3333 to confirm the dates for open studios or (617) 776-3410 for driving directions.

Occasions

Anniversary Recharge

THIS WEEKEND IS DESIGNED to celebrate a special event in your life together—a moment so important that you want to mark the occasion with an air of ceremony and formality. It could be the day you met, the day you decided to merge your households, even the day you paid off the house. In memory of the best of times, you want to create another occasion to remember by treating yourselves to attentive service, sybaritic pleasures, and every conceivable comfort. Add the restorative power of spa treatments, and you'll be set to charge forward together to the next milestone.

PRACTICAL NOTES: Almost every pleasure on this trip is in great demand, so be sure to book all of them as far as possible in advance. Biba serves brunch only on Sunday, so this trip works best as a Saturday–Sunday combination.

DAY ONE: morning

Your adventure begins with precisely the service you knew was possible but have perhaps never quite experienced—all in a style to which you would like to become accustomed. When the gentleman in the deep brown, modernistic uniform greets you (and whisks away your vehicle for safekeeping) and the similarly attired bellhop masterfully takes charge of your luggage, you'll realize you have entered a world where your needs will simply (and swiftly) be taken

129

$\mathcal{R}$om**ance**
AT A GLANCE

♦ Experience the dazzling contemporary elegance of Boston's luxury boutique hotel, **XV Beacon** (15 Beacon Street; 617–670–1500 or 877–XV–BEACON) at the pinnacle of Beacon Hill.

♦ Pamper yourselves with more than four hours of spa treatments at **Bella Santé,** The Spa on Newbury (38 Newbury Street; 617–424–9930). Pull out all the stops with the "Royal Treatment" for her "Fit for a King" for him.

♦ Revel in the sensual pleasures of the table, as crafted by celebrated chef Robert Fathman, at **The Federalist** (XV Beacon, 15 Beacon Street; 617–670–1500).

♦ Enjoy a bold and brilliant brunch at **Biba** (272 Boylston Street; 617–426–7878) in the care of one of America's leading chefs, Lydia Shire.

♦ Feel like royalty-for-a-day on a sightseeing tour of **Back Bay** or **Beacon Hill.** You can sit back in plush and cozy seats as your carriage horse prances through town.

care of. Enter the Beaux Arts structure in the rarified heights of Beacon Hill wealth and power, and you will suddenly discover Boston's first twenty-first century hotel, dazzling with its crisp minimalism.

In all fairness, **XV Beacon** (15 Beacon Street; 617–670–1500 or 877–XV–BEACON; double room rates beginning at $295 on weekends; $395 on weekdays) opened its doors on the last day of 1999 to usher in what was popularly called the beginning of the new millennium, but the style couldn't be more forward-looking. The $25-million renovation of the ten-story former office building kept the best of the original features—a facade of cast-iron, brick, and limestone; a striking white marble staircase; and the original cage elevators. But most of the interior bespeaks a design with minimalist lines and sumptuous textures: floor-to-ceiling mahogany paneling, impressive original contemporary paintings, and top-of-the-line furnishings that blend select antiques with the best contemporary pieces.

There are a maximum of seven rooms on each floor, which produces a feeling of intimacy, almost like a private residence. The rooms have an airy spaciousness (derived in part from the extremely high ceilings), yet nothing has been overlooked. Each room has a queen-size canopy bed, a gas fireplace, and surround-sound stereo.

There are also touches for business travelers that you needn't worry your pretty heads about (a work desk, high-speed Internet access, three phones, loaner cell phones with call-forwarding when someone rings your room, a combination color fax and copier, and more).

DAY ONE: afternoon

You will have made arrangements in advance for treatments today at **Bella Santé,** The Spa on Newbury (38 Newbury Street; 617–424–9930), a full-service spa and beauty treatment center just above the jeweler Cartier. Treatments begin with a simple fifty-minute massage ($80) and continue into the esoteric wonders of mud, acupuncture, and herbal and stone treatments derived from Asian origins. We suggest going for the gold to achieve complete and absolute physical recharge. The five-hour "Royal Treatment" for women ($377) includes a deluxe facial, an eighty-minute massage, body skin treatments, and manicure and pedicure. The comparable men's package, "Fit for a King" ($322), skips the body treatment and features a facial tailored to the special needs of a man's skin. One thing we adore about Bella Santé is that patrons must switch off cell phones, pagers, and other annoying devices. Make sure you arrive at least fifteen minutes early to change and get in the mood. Treatments *always* begin at their scheduled time.

So that means you should leave some extra time as you stroll over (or have yourselves dropped off by XV Beacon's complimentary Mercedes town car) to pay a visit to **Shreve Crump & Low** (330 Boylston Street; 617–267–9100), jeweler to the well-heeled Bostonians long before there were robber barons. Have you considered matching rings to mark your special occasion? Perhaps matching gold watches? Well, it doesn't hurt to look . . .

LUNCH

When you made your reservation for the spa treatments they asked if you would like a light lunch included with the packages. You, of course, said, "Yes, thank you. That would be nice." It will definitely be light, but you'll have ample opportunity to indulge your appetites later on.

Engaging 21ST Century Style

Noted Boston interior designer Celeste Cooper created individualized decor for every room at XV Beacon, working with her signature palette of taupe, cream, and espresso. To see more of the shrouded chairs, the contrasting stainless steel and rich wood, the luxurious yet practical fabrics, visit the upscale home design store on the other side of Boston Common, **Repertoire** (114 Boylston Street; 617–426–3865). Not only can you apprise, appreciate, and appraise the bedroom and living room furniture with which you've already grown somewhat familiar, but you can also see how Cooper's design sensibility informs her selections to address the aesthetic challenges of kitchen and bath.

DAY ONE: evening

After you have been knuckled, kneaded, buffed, and fluffed, you'll want to stroll back to your room agleam with your rejuvenation to take advantage of feeling so good—and to let all the world see it. You have, of course, arranged with the in-house florist to prepare a stunning arrangement of exotic flowers that will be waiting for you when you arrive. Change out of your street clothes into the soft robes and enjoy some time in front of your fireplace, perhaps popping the cork on the bottle of Krug champagne in the room bar as a relaxing aperitif. You don't have to be in a rush to dress for dinner, as you're not going far.

DINNER

The Federalist (XV Beacon, 15 Beacon Street; 617–670–1500; expensive) is one of the most sought-after reservations in Boston, so be sure to request a table when you make your hotel reservations. What Bella Santé did for your exteriors, The Fed will do for your tastebuds—that is, indulge them with a surfeit of sensual pleasure. Chef Robert Fathman is one of the younger rising stars in the constellation of Boston's top chefs, and he's known for his ability to pull out all the stops with wonderfully complex, updated French cuisine. The owners named the restaurant not for the Boston co-creator of the Federalist papers, John Adams, but for his Virginia counterpart, the renowned international gourmet (and, incidentally, American president) Thomas Jefferson.

Tom would have approved, particularly of the wine list, which is dominated by old-growth Bordeaux and *grand cru* Burgundies, augmented by some of the gigantic Rhônes (Chateauneuf-du-Pape, for example) and the best of the modern Californians (Opus One, among others). He would likely have nodded enthusiastically at the dollops of caviar that garnish many plates (such a treat was even more prohibitively expensive in his day). In fact, we'd bet that Jefferson would have been so overwhelmed by the exquisite menu that he would have opted for the chef's tasting menu, which consists of eleven small courses. You ate an ascetic spa lunch, so go ahead and treat yourselves.

DAY TWO: morning

After that magical day and epicurean feast, you might just feel like sleeping in. Whoever wakes first can go to the Federalist bar downstairs to bring back coffee, and you can peel some of the fruit in your basket for a snack while you stretch and yawn. Plunk into the chairs in front of the fireplace and enjoy its hypnotizing flicker. If you feel the need to be virtuous after last night's excesses, you could head down to the basement for a workout together in the fitness room. Even if you're not feeling virtuous, a little exercise might help you recapture your appetites.

BRUNCH

You'll need them to tackle the Sunday brunch at **Biba** (272 Boylston Street; 617–426–7878; moderate for brunch or lunch, expensive for dinner), where chef-owner Lydia Shire makes every meal an adventure. Shire is the queen bee of the Boston culinary scene, having directly or indirectly trained most of the city's best-known chefs. Her own cooking style is bold, and the decor at Biba matches the assertiveness of Lydia's menu, which she changes whenever she feels like it. Look for things you will recognize prepared in ways you never considered—eggs Benedict laced with pepper, buckwheat pancakes, Lydia's own chorizo sausage. Love is a matter of trust. Lydia Shire loves food and loves cooking. Keep an open mind and you will have a brunch as memorable as the occasion you're celebrating.

As a highlight for your afternoon, we suggest that you engage the services of **Elegant Touch Carriage Corp.** (800–497–4350) for a tour of Back Bay or Beacon Hill in a horse-drawn carriage. Ask your concierge to call ahead to make a reservation. Like as not, your elegant white carriage will be drawn by a genial giant bay gelding. An hour of touring, complete with champagne, is $100.

For More Romance

If you're extremely lucky (Saturday reservations are *very* hard to get) you could swap your Federalist dinner for a night of dining and dancing. From 1933 to 1946, **The Ritz Roof** restaurant operated on the seventeenth floor of the Ritz-Carlton, (15 Arlington Street; 617–536–5700). Guests dined and danced under the stars while musicians such as Benny Goodman, Tommy Dorsey, and Artie Duchin performed in an elegant half-shell bandstand. Alas, a 1946 hurricane destroyed the restaurant, leaving the Ritz Roof as a legend that only a dwindling number of lucky souls had experienced. But in 1993, The Ritz revived the elegant tradition of dining and dancing under the stars, at least from Memorial Day to Labor Day on weekend evenings. The spirit of the 1930s and 40s has been revived with the seven-piece Ritz-Carlton Orchestra performing classic melodies of the Big Band swing era. Dine on a four-course meal, selecting from the grill menu, and then plan to dance the night away under the stars. The package is $85 each. On rare occasions, some people go home early, so you might be able to go just for the dancing ($20 each) if you call the restaurant that evening around 9:30 P.M. (In 2002, the Ritz closes for renovations.)

Shop the art galleries of **Newbury Street** (see "the Artist's Touch: September Weekend) or stroll and shop on Charles Street (see "When Harry Met Sally [on Beacon Hill]").

The Right Foot
FIRST NIGHT

HE CUSP OF THE YEAR is a time to tally the good times of the year past and to plan for even better in the year to come. In their heyday, the Romans stopped everything for a multi-day party on the theory that the past deserved a send-off and the future a hearty welcome. (It also made their calendar come out even.) Two millennia later we've trimmed the party down to one night—but, oh, what a night! Before you indulge in a bottle of champagne and a great hotel room, try joining the entire city of Boston in appreciation of the old and anticipation of the new.

From its early days on the Boston Common, First Night has grown into the largest New Year's Eve party in the United States and Canada. With the stunning winter city as a backdrop, First Night showcases about 1,000 performers and artists and attracts more than 1.5 million participants. The extravaganza has worked so well that more than 130 other cities have copied it. But Boston's First Night remains first and—we think—best. You'll spend some time on the city streets and in concert halls, joining the revelry and excitement. Then you can withdraw to your private window to watch the fireworks burst over the harbor and usher in the new year in style.

PRACTICAL NOTES: Be sure to bring warm, comfortable clothes and shoes or boots. Bring a bottle of champagne to leave chilling in your room while you partake of the festivities. *The Boston Globe Calendar* published the Thursday before New Year's Eve has a full list of activities and a map. First Night buttons, which give you access to indoor events, are for sale throughout the city for about $15.

◆ Perch in a harbor view room at **Harborside Hyatt Conference Center & Hotel** *(101 Harborside Drive; 617–568–1234 or 800–233–1234), with stunning views of Boston's inner harbor backed by the city skyline.*

◆ *Join Bostonians (and other visitors to the Hub) in the explosive revelry of the world's original **First Night** celebrations to welcome in the New Year.*

◆ *Asian tradition dictates that a noodle dinner on the eve of the New Year guarantees long life and prosperity. Enjoy yours in delicious Vietnamese soup at **Pho Pasteur** (8 Kneeland Street; 617–451–0247).*

◆ *Cozy up in your bathrobes and press your noses to the glass of your window as you watch the **First Night fireworks** burst in front of you over Boston Harbor.*

◆ *Start the year on a harmonious note by attending a **First Day concert** performed by Boston Baroque.*

DAY ONE: afternoon

You'll want to check into your room at the **Harborside Hyatt Conference Center & Hotel** (101 Harborside Drive; 617–568–1234 or 800–233–1234; $179–$315; special packages available) by early afternoon. When making your reservation, specify an odd-numbered room on as high a floor as possible, as these rooms provide an extraordinary view of the inner harbor with downtown Boston as a backdrop. That little fact becomes very important this evening. A fourteen-story, 270-room airport business hotel might seem a strange choice for a celebratory getaway, but the Harborside has the feel of a luxury ocean liner, an impression enhanced by the shipboard motif in window shapes, curved trim, and other details. And downtown is only a seven-minute water-shuttle ride away.

After you've settled in—and once you can tear yourselves away from the view—spend some time studying the **First Night** schedule to choose among the various concerts, theater presentations, poetry readings, exhibitions, and other events. The choices can seem overwhelming, so try to settle on your preferred options in advance. We find that the best way to enjoy the full flush of First Night is to spend a few hours on the streets, caught up in the throng of people and activities and enjoying outdoor events and displays. We select only a few indoor performances, which generally last thirty to forty-five minutes. Sometimes, we even just elect one space and sample from the succession of activities happening there. Since seating (and standing room) is solely on a first-come, first-served basis, have some backup choices.

Truth be told, you could wander through the streets for serendipitous encounters with performances and still have a great time because everyone around you is in high spirits. This upbeat mood makes First Night a good time to try something you've never experienced—a chamber music performance if you're country and western fans, a Japanese court dance if you like Broadway chorus lines, or a poetry slam if your literary tastes usually run to Stephen King.

Children's events begin at 1:00 P.M., but the real kickoff to the festivities is the **Grand Procession,** which begins at 5:30 P.M. from the Hynes Convention Center and proceeds up Boylston Street, turns onto Charles Street, and concludes at the corner of Charles and Beacon about an hour later. This colorful and festive procession combines the imagination of Mardi Gras with the fervor of Independence Day as costumed and masked people and puppets weave in and around bands as the entire menagerie progresses from one end of Back Bay to the other.

You should head over to the city by mid-afternoon. Fortunately for you, the water shuttle is just outside the hotel door. For $10.00, you whisk across the harbor, Boston looming ever larger, until you're presented at Rowes Wharf. Before you head up to the main activities, walk over a wharf to see the ice sculpture in front of the New England Aquarium. Then double-back on Atlantic Avenue for a few blocks to South Station to hop the subway's Red Line—two stops to Park Street (the Boston Common), where you can exit or switch to the Green Line for four stops to Hynes/Auditorium (the upper end of Back Bay). Most of the First Night activities take place between those two stops.

Unless you're in a big hurry, get off the T at Park Street so you can marvel at the ice sculptures in the **Boston Common,** then walk down Boylston Street to see the most elaborate ones of all in Copley Square. Many are works in progress, so if you keep passing by as the day wears on, you'll get to see a form emerge from the white ice. The Common almost always features a variety of activities, including some to get even the most retiring passersby involved. Stop to add your resolutions to a list containing the intentions of thousands of others.

With more than a million people out on the streets, there will be a crowd probably wherever you go. But for the procession, the route seems to be *most* crowded near the beginning. We like to watch from the corner of Boylston and Charles for an optimum view as the marchers make the turn for the home stretch along Charles to Beacon. By this point virtually all of the marchers are euphoric; just watch out for bandit kissers. (The best protection is a lingering embrace of each other.)

DAY ONE: evening

DINNER

Once the procession has passed, hotfoot it over to **Pho Pasteur** (8 Kneeland Street; 617–451–0247) to get in line for a table. Asian traditions suggest eating soba noodles on the eve of a new year as a guarantee of long life. Your noodles needn't be buckwheat, since this Vietnamese noodle soup restaurant offers a wide-ranging menu that includes many types of noodles. And the price is right: dinner for two around $25.

Most of the performances geared for adults take place in the evening. You'll want to stroll along Newbury Street, where local dancers and choreographers create special works to perform in lighted store windows. If you're dance aficionados of the spectator variety, make your way to the Boston Ballet Building on Clarendon Street in the South End, where a variety of local companies perform in the Ballet's studios. If you're dance fans of the participant persuasion, check out the Hynes Convention Center on Boylston Street, where you might find options in the exhibit halls that range from country line dancing to ballroom dancing to shaking to the strains of oldies rock.

Boston's beautiful churches are often venues for classical concerts that take advantage of their magnificent organs. (Boston was a center for organ manufacturing in the last century.) For example, recent First Nights have included organ recitals by the American

Guild of Organists at Trinity Church (Copley Square) and works for tympani and organ at Old South Church (Boylston Street at Copley Square).

When you've had enough and it's time to be alone together (say, around 10:30 or so), head back to your hotel. The water shuttle stops at 8:00 P.M. in winter, so take the subway—the Green Line to Government Center, then the Blue Line to the airport. When you arrive, call the Harborside (617–568–1234), and they'll send a van to pick you up.

The idea is to settle in with your harbor-front view and your cold champagne in time to watch the New Year's Eve countdown on the Custom House Tower. (If you're in doubt about which tower this is, see the photographs of the Boston skyline on the mezzanine level. The Custom House is the only tower in the 1950s photo, and you can locate it—now dwarfed—in the same spot in the 1993 shot.) When midnight comes, the fireworks display begins over Boston Harbor from a barge anchored off Long Wharf. Times Square, eat your heart out!

Three Good Resolutions

for the Year to Come

1. Try something together that neither of you has ever done.

2. Be a sport and try an activity that your mate loves.

3. Come back to Boston in the spring, summer, and fall (see other chapters).

DAY TWO: morning

BREAKFAST or LUNCH

It's a new year now, so start it off right: Sleep late. Then enjoy a pot of coffee (every room has a coffeemaker and coffee) in your room, followed by a brisk walk along the ¾-mile harborside path just outside the hotel. Doesn't that feel good? Then order a hearty breakfast at the **Harborside Grill**, a very pleasant restaurant that makes the best of the hotel's great views. Maybe a garden omelet or crepes with strawberries entices you? On Sunday the hotel features a buffet breakfast. Ask if it's being served on New Year's Day. If it's already lunchtime, you can opt instead for sandwiches or one of the light entrees from the "cuisine naturelle" menu—perhaps the couscous with tomato and asparagus.

DAY TWO: afternoon

Bostonians have a number of New Year's Day traditions, one of which is to attend the annual **First Day concert** presented by the Grammy-nominated Boston Baroque orchestra at 3:00 P.M. at Sanders Theatre in Cambridge. For information, call Boston Baroque at (617) 484–9200. For tickets, call the Harvard box office at (617) 496–2222. Baroque music is characterized by order, ornament, and clarity—sort of like true love.

FOR MORE ROMANCE

Instead of the concert, you can join the annual First Day hikes at **Blue Hills Reservation** (617–698–1802). Meet at noon at the Houghtons Pond parking lot on Hillside Street in Milton, where chowder and beverages are served around a bonfire before the hikes begin at 1:00 P.M. Choose from up to six ranger-led hikes ranging from one hour to more than two hours. Or, if you'd rather set off alone, it's about a forty-five-minute walk around Houghtons Pond. From Boston take the Southeast Expressway, veering south on the combined I–93, I–95, and Route 128 to Exit 3 (Houghtons Pond). As you come off the ramp, turn right and continue 0.6 mile to a stop sign. Turn right onto Hillside Street.

Hearts and Flowers

A Celebration of Spring

JUST WHEN WINTER SEEMS AS IF it will never end, the Massachusetts Horticultural Society bestows a magnanimous gift of hope and beauty on the region by sponsoring the New England Spring Flower Show. This celebration of rebirth of the natural world is a great opportunity for the two of you to shake off the doldrums of winter and look ahead to a fresh world where beauty is magically commonplace. On a less philosophical note, it's also a great chance to get away and do some planning of how you might brighten your own home inside and out.

PRACTICAL NOTES: The New England Spring Flower Show is held in mid-March. Contact the Massachusetts Horticultural Society at (617) 536–9280 for more information and exact dates. You'll enjoy the show most if you make advance drawings of your home landscape, complete with notations on levels of sun and shade. If possible, follow this itinerary on weekdays to avoid the decidedly unromantic crush that descends on the show on weekends. A car is necessary for this itinerary.

DAY ONE: morning/afternoon

See if you can check in early at the **Doubletree Guest Suites** (400 Soldiers Field Road; 617–783–0090 or 800–222–8733; $190–$260), which perches high above the Charles River at the Cambridge exit from the Massachusetts Turnpike—speedily convenient to both downtown Boston and Cambridge. The prime views are either of downtown or of the Charles River. This is principally a business

◆ *For comfort and convenience, stay at the* **Doubletree Guest Suites** *(400 Soldiers Field Road; 617–783–0090 or 800–222–8733).*

◆ *Luxuriate in an early taste of spring and revel in the beauty of nature at the* **New England Spring Flower Show** *(Bayside Expo Center; 617–536–9380), one of America's oldest and largest flower exhibitions.*

◆ *Dine on the boathouse grill cuisine of* **Scullers** *(400 Soldiers Field Road; 617–783–0090) and hold onto your table for an evening of contemporary jazz.*

◆ *Step into a Venetian-style palace to view Boston's best year-round flower display: the courtyard at the* **Isabella Stewart Gardner Museum** *(280 The Fenway; 617–566–1401).*

◆ *Visit the historic* **Lyman Estate Greenhouses** *(185 Lyman Street, Waltham; (781–893–7232) to wander indoors among blooming bougainvillea, orchids, and a few late camellias.*

hotel; suites have a separate sitting area that most business types use as an office on the road, but which also makes a good spot for spreading out your home landscape plans. The hotel also provides frequent shuttle service to points in downtown and corporate Boston and Cambridge, should you decide to prolong your stay for more sightseeing from another itinerary.

Once you're checked in, get on the Turnpike across the street and follow the signs toward Boston, exiting southbound on the Southeast Expressway (I–93 south). Take exit 15 from the expressway, make a left at the end of the ramp, and follow the signs less than a mile to the **Bayside Expo Center.** This facility plays host to the **New England Spring Flower Show,** which has become so large that no other center in the region can accommodate it. The Massachusetts Horticultural Society has sponsored the show for more than 125 years, making it the oldest annual flower exhibition in the United States and the third largest in the world. The organizers say that the "New England Spring Flower Show is a social celebration of the beauty, utility, necessity, and glory of the plant world." And it's done in outstanding style. Prepare to be overwhelmed with five and a half acres of exhibits and competitions and a full schedule of lectures, demonstrations, and other activities.

With such daunting offerings, you will want to check the day's schedule first to see what lectures or demonstrations are taking place and plan your visit accordingly. Among the offerings will be such presentations as "Designing Small Spaces and Courtyards," "Designing with Herbs and Vegetables," "Beautiful Easy Flowers," "Perennial Garden Design," "Water and Tub Gardening," "Orchids for the Home," "Growing Your Own Dried Flowers," and "The Old-Fashioned American Garden."

With your plan of assault in place, you can begin to explore the exhibits. The Flower Show is a showplace for New England nurseries, landscape designers, botanical gardens, garden clubs, and regional chapters of national and international societies developed to promote particular types of plants (rhododendrons, African violets, hostas, bromeliads, orchids, and many others). In 1929, the Flower Show began using mocked-up house fronts as an integral part of garden settings. This proved so popular that it remains an important feature of the show. Designers go all out here, hoping to win one of the many awards given at the show. (A New England Flower Show ribbon is a powerful marketing tool because the standards are so high and the competition so fierce.) In recent years, the exhibition has included a large and popular section on interior design using plants and cut flowers to create a mood or enhance a setting. This is more than an opportunity to ooh and aah over spectacular displays—it's a chance to get new ideas for keeping your lives filled with excitement and grace through green and blooming plants.

LUNCH

The show is so all-encompassing that you won't want to leave to find a bite to eat, which, in any case, would take you several miles away. But Bayside Expo does have a cafeteria, and, since Flower Show patrons are assumed to have impeccable taste (well, it's true, isn't it?), the selections are a cut above the hot-dog-and-fries fare of many shows.

If the displays inspire you, move along to the Flower Show's marketplace, where you will be able to buy everything from fencing, unique garden antiques, garden furniture, and arbors to perennials

Saying It with Flowers

The language of flowers is long and complex, stretching back to the Greeks and Romans, who saw flowers in general as the goddess of spring personified and attached myths to specific flowers. But no era was so giddy over flowers as that of the Victorians, who developed an entire code of communication based on bouquets, nosegays, and even single blossoms. In 1879, a "Miss Corruthers" of Inverness, Scotland, literally wrote the book on floral symbolism that became the standard source in Britain and the United States to communicate many sentiments that the propriety of the times would not otherwise allow. Arbutus signaled "thee only do I love," while the carnation (especially red carnations) bespoke "pure and deep love." The daisy said "I will think about it," while the geranium announced "I prefer you." A hyacinth was the symbol of constancy, the purple lilac the sign of the first emotions of love, and the morning glory the sign of affection. Roses have a language of their own: red for love, white signifying silence, yellow meaning unfaithfulness. A yellow rose might be met with a bouquet of violets—a protest of faithfulness and constancy. The bright jonquil—so available this time of year—is a sign of desire.

and annuals, cacti, bulbs, hand-thrown pottery, dried-flower arrangements, herbs, and birdhouses. In most cases, you can arrange to have everything except the live plants shipped to your home address. Be careful buying blooming plants, as you'll have to warm the car before transporting them to avoid blossom drop.

Seeing all these floral possibilities in practice might leave you perplexed. Fortunately, the Horticultural Information Station is staffed by Massachusetts Horticultural Society Master Gardeners to answer your garden questions. They also provide free pH soil testing (assuming you brought a sample) and help diagnose plant problems (if you brought the troubled plant).

DAY ONE: evening

DINNER

Your hotel happens to feature an excellent seafood grill restaurant and one of the top jazz rooms in Greater Boston, **Scullers** (617–783–0090; moderate), which offers a dinner-show package that's hard to beat. For the price of concert tickets plus $28 each, you get dinner of chowder, soup or salad, a selection of entrees, dessert, and coffee. Ask for a window table in the softly elegant dining room so you can look out on the Charles River. The Scullers menu resembles a boathouse grill—plenty of delectable fish such as salmon steaks and skewered scallops, as well as herb-infused lamb.

Scullers diners also receive reserved seating for the second show in the jazz room, where mostly regional groups (the Mili Bermejo Quintet, for example) or new artists (such as Nestor Torres on jazz flute) play Tuesday through Thursday and nationally known performers (Eddie Palmieri, Shirley Horn, and the Artie Shaw Orchestra) headline on weekends.

DAY TWO: morning

BREAKFAST

When you finally arise, you'll discover a coffeepot in your suite to jump-start your nervous systems before heading downstairs to Scullers for a pleasant if conventional breakfast (spread your English muffins with some honey, the distillation of last year's flowers) to fortify you for more floral research. Scullers by day is a bright and gleaming place—maybe too bright if the show ended late last night. If so, ask for a table on the upper level out of the sun.

From your hotel, take Storrow Drive inbound to the exit for The Fenway and follow the signs—first to the right, then toward the left—at a large traffic circle. When you pass Emmanuel College on the right, you know you are getting close to the **Isabella Stewart Gardner Museum** (280 The Fenway; 617–566–1401; open Tuesday through Sunday 11:00 A.M. to 5:00 P.M.; adults $10; $11 Saturday and Sunday). Mrs. Gardner left a legacy of a wonderful art collection (see "The Painters' Passion: A Fine Arts Weekend"), but she also left behind what might be the city's best year-round green space, and certainly one of the most popular: the soaring four-story inner courtyard of her Venetian-style palazzo. Enamored as she was of Venetian architecture, Mrs. Gardner had the courtyard enclosed in glass so that light could filter down to the plants but they would be protected from the elements of Boston's cold winters. Amid the statuary and Italian tilework is a changing array of green and blooming plants. This time of year expect the air to be filled with the scent of jasmine, which will be in bloom along with azaleas and calla lilies. The museum employs a whole gardening staff just to keep up the courtyard and grounds. A full complement of greenhouses stands behind the palace.

LUNCH

Before departing on a foray to get ideas for your houseplant collection, treat yourselves to soup and salad in the **Gardner Café**. The cafe is right near the museum gift shop. A hand-painted silk scarf inspired by the flowers in the courtyard by Boston artist/designer Peggy Russell might make a perfect memento to tide you over 'til spring.

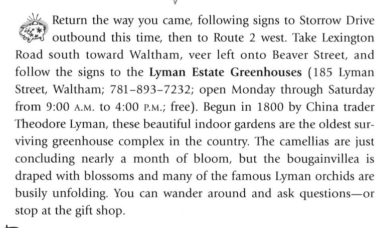

Return the way you came, following signs to Storrow Drive outbound this time, then to Route 2 west. Take Lexington Road south toward Waltham, veer left onto Beaver Street, and follow the signs to the **Lyman Estate Greenhouses** (185 Lyman Street, Waltham; 781–893–7232; open Monday through Saturday from 9:00 A.M. to 4:00 P.M.; free). Begun in 1800 by China trader Theodore Lyman, these beautiful indoor gardens are the oldest surviving greenhouse complex in the country. The camellias are just concluding nearly a month of bloom, but the bougainvillea is draped with blossoms and many of the famous Lyman orchids are busily unfolding. You can wander around and ask questions—or stop at the gift shop.

FOR MORE ROMANCE

There's no better place to research the art of growing things than at the **Massachusetts Horticultural Society Library**, located at the Society's headquarters in Horticultural Hall (300 Massachusetts Avenue; 617–536–9280). Within weeks of its founding in 1829, the Society launched its library, which has developed into the largest and finest horticultural collection in the country and one of the best in the world. Society members actually have borrowing privileges, but nonmembers are welcome to browse and use the resources. While you're there, take note of Horticultural Hall itself, a grandiose 1901 English Baroque building decorated with garlands and wreaths. One of the buildings that helped to establish the Fenway area as a cultural center, it is open Monday through Friday from 9:00 A.M. to 4:30 P.M.

You might want to check out the early signs of spring along Boston's famous green pathway, the Emerald Necklace (see "Budget Boston: Biking through the Parks"). Another of Boston's unique floral treasures is the collection of **Glass Flowers** at the Botanical Museum at Harvard University (see "In the Groves of Academe"). Handblown and shaped by Leopold and Rudolph Blaschka between 1887 and 1936, the 3,000 models of 850 plant species are extraordinary examples of the glassblower's art. Each species is illustrated with a scientifically precise life-size model as well as magnified parts.

The **Wellesley College Greenhouse** (Routes 16 and 135, Wellesley; 781–283–3074; open daily from 8:30 A.M. to 4:00 P.M.; free) is a little-known cluster of sixteen connected greenhouses, where climates can range from desert to tropical forest.

Echoes of Camelot

IRISH ROOTS OF AMERICAN ROYALTY

A WHOLE GENERATION OF COUPLES ONCE MODELED themselves after John Fitzgerald Kennedy and Jacqueline Bouvier Kennedy. When they entered the White House in 1961, America was launched on a thousand days of Camelot—a new golden age presided over by a couple who seemed to embody what the country wanted to be. In Boston, the inauguration of President Kennedy marked the apotheosis of everything Irish-American, for in no other place did the Irish so completely come to dominate local life than in Boston. This itinerary visits Kennedy's Boston roots, plumbs a bit of the enduring Irish presence in Boston, and concludes with a tour of Kennedy's legacy. Walk in the footsteps of Jack and Jackie in Boston and feel something of their grace and glamour as well as their humanity.

PRACTICAL NOTES: Although you could visit all these sites by public transportation, you'll find it much easier to get around with your own automobile. The John F. Kennedy National Historic Site is open early May through Columbus Day.

DAY ONE: afternoon

You'll relax in comfort and style at **A Cambridge House Bed & Breakfast Inn** (2218 Massachusetts Avenue, Cambridge; 617–491–6300 or 800–232–9989; double room rates $149–$279). This gracious urban inn sits in the strongly Irish neighborhood of North Cambridge, the home of former Speaker of the House, Thomas P. "Tip" O'Neill, one of Greater Boston's politicians in the grand Irish style. You might remember him for his pronouncement that "All

*R*oₘₐnᴄe
AT A GLANCE

◆ *Ease yourselves into the plush Victorian comforts of **A Cambridge House Bed & Breakfast Inn** (2218 Massachusetts Avenue, Cambridge; 617–491–6300 or 800–232–9989) in the North Cambridge neighborhood where Thomas P. "Tip" O'Neill said "All politics is local."*

◆ *Visit the modest Brookline home where the Kennedy clan lived in the days before they acquired wealth and power. You'll hear a recording of Rose Kennedy talking about the early days at the **John F. Kennedy Birthplace** (83 Beals Street, Brookline; 617–566–7937).*

◆ *Kick up your heels and settle in for contemporary Irish cuisine (and fine Irish malt brews on tap) at **Kinsale** (2 Center Plaza, Boston; 617–742–5577). The food rivals the best of the Irish pubs in Dublin and Belfast, and the music will carry you off to the Emerald Isle for the night.*

◆ *Revisit the power, glory, and sorrow of the days of Camelot by touring the moving exhibits of **The New Museum at the John F. Kennedy Library** (Columbia Point, Boston; 617–929–4523).*

politics is local." O'Neill's congressional seat was held by Joseph Kennedy, son of the former Attorney General Robert "Bobby" Kennedy and nephew of the late president.

This grand early twentieth century home is elegantly decorated in Waverly fabrics and wall coverings and filled with antiques and representative period furnishings. We suggest you ask for the sumptuous Isaac MacLean Room on the second floor in the front, where you'll recline on a queen-size canopy bed and enjoy the lavishly tiled working wood-burning fireplace and a sybaritic bathroom that features a luxurious sunken tub. The inn also provides free off-street parking—a great convenience that many Cambridge residents don't enjoy.

Plan to spend the afternoon at the **John F. Kennedy National Historic Site** (83 Beals Street, Brookline; 617–566–7937). From your B&B, proceed down Massachusetts Avenue through Harvard Square to JFK Street. Turn right and cross the bridge on North Harvard Street, continuing as it veers left to Franklin Street, which in turn becomes Harvard Street. After crossing Commonwealth Avenue, Beals Street will be the sixth street on the left.

In 1914 Joseph P. Kennedy purchased the nine-room Colonial Revival house at 83 Beals Street in anticipation of his marriage to Rose Fitzgerald. Joseph Kennedy had already begun his career in business and finance when he married Rose Fitzgerald, the daughter of John "Honey Fitz" Fitzgerald, one-time mayor of Boston and member of Congress.

When Rose and Joe returned from their wedding trip, they moved into the Beals Street house. Four of their nine children were born while they lived here, including John Fitzgerald Kennedy, who came into the world on May 29, 1917, in the master bedroom on the second floor. The growing family moved to a larger house in 1921. In 1966, the family repurchased the Beals Street home as a memorial to the late president, and Rose Kennedy supervised the restoration and refurnishing of the home to the way it appeared in 1917. A recording of Rose Kennedy's reminiscences of life in the house is included as part of the tour. Calling the home "just right, beautiful, and comfortable," she recalls on the tape, "We were very happy here. . . . Although we did not know about the days ahead, we were enthusiastic and optimistic about the future."

Open April through October on Wednesday through Sunday, 10:00 A.M. to 4:30 P.M., the home is now a National Historic Site. Admission is $2.00. The U.S. Park Service provides a very good descriptive brochure, which also includes a walking tour of other sites of importance to the early years of the Kennedy family. They include the home at 51 Abbottsford Road, where the Kennedys moved when they outgrew the Beals Street home. Close by is St. Aidans Roman Catholic Church, where the children were baptized and John served as an altar boy. Also in the neighborhood is the Edward Devotion

Tapping the Power of Women

Tip O'Neill observes in his memoirs that John F. Kennedy was the first politician to actively court the votes of women: "Women had been active in politics before, but nobody paid them as much attention as Jack did. He had what we called a warm hand, and the women would melt when he looked into their eyes. He certainly knew how to charm the ladies, and he always made a point of appealing to what he called, correctly, 'womanpower, the untapped resource.'"

School, the first school attended by John and his older brother, Joseph, Jr.

On your way back to the inn you might want to stop off at **Irish Imports Limited** (1737 Massachusetts Avenue, Cambridge; 617–354–2511) to browse a bit. Open Monday through Saturday from 10:00 A.M. to 6:00 P.M., this shop on the Harvard Square side of Porter Square has been supplying fine Irish clothing and gift items for a quarter century. You'll see rugged handknits, cozy throws, and crisp linens as well as fine outerwear in wool, mohair, and cashmere. A shawl for milady? A fedora for milord? You'll also find a fine selection of Irish books—poetry, drama, fiction, history, and picture books—as well as contemporary and traditional Irish music. No harps, but they do carry tin whistles.

In any event, you'll want to be back at the inn in time to enjoy hors d'oeuvres and beverages laid out in front of the fireplace in the parlor from 5:30 to 7:30 P.M. The inn attracts many visitors from Europe (including, at one point, an English duke and duchess) as well as many scholars and others who are visiting Harvard University, so you will be certain to have some interesting conversation.

DAY ONE: evening

DINNER

One of the great advantages of your lodging is the ready access to the MBTA's Red Line public transit—especially useful for an evening of good food, fine beverages on tap, and more than a little music at **Kinsale** (2 Center Plaza, Boston; 617–742–5577; moderate). You can't get more Irish than a pub built in Ireland and shipped over, brick by brick, in seaborne containers. The easiest way to get to Kinsale is to take the T to the Park Street station, then walk past Park Street Church and the Old Granary Burying Ground along Tremont Street. Kinsale is a short distance down on the left on Tremont Street across from the head of Court Street.

If "Irish pub" conjures images of old codgers with briar pipes and a dreadful menu with fifty-seven kinds of potatoes, you'll be in for a pleasant surprise. Kinsale is Irish through and through—and as lively and modern as any fine pub in the heart of Dublin or Belfast. The old overcooked, oversalted, old-fashioned cuisine for which

Ireland was once justly maligned simply can't be found here. Instead, try such hearty dishes as stout-braised short ribs of beef or fresh salmon steaks brushed with an Irish whiskey glaze.

You can still get some suggestions of old-time authenticity, of course, with the colcannon that accompanies many meals (potatoes mashed with green cabbage). Die-hard Irish-Americans can even order the "Immigrant's Boiled Dinner," Kinsale's nod to corned beef and cabbage with baby carrots and boiled potatoes. To slake your thirst, Kinsale has Guinness on tap (of course) as well as a bevy of other ales, stouts, and porters.

Time your arrival so you can finish dinner before the live music begins (Wednesday and Thursday at 7:30 P.M., Saturday at 9:00 P.M., Sunday at noon). You can count on many a whoop and holler to rollicking contemporary Irish tunes.

DAY TWO: morning

BREAKFAST

Ellen Riley, your hostess at the B&B, lays out a full breakfast spread, alternating each day between sweet and savory dishes. Help yourselves and pull up some chairs—some of them from her great-grandfather's North Cambridge home—to enjoy your meal at one of the skirted tables in the front room, now designated the dining room. When you're done, take along a piece of fruit to enjoy later in the day.

Then check out and drive to **The New Museum at the John F. Kennedy Library** (617–929–4523), which sits in South Boston on the rocky peninsula of Columbia Point. The museum is open daily from 9:00 A.M. to 5:00 P.M., but before you go in, walk around the beautiful and dramatic nine-and-a-half-acre site. This windswept point jutting into Dorchester Bay is landscaped with pine trees, shrubs, and roses in a manner that hints at President Kennedy's Cape Cod compound. Kennedy's 26-foot sloop *Victura* sits cradled on the lawn, oriented toward the entrance to Boston Harbor.

The soaring architecture of the museum, a triumph of white concrete and glass designed by I. M. Pei and Partners, dominates the site. Head inside (admission is $8.00), and you will see how the museum takes full visual advantage of its position on a precipice, high above the water and looking out to the lonely sea through a 50-foot-high glass wall.

Perhaps understandably, the original 1979 museum exhibitions at the John F. Kennedy Library were essentially extended elegies to a fallen leader, displays that were unabashed in their hero worship and which depended heavily for their effect on the visitor's memory of the Kennedy years. The "New Museum" no longer assumes that visitors have personal memories of the Kennedy administration; instead, it presents the period as closely as possible with a real "you are there" sense of immediacy. Exhibits follow a chronological path through Kennedy's life, political career, and the challenges and triumphs of his brief presidency. Kennedy was the first modern political master at using the media to present his message and himself. The extensive film, newsreel, and television clips capture his charisma and his power—really one of the most effective and moving presentations of a personality we have ever witnessed.

In talking about the use of the late president's voice in twenty exhibits and in three theaters, his daughter Caroline (president of the Kennedy Library Foundation) explained that the purpose was to present JFK's ideas without interpretation or analysis. "Our objective was to have President Kennedy speak directly to the visitor and convey the optimism and vigor he represented to a world confronting a dangerous time."

Be prepared for strong emotions as you go through the museum, which, incidentally, devotes only one small exhibit area to the assassination. Wherever you stop (each area has film clips you might want to see), some of your fellow visitors might find themselves in inexplicable tears. This visit will take the better part of the day, so plan on enjoying the fruit you brought from breakfast to accompany a sandwich and soft drink from the Museum Café.

FOR MORE ROMANCE

For other sites associated with the Kennedy Family, see "The Snug North End" and "One if by Land: The Heart of Old Boston." If you have time, stop in Harvard Square. Kennedy graduated from Harvard University, living in room 32 in Weld Hall as a freshman and in room F-14 in Winthrop House as an upperclassman. The

Winthrop House room is now reserved for visitors to Harvard's John F. Kennedy School of Government on JFK Street next to JFK Park.

In his days as a Congressman, Kennedy often treated himself to lobster stew at the **Union Oyster House** (41 Union Street, Boston; 617–227–2750), and you might want to try this traditional dish prepared the way he liked it. His favorite spot—he would nail it down from noon to 5:00 P.M. on Sunday to read the papers—was Booth 18 on the second floor. Go ahead—have a waitress snap your picture here.

Take the section of the Harbor Walk from the JFK Library and sit on the benches under the Fathers Rest Pavilion. The stanchion here recapitulates the Brothers Grimm's version of the fairy tale called "The Fisherman and His Wife," the story of a talking flounder, a timid fisherman, and his overreaching wife. Its moral is to be satisfied with good fortune and not to ask for too much.

Laissez Les Bon Temps Rouler

Bastille Day in Boston

VEN EUROPEANS WILL TELL YOU that Boston is more European than any other city in America. Maybe it's the architecture. Maybe it's the attitude that we weren't born yesterday. Maybe it's our sense that we *do* have culture and we are proud of it. And maybe it's that we love to adopt European festivities and pretend that our Old World roots have sprung new green shoots. You can rediscover your *vrai amour* on the streets of Boston. Think of the city as a kissing cousin to Paris as you help mark the French *fête nationale*, Bastille Day, with a weekend of activities. You don't have to speak French to partake in the joie de vivre and celebrate life, liberty, and the pursuit of happiness *à la français*.

PRACTICAL NOTES: Bastille Day, July 14, celebrates French independence by marking the storming of the Bastille at the beginning of the French Revolution. In Boston, it's usually celebrated with activities on the Friday, Saturday, and Sunday nearest to that date. Confirm arrangements with The French Library and Cultural Center (617–266–4351; tickets for Street Dance Festival are $20) and The Hotel Meridien (617–451–1900; reservations for Bal Musette and Sunday brunch are required).

DAY ONE: afternoon

Your lodging choice is obvious: **The Hotel Meridien** (250 Franklin Street; 617–451–1900 or 800–543–4300; $435–$695; weekend packages begin at $229). You might be surprised to find this elegant

Romance
AT A GLANCE

♦ Reside in European comfort at **The Hotel Meridien,** Boston's French hotel (250 Franklin Street, Boston; 617–451–1900 or 800–543–4300). There's good reason that the hotel in this graceful stone building is a member of Leading Hotels of the World.

♦ Join the Bastille Day revelers at the **Back Bay block party** sponsored by the French Library and Cultural Center (53 Marlborough Street, Boston; 617–266–4351).

♦ Sample the lesser-known delights of Alsace with a light and playful lunch at **Sandrine's Bistro** (8 Holyoke Street, Cambridge; 617–497–5300).

♦ Select your special parfum d'amour from hundreds of choices at **Colonial Drug** (49 Brattle Street, Cambridge; 617–864–2222).

♦ Browse among French books and magazines in Harvard Square at **Schoenhof's** (76A Mount Auburn Street, Cambridge; 617–547–8855) and **Out of Town News** (Zero Harvard Square; no phone). Imagine posing for the French edition of Vogue in an article on lovers.

♦ Continue the celebration with dinner and dancing at **Bal Musette** in the gracious ballroom of The Meridien.

♦ Have a final taste of French cuisine at Sunday brunch at the Gallic groaning tables of the **Cafe Fleuri** (617–451–1900) in The Meridien.

outpost of la belle France housed in Boston's former Federal Reserve Bank in the financial district. The national architectural landmark building, a 1922 Renaissance Revival granite and limestone structure modeled after the Palazzo della Cancelleria in Rome, was completely renovated in 1981 under the watchful direction of one of France's most exacting hoteliers. The result weds a gracious use of historic space and attention to detail to modern-day comforts and furnishings. As part of the renovation, a glass mansard roof was built to add three floors to the original six-story structure. As a result, nearly a third of the 326 guest rooms feature sloping glass windows that provide dramatic views of downtown Boston and the scenic Post Office Square. Don't worry: It's OK to treat yourselves like French aristocrats, even on Bastille Day.

If the weather is pleasant, plan to stroll from your hotel to the festivities in the Back Bay. You should break your walk at about the halfway point with a Dubonnet in the Terrace Bar of **Maison Robert** (45 School Street), a French restaurant that has been an important fixture on Boston's culinary scene for many years. (See "One if by Land.") You'll be sitting directly behind a statue of the first American ambassador to France, the Boston-born Ben Franklin.

DAY ONE: evening

Your destination, **The French Library and Cultural Center,** occupies two historic mansions in the Back Bay (53 Marlborough Street; 617–266–4351). The library was established after the Second World War to promote cultural relations between the United States and France. (They gave us Truffaut; we gave them Jerry Lewis. They provided Charles Boyer and Brigitte Bardot; we replied with EuroDisney.) At present, the French Library is the largest institution of its kind in New England, serving the culturally diverse Francophone and Francophile communities of Boston and New England with an impressive library of books and periodicals and a year-round schedule of programs ranging from French language lessons and cooking lessons to art and photography exhibitions and film screenings.

Since 1975, the French Library has thrown one of the two or three best parties of the year in honor of the French Revolution: the **Bastille Day Street Dance Festival.** The City of Boston cooperates by closing down Marlborough Street between Berkeley and Clarendon Streets. A fund-raising dinner inside the Library opens the festivities, but at 7:00 P.M. the block opens to partygoers with reservations. Trees and fixtures strung with lights all along the street transform this tony urban neighborhood into a *très française mise-en-scène* of sidewalk cafes and wine bars, where you will pick up snacks that serve as tonight's dinner. Street artists set up easels, and *les accordéonistes* stroll about, swinging with gusto into the chorus of "*Non, je ne regrette rien.*" As darkness sets in, the dance band gets going, and there is literally dancing in the streets until curfew rings in at 11:30 P.M.

When you return to your hotel, you might want to end the evening with a quiet nightcap at **The Julien Bar.** You'll see immediately why this room was named Boston's "Best Fancy Bar" by *Boston Magazine.* It served at one time as the reception room for the governors of the Federal Reserve Bank. Soak in the elegant detail of the carved doorways and the gilded coffered ceilings. Those murals on the paneled walls are by N. C. Wyeth.

DAY TWO: morning

Allow yourselves a casual morning. Perhaps check out the hotel's health club, which has a number of exercise machines. But you danced hard all night, so take it easy with a slow, stretching swim in the indoor pool (perhaps a languorous backstroke), or a whirlpool or sauna. Coffee, tea, and fruit are all available poolside. After all, you want to stay fit for another night of dancing.

How to Test Perfume

The knowledgeable staff at Colonial Drug advises the best way to test perfume. Using a blotter stick, dab no more than three scents, one on the inside of each wrist and a third on the inside of one elbow. Don't rub. Rubbing bruises the top notes of a scent, just as crushing a flower coarsens its perfume. Allow a full minute for the fruit alcohols to evaporate, then raise the sample spot a few inches below your nose and inhale. Keep in mind that perfume will evolve on your skin as the aromatic impression blends with your skin chemistry to create your individual signature fragrance.

When you leave your hotel, stroll around the Financial District. On a weekend, it's free of the usual bustle of office workers, so you can better appreciate the striking architecture in Art Deco style, which originated in France. No doubt you've already noticed the charming **Post Office Square Park**. This lively bit of greenery and frivolity is all the more admirable when you know that it was created on the site of a decrepit old parking garage. It's still used for parking, but the only evidence is the glass gazebos that serve as entries to a new seven-level underground parking facility. Other gazebos hold a cafe and a flower stand. You'll find benches aplenty for sitting, and you might even shift around for different views of the surrounding buildings or the charming plantings. The tall specimen trees are on loan from the Arnold Arboretum (see "Budget Boston: Biking through the Parks).

When you've soaked in enough ambience and you're ready to go, walk up Franklin Street to Downtown Crossing and take a Red Line subway train to Harvard Square in Cambridge.

DAY TWO: afternoon

LUNCH

Headed by the former executive chef of the Meridien, **Sandrine's** (8 Holyoke Street; 617–497–5300) is Harvard Square's very own Alsatian bistro, named for chef Raymond Ost's daughter. Sure, you can indulge in a choucroute (I adore you, my little cabbage) or a sausage like weisswurst, but Ost's specialty is a hearth-baked, unleavened bread topped with herbs, meats, and cheeses. It's called *flammeküche* (FLAM-uh-koo-shuh), and it's traditional to Alsace. Just don't let Ost hear you call it pizza.

This seems a weekend of surprising discoveries. Another is on the opposite side of the Square. **Colonial Drug** (49 Brattle Street; 617–864–2222) also bills itself as the specialist in hard-to-find fragrances. And it's true. You'll find more than 1,000 fragrances—from Arpège to Zibeline—at this Harvard Square *parfumerie*. Among them is the complete Jean Patou collection, created between 1925 and 1964 to mark special occasions in modern French life. Others are designated for specific stages of a relationship—like "Amour, Amour" for the moment of flirtation. Be sure to sample "Moment Suprême," a spicy and assertive scent that Patou claimed "elegantly combines the excitement of Waiting, the Temptation of every sense, the very Power of Desire, and the Pleasure of blissful moments." We're not exactly certain what M. Patou was talking about, but it certainly smells good. If the Patou scents captivate you but you can't choose, Colonial offers a sampler box of tiny bottles for $80. Also worth checking out is "Tabac blond," a scent created by Caron for Marlene Dietrich that combines elements of cured tobacco and leather. Its subtle and memorable scent belies its unfashionable origins; Colonial also sells "Derby," a similar Caron scent for men. If they suit your skin chemistry, you could have complementary scents.

Do you read French? Maybe just a little . . . ? Then by all means visit **Schoenhof's Foreign Books** (76A Mount Auburn Street; 617–547–8855). This bookseller, established in 1856, carries such a good line of foreign books that many of its customers order by fax from overseas. The French section holds a full line of classic and contemporary literature as well as books on tape and some of the hardbound great comic books for kids in the Tintin and Asterix the Gaul series. One of our favorite authors—who certainly knew all about the arts of love as well as more "lofty" subjects—is Colette, whose works cover an entire shelf here. On your way back to the subway station, stop at **Out of Town News** (Zero Harvard Square) for French newspapers (*Le Monde* or *Le Figaro*, depending on your politics) and great French magazines of style and fashion, like the French *Vogue* and *Elle*.

DAY TWO: evening

DINNER

The Hotel Meridien continues the Bastille Day celebrations tonight with the **Bal Musette,** a French dance with popular music ($39 per person). The brasserie-style restaurant, the **Café Fleuri,** situated beneath the soaring six-story glass atrium, serves as the locale for this French country-style buffet dinner accompanied by a cabaret singer and followed by dancing.

DAY THREE: morning

BRUNCH

As you have no doubt already concluded, the French consider the preparation of food to be an art form whose greatest expressions are Gallic. The buffet brunch ($39) at the Café Fleuri has been named "Best Sunday Brunch" by *Boston Magazine* ten times. Although the regular Sunday brunch has strayed from its French origins, on Bastille Day weekend the brunch features many French specialty items, and the room is filled with festive decorations. French jazz musicians play throughout the meal, and can-can dancers perform.

FOR MORE ROMANCE

For another, somewhat less luxurious hotel option in the same neighborhood as the Meridien, try the fifty-four-room **Harborside Inn of Boston** (185 State Street; 617–723–7500; $135–$200; suites $210–$330). This brick-and-granite beauty near Faneuil Hall features hardwood floors, oriental rugs, and Victorian-style furnishings.

Although positioned more as a B&B than a hotel, all rooms have queen-size beds, climate control, and telephone with voice mail.

See the wonderful collection of Impressionist and Post-impressionist paintings at the **Museum of Fine Arts** (see "The Painters' Passion: A Fine Arts Weekend").

During July, the Museum of Fine Arts and the Cultural Services of the French Embassy in Boston sponsor a **French Film Festival;** call 617–369–3770 for details.

Holiday Shopping in the Hub

THE PRAGMATIC ROMANTIC'S ANSWER to the stresses of the holiday season is to turn obligations into adventure. December can be a terrific time for the two of you to get away to Boston. Pull the plug on holiday hassles by settling in for a little luxury as you complete your shopping chores, remembering to select a special something for each other. At the same time, you can immerse yourselves in the holiday spirit with classic Christmas season music, dance, and theater.

PRACTICAL NOTES: Timing is everything. The holiday shopping season switches into high gear in Boston the day after Thanksgiving, but some of the performing arts adhere to a less comprehensive schedule. Double-check performance dates of those that interest you most.

DAY ONE: afternoon

It's beginning to look a lot like Christmas when you enter the broad lobby of the **Four Seasons Hotel** (200 Boylston Street; 617–338–4400 or 800–332–3442; $450–$625), where the interior lights and garlands echo those throughout the city. The Four Seasons is not only Boston's most easygoing luxury hotel, it also offers thoughtful packages available from Thanksgiving through the end of December. Key to all the packages are town car service to your shopping destination and a plate of holiday cookies at turn-

Romance AT A GLANCE

◆ Settle yourselves into easygoing luxury in the heart of the city at the **Four Seasons Hotel** (200 Boylston Street; 617-338-4400 or 800-332-3442) with a room overlooking the Public Garden.

◆ Snap up bargains at the original **Filene's Basement** at Downtown Crossing, then switch to the other end of the sliding scale as you seek a "perfect something" in the shops of Back Bay.

◆ Take afternoon tea by the fireplace (or at a window where you can see and be seen) at the **Bristol Lounge** (Four Seasons Hotel, 200 Boylston Street; 617-338-4400).

◆ Spice up the holidays with a dinner of innovative New Italian cuisine in the dramatically designed dining room at **Pignoli** (91 Park Plaza; 617-338-7500).

◆ Attend an evening performance of Langston Hughes' gospel song-play **Black Nativity** in historic Tremont Temple (88 Tremont Street; 617-442-8614).

◆ Celebrate the completion of shopping by dining in your hotel on the exquisite classic French cuisine of **Aujourd'hui** (Four Seasons Hotel, 200 Boylston Street; 617-338-4400).

◆ Relive a child's sense of holiday season wonderment with a matinee performance of **The Nutcracker.**

down. Rates range from $550 to $605. (Rooms with a view of the Public Garden command the higher prices.)

Ease into shopping mode by spending the afternoon at **Downtown Crossing,** where **Macy's** (formerly Jordan Marsh) and **Filene's** face each other at the corner of Washington and Summer Streets. These department stores vie to outdo each other with holiday season window displays. Both stores have a broad range of excellent merchandise, but neither quite captures the jangling excitement of your primary Downtown Crossing destination: **Filene's Basement,** pioneer of the "automatic markdown." Each item is tagged with a date of arrival and a sale price significantly below retail. Automatic discounts begin at 25 percent after two weeks, 50 percent after three weeks, 75 percent after four weeks. After five weeks, remaining goods are donated to charity. Shopping for clothing at "The Basement," as it's often called, is as much a Boston tradition as Christmas caroling on Beacon Hill. You could end up with a designer label at a price you can brag about for weeks to come. Lest the idea of a bargain seem unromantic, consider that some of the city's most blue-blooded Brahmins are regularly clad from toe to head in socks and suits and even minks from Filene's Basement.

An afternoon in the Basement can be wearing—what to choose? what to choose?—so head back to your hotel, trailing your Basement bags behind you, for afternoon tea in the **Bristol Lounge** ($22.50). Aim for a window table to watch passersby or a couch next to the fireplace so that you can snuggle if the weather seems especially nippy. Full tea comes with a pot of tea, little sandwiches, fruit and nut breads, pastries, raisin scones, and sides of whipped cream, raspberry jam, and lemon curd.

The Perfect Gift

The perfect gift is one that comes out of the blue with no occasion or reason attached (except "I love you"): the unexpected foot rub, a scalp-tingling shampoo, a deliciously sexy message whispered in his or her ear as you come off the elevator into the lobby, a sly and knowing wink just as the hubbub of shopping seems to become too much. Too many couples ruin their gift shopping by trying to buy the perfect gift. Spend your money together on something you'll use and appreciate together (a new stereo, perhaps). If you've been struck by an inspiration to buy something your lover would love, hold that thought for when she or he least expects a gift.

DAY ONE: evening

DINNER

Several days ago you made an early dinner reservation just around the corner from the hotel at **Pignoli** (91 Park Plaza; 617-338-7500; expensive). The stunning New Italian fine dining here is a collaboration of legendary Boston chef Lydia Shire and chef de cuisine Susan Regis. Your hearts will start pounding as soon as you walk into the innovative and colorful room. The look is chic to the max, and the plates are as pretty as the decor, concentrating intense flavors in artistic arrays. Start with an endive, pear, and seared foie gras salad, move on to a roast duck with strudel of braised greens and sweet potato jam, and conclude with a pumpkin crème caramel. The pronouncement most commonly voiced in Pignoli is "I never knew _____ could taste so good!"

To keep with the spirit of the season, spend the rest of your evening enjoying a Boston holiday tradition: *The Black Nativity*, Langston Hughes's gospel song-play presented by the National Center of Afro-American Artists at Tremont Temple (88 Tremont Street; 617-442-8614). The performers are a mix of amateurs and professionals, but it can be hard to tell which is which as their voices rise to hosannas on high. Before you retire for the night, hang out your 9:00 A.M. order for continental breakfast tomorrow morning.

DAY TWO: morning

Enjoy a quick breakfast of croissants, jams, juice, and coffee to prepare for a full day of shopping that begins with continental high style in the same block of Boylston Street where your hotel sits. Pay special attention to **Adesso** (200 Boylston Street; 617-451-2212) for avant-garde home furnishings (could Jean use that chic desk lamp or what?). Look for designer clothing at **Sonia Rykiel** (280 Boylston Street; 617-426-2033) and **Escada** (308 Boylston Street; 617-437-1200), for to-die-for footwear at **Arche** (314 Boylston Street; 617-422-0727), or for the eternal all-purpose silk scarf at **Hermès** (22 Arlington Street; 617-482-8707). In a single block you can cross off the most stylish names on your holiday list.

As you continue along Boylston Street another Boston institution looms at the corner of Arlington Street: **Shreve Crump & Low Co.** (330 Boylston Street; 617-267-9100). Shreve has been jeweler to Boston's aristocrats since time immemorial, the very embodiment of good taste in precious metals, crystal, and, of course, jewels. Let your conscience and pocketbook be your guide, but, as the advertising slogan says, diamonds *are* forever. At least pick up a memento of your trip: a sterling silver swan boat pin.

On the same block you might stop in the **Women's Educational & Industrial Union** (356 Boylston Street; 617-536-5651), which has a good selection of needlework and interesting small antiques (including a lot of tableware) on the second floor. Directly opposite, **The Booksellers at 355 Boylston Street** (617-421-1880) can supply rare books and prints for any bibliophile you want to please. Also along the street (you can't miss the bronze teddy bear out front) is **F.A.O. Schwarz** (440 Boylston Street; 617-262-5900) for the children on your list.

At Dartmouth Street, you can turn left, walking diagonally across holiday-bedecked Copley Square to **Copley Place.** As you ascend the escalator with water cascading on each side, you'll comprehend immediately that this is no run-of-the-mill shopping center. And the blitz of holiday decoration, especially in the two-story atrium, puts most mall decorating schemes to shame. But this is a center anchored by **Neiman Marcus** (617-536-3660) on one end and **Tiffany & Co.** (617-353-0222) on the other. Not everything at the latter requires the riches of a robber baron, but every purchase is packaged in Tiffany's signature light blue box.

Between these two upper-crust extremes are all manner of fine boutiques, including **Gucci** (617-247-3000) for bags, shoes, scarves, and ties; **Louis Vuitton** (617-437-6519) for luggage that epitomizes the phrase "traveling in style"; and the **Custom Shop** (617-353-0291), which specializes in custom-made shirts and limited edition color-coordinated neckties. You'll also find excellent gift shopping in **Mont Blanc: The Art of Writing** (617-267-8700), purveyor of luxury pens and other writing implements; and **The Artful Hand Gallery** (617-262-9601), a well-curated contemporary crafts gallery that always has an extensive display of stemware and artists' jewelry. Look for lots of original craftsmen's Christmas ornaments.

When you're through being dazzled at Copley Place, follow the enclosed overhead walkway to **The Shops at Prudential Center,** another large, if less glitzy, shopping center with an immense Christmas tree in its outdoor center plaza.

DAY TWO: afternoon

LUNCH

The Pru has one of the largest, most attractive branches of yet another Boston institution, **Legal Seafoods** (617-266-6800), an excellent spot for lunch before you pick up the gift shopping gauntlet again. A recent complete renovation created lots of tables with window views. Keep the meal simple: a clam or fish chowder and a salad.

Within the Pru, you might find some good gifts at **Crane & Co. Papermakers** (617–247–2822), where you can purchase initialed note cards or—for those teenagers who would rather receive money—note cards made from recycled U.S. currency. **World of Science** (617–247–1341) proffers good gifts for kids—crystals, garden kits, and educational toys—whereas museum reproduction jewelry and other artistic items are the province of **The Museum Company** (617–267–0071).

As you leave the Pru, cross Boylston Street and continue one block over to Newbury, Boston's poshest outdoor shopping street. Clothing designers run the gamut from ultra-chic to school-tie traditional, including **Emporio Armani** (210 Newbury Street; 617–262–7300); **Rodier Paris** (144 Newbury Street; 617–247–2410); **Brooks Brothers** (46 Newbury Street; 617–267–2600); and **Gianni Versace** (12 Newbury Street; 617–536–8300).

But couture is only half the story. **Newbury Street** is great hunting ground for amusements to match all interests and tastes: **John Lewis Jewelers** (97A Newbury Street; 617–266–6665) features a broad selection of sterling bracelets and chains in varying levels of ornament (and price); **Kitchen Arts** (161 Newbury Street; 617–266–8701) carries all the ultra-chic kitchen design concepts from industrial-grade mixers to elegant balloon whisks and French restaurant toques that make every home cook feel like a Michelin-star chef. Pop into **Desana** (211 Newbury Street; 617–450–9699) for a world of custom-blended fragrances that can be applied to products ranging from body talc to hand lotion to true perfume and cologne. **Toppers** (230 Newbury Street; 617–859–1430) carries fanciful women's hats. Two shops with a broad selection of fine crafts are the **Society of Arts and Crafts** (175 Newbury Street; 617–266–1810) and **Alianza Contemporary Crafts** (154 Newbury Street; 617–262–2385).

For the *House Beautiful* subscribers on your list, be sure to examine the French provincial fabrics and accessories at **Pierre Deux** (111 Newbury Street; 617–536–6364); the nostalgic dishware at **LouLou's Lost & Found** (121 Newbury Street; 617–859–8593); and the contemporary ceramic dishware at **Bellezza** (129 Newbury

Street; 617-266-1183).

Somewhere in this jaunt you'll probably reach overload on packages—a good time to call the town car to have them returned to the hotel. You'll also need a break. We suggest a cappuccino and pastry—or a drink—at **Stephanie's on Newbury** (190 Newbury Street; 617-236-0990).

DAY TWO: evening
DINNER

This is an evening to celebrate the spirit of the season. The two of you have been thinking of family and friends all day as you completed your shopping. Now concentrate on each other. What better place to celebrate than the hotel's **Aujourd'hui Restaurant** (expensive), which is the only AAA Five Diamond restaurant in Boston and is regularly designated by *Zagat's* as the best fine dining in this competitive city. Like the hotel, the restaurant features perfection without mannered fanfare. You could begin with an appetizer of seared tuna, sesame cracker and tobiko; linger over a venison loin or a tenderloin of veal; and finish with warm apple crisp served with a vanilla bean ice cream made on the premises.

DAY THREE: morning
BREAKFAST

Enjoy another light room-service breakfast, or, if you're not still full from the night before, venture back to Aujourd'hui for Sunday brunch.

You can't leave Boston without partaking of *The Nutcracker,* so take in a matinee performance. Two options are right within walking distance in the Theater District. The **Boston Ballet** performs an extravagant interpretation at the Wang Center for the Performing Arts (270 Tremont Street; 617-695-6950). Alternately, the **Ballet Theater of Boston** offers a more intimate presentation at the Emerson Majestic Theater (221 Tremont Street; 617-824-8000).

FOR MORE ROMANCE

If you're in town the first weekend in December, you can shop at the very high quality juried crafts exhibition **Crafts at the Castle,** which benefits Family Service of Greater Boston. It's held at Park Plaza Castle, Arlington Street and Columbus Avenue. Call (617) 523-6400 for information.

Other Boston holiday traditions include: **The Christmas Revels** at **Sanders Theatre in Cambridge** (617-496-2222), *Handel's Messiah* performed by the **Handel & Haydn Society** at **Symphony Hall** (617-266-3605), and *A Child's Christmas in Wales* presented by **Lyric Stage** (617-437-7172).

Well-Seasoned
Day Trips

Bird-Watching at Plum Island

HEN THE SUN CROSSES THE EQUATOR for the vernal equinox, it's time to take a long trip and start courting. Birds have that instinct hard-wired into their genes; humans have to make a conscious effort. This day trip from Boston focuses on one of the great birding grounds of North America during its most pleasant season of the year, springtime. As a bonus, you get to hop almost magically from the wilds of a wildlife refuge into the charming heart of a picturesque sea captains' village for dining and shopping before you return to the city.

PRACTICAL NOTES: You'll find a set of binoculars and a bird-identification guide helpful; if you're bringing a camera, a telephoto lens will be handy but not essential. Insect repellent, long pants, and high socks are wise precautions. Even on a warm day, you'll appreciate having windbreakers, as Plum Island is a rather exposed barrier island. The best season for this trip is during the March 1 through June 7 peak bird-migration season. Refuge beaches begin closing April 1 to protect the nests of the endangered piping plover, although the birds are visible from observation towers near the beach. Regardless of the closed beaches, you will enjoy the activities of the many other birds that frequent the island's other habitats.

DAY ONE: morning

After a solid breakfast at home, set out for Newburyport and Plum Island. From downtown Boston, take the Central Artery north to

Romance AT A GLANCE

◆ Visit one of the greatest birding grounds on the east coast of North America, the **Parker River National Wildlife Refuge** on Plum Island, to observe shore birds, water-fowl, ospreys, and the spring warbler migration.

◆ Enjoy a lunch of traditional chowder, fried fish, and dense desserts in a snug wooden booth at Newburyport's atmospheric **Grog** (13 Middle Street, Newburyport; 978-465-8700).

◆ The historic downtown and waterfront of Newburyport are studded with dozens of small independent shops, boutiques, and antiques dealers. Spend a while investigating antiquarian books at **Old Port Book Shop** (18 State Street, Newburyport; 978-462-0100).

◆ Combine a casual dinner with seeing a movie from your table at **Stage Two Cinema Pub** (109R Main Street, Amesbury; 978-388-6555 for information, 978-388-3676 for reservations).

Route 1. Follow Route 1 to I–95 north and continue to exit 57 (Historic Newburyport District). The road you're on becomes High Street. Turn left onto Rolfe's Lane, following the signs for Plum Island and **Parker River National Wildlife Refuge** (open daily sunrise to sunset; $5.00 per car).

The refuge (one of 500 around the country administered by the U.S. Fish and Wildlife Service) contains 4,662 acres of sand beach and dunes, bogs, tidal marshes, and small freshwater ponds and springs. These diverse habitats make the refuge home to a wide variety of wildlife. The most commonly seen large mammals are deer and muskrat, but most people come to see the birds, including the large nesting colony of piping plovers.

After you enter at the gate, pull into the first parking lot on the left to pick up literature at the Information Center, staffed by volunteers primarily on weekends during spring. Even when the center is closed, a weatherproof box at the door should have copies of a one-page map of the reservation and the bird checklist. The odd birdhouses near the center are designed for purple martins, a large, swallow-like bird that becomes increasingly common as insect life picks up in the spring.

While you're here, walk to the crest of the dunes for a view of the beach. This particular beach is a favorite nesting area for the piping plover, a bird more remarkable for its rarity than its appearance.

In fact, without a bird-identification guide, you may be hard-pressed to tell the piping plovers apart from the black-bellied and semipalmated plovers that share their habitat.

But there will be no shortage of birds to see, many of them in courting pairs at this time of year. In fact, some seventy species nest in or near the refuge, and 302 different species are seen each year. (True exotics or, in birders' terms, "accidentals," add another thirty-nine to the list of birds sighted here since 1975.) Plum Island in general and Parker River Refuge in particular constitute a birder's heaven.

To begin your search, drive down the single road to parking lot 4 (lots 2 and 3 will likely be closed to keep people off the beaches). This lot is the access point for the Hellcat Swamp Trail, an unappealing name for an extraordinary boardwalk that winds through the wooded wetlands at the edge of a tidal marsh. This is prime territory for spotting the migrating warblers and vireos, so walk slowly without any quick motions and keep the noise down. You'll almost certainly be rewarded by good views of the red-eyed vireo, the yellow warbler, the common yellowthroat, and the American red-start—all of which nest here. You'll likely see yellow-rumped warblers, blackpoll warblers, and black-and-white warblers as well.

And they will be . . . well, warbling. This is mating season, and the males are staking out territory in the ornithological equivalent of chest-thumping. When you hear the song, look up—at least two-thirds of the way up the tree canopy—until you spot the singer. (This is the best way to learn to identify bird songs, by the way.) Then look very carefully lower in the canopy for the same type of bird with the contrast and color turned down. This is the female. If she likes the sound of this show-off, she may join him on his lofty perch.

When you return to the parking lot, turn right to take the broad path on a dike out to the marshes. Suddenly you're in an entirely different habitat, with open water as well as tidal marsh. The marsh grasses should be a bright, almost iridescent green, showing their new growth. But you'll be too busy ogling some of the most dramatic of the reservation's birds—the herons and egrets fishing in the shallows. These long-legged birds have what seems to be infinite patience as they stand and wait, stand and wait—and then lunge for fish, frogs, newts, or salamanders. During the morning hours, you're most likely to see great blue herons, green herons, and snowy egrets (in descending order of size). The egrets look for all the world like miniature white flamingos, except that they tend to be solitary fishers, unlike their southern cousins.

Sharing these waters with the great fishers are a plethora of ducks and geese, including the increasingly ubiquitous Canada geese. Swimming among them will be a few mute swans, those great and beautiful birds of legend and lore. One true story told of the mute swans is that they mate for life, forming a tight monogamous union until death do them part. The best view of these waterfowl is usually from the observation tower at the end of the embankment path. Circling overhead and occasionally swooping from the sky into the swamp will be some of the various hawks that winter over here, especially the northern harrier and the American kestrel.

If you continue down the reservation road (which quickly becomes a rutted path that will pretty much guarantee that you don't exceed the 25 miles-per-hour speed limit), you can park at lot 6 to get a look at one of the broad barrier beaches that usually remains open during plover nesting season. At the water's edge, you'll see plovers and sandpipers skittering along the wet sand, perhaps an osprey (a fish eagle) diving off the coast for herring, and great numbers of various gulls, terns, and cormorants.

DAY ONE: afternoon

To see all these winged creatures, you've probably lingered long enough to be famished. Return the way you came, except follow the signs to Water Street to head into historic **Newburyport.**

LUNCH

Your hunger can be sated nicely from the cozy confines of a wooden booth at the downtown Newburyport pub **Grog** (13 Middle Street, Newburyport; 978–465–8700; inexpensive). The street-level dining room has surprising decorum (the nighttime party bar is downstairs), and you can hardly go wrong with a bowl of local clam chowder or lobster bisque, a plate of fried haddock, and a strapping dessert such as tollhouse pie. Wash it down with a locally brewed Ipswich Ale.

You'll want to linger a while in this intriguing little village. State Street is lined with shops, including the superb **Old Port Book Shop** (18 State Street; 978-462-0100), which includes selections from several Massachusetts and New Hampshire antiquarian book dealers as well as the operators' own offerings of rare and collectors' books. Head toward the foot of State and turn right onto Water Street, where you'll pass several small and a few large antiques dealers en route to The Tannery marketplace. Here you can come full circle on your day by browsing among the guides, binoculars, and other paraphernalia at **The Birdwatcher of Newburyport** (50 Water Street, The Tannery; 978-462-BIRD).

You can take your time investigating the shops of Newburyport, but around 6:00 P.M. you should hop in the car and drive across the river to Amesbury.

Sky Watching

Own up—when's the last time the two of you watched cloud formations? You have the perfect opportunity on Plum Island because you can stretch out on your backs together on the beach and watch the clouds scud by, especially in the afternoon. What do you see? What do you imagine? At this season you'll probably see both stratus clouds (high and streaky) and cumulus clouds (lower and heaped). Fair-weather cumulus clouds have flat bottoms, which mark the altitude where water in the atmosphere condenses. If the bottoms are rounded or indistinct, grab your umbrellas.

Head west on Merrimac Street (the opposite direction from Plum Island) and stay on the road until it hits a T intersection. Turn right and you'll cross a small bridge. Keep to the left and make a left turn onto Amesbury's Main Street. Keep following the road about 3 miles into the middle of town, where you'll find **Stage Two Cinema Pub** (109R Main Street, Amesbury; 978-388-6555 for information, 978-388-3676 for reservations) at the back of a package store parking lot. Good, inexpensive fun accounts for the enduring popularity of this local institution (they've been around since the mid-1980s). By arriving before 6:00

P.M., you'll save $1.00 each off the admission price of a show, which is already a bargain at $4.00.

The films are what used to be called "B" movies in the days of double features—light fare akin to what you might see on an airplane. Seating is at funky plastic-laminate tables with a mix of malt-shop banquettes, plain cafe chairs and a few reclining seats. You might prefer a booth at the back in case you want to make out when the lights go down. The meals are classic burger-and-fries fare, reasonably priced, and beer and wine are also served at your screenside table.

FOR MORE ROMANCE

If you'd prefer more highbrow entertainment (well, not too highbrow) for the evening, contact the **Firehouse Center for the Arts** (Market Square, Newburyport; 978-462-7336) to find out what theatrical, music, or dance production will be going on during your visit. If you're coming in May, you might want to participate in the **Spring Plover and Wildlife Festival.** Call the Friends of the Parker River National Wildlife Refuge (978-462-2975) for dates and details.

Literary Concord
THE LIVES OF THE AUTHORS

IN THE MIDDLE THIRD of the nineteenth century, **Concord, Massachusetts**, was America's equivalent of Periclean Athens— source of a sudden and unexpected outburst of intellectual and artistic creativity. The men and women responsible were in many ways absolutely ordinary citizens of this small town, yet in their writings they created a uniquely American literature that continues to ring through the ages. Take a day together to touch their lives, keeping in mind this thought of Henry David Thoreau: "A written word is the choicest of relics. It is at once something more intimate with us and more universal than any other work of art. It is the work of art nearest to life itself."

PRACTICAL NOTES: Although Concord is only about 12 miles from Boston, we recommend driving to expedite getting around. Commuter rail is also an option if you don't mind a bit of hiking around town, though you'll probably have to skip Walden Pond. In either case, time your visit between May and October to be sure all the sites will be open. If you can visit on a weekday, Walden Pond will be less crowded.

DAY ONE: morning

It's a quick drive to Concord if you wait until after rush hour. Head west on Route 2 by getting on Memorial Drive, which follows the Charles River in Cambridge. Continue west for about 10 miles to the Concord exit. As you drive into town, stop at the Visitor Information booth on Heywood Street, 1 block east of Concord

Romance
AT A GLANCE

♦ Visit the home of Concord's most eminent sage, **Ralph Waldo Emerson House** (28 Cambridge Turnpike, Concord; 978–369–2236) and the abode that the mercurial Louisa May Alcott describes in Little Women, the **Orchard House** (399 Lexington Road, Concord; 978–369–4118).

♦ Enjoy a great lunch drawn from the exquisite Portuguese cuisine at **Guida's Coast Cuisine** (84 Thoreau Street, Concord; 978–371–1333).

♦ Pay your respects to Concord's great artistic figures on Author's Ridge at **Sleepy Hollow Cemetery.** Leave a plain smooth stone for Ralph Waldo Emerson, a penny for sculptor Daniel Chester French.

♦ Follow the trail through the woods at **Walden Pond Reservation** to visit the site of Henry David Thoreau's famous cabin.

Center. Open weekends in April and daily May through October, this booth has a $1.50 map of all the major sites.

The **Emerson House** (28 Cambridge Turnpike; 978–369–2236), a solid white Federal house with black shutters and a large American flag out front, should be your introduction to the domestic lives of the authors. Ralph Waldo Emerson lived here during the most productive part of his life, from 1835 until he died in 1882. Operated by his descendants, the house is kept much as it was in Emerson's day, right down to many of his books, personal effects, and furnishings. (His study room is across the street at the Concord Museum.) Emerson was the sun in Concord's solar system of literary planets. In his orbit spun the curmudgeonly Henry David Thoreau, the dreamer A. Bronson Alcott, his talented and dramatic daughter Louisa May, and a dozen lesser lights. Nathaniel Hawthorne spun in and out of Emerson's gravitational field like a periodic comet, absent for years in Salem and Europe, then reappearing to light up the sky.

The "Sage of Concord," as Emerson was known, was the social as well as the intellectual center of the Concord literati. During his years in "exile" at Walden, Thoreau came to dinner every Sunday at the Emerson House. Every literary and scholarly visitor to Boston made a pilgrimage here to talk with Emerson. Imagine the conversations around that dinner table! You can visit the house mid-April through mid-October on Thursday through Saturday from 10:00 A.M. to 4:30 P.M. and on Sunday and holidays from 2:00 to 4:30 P.M. Adults pay $5.00.

The incurable storyteller Louisa May Alcott, the sensible daughter of a utopian dreamer, stands in counterpoint to Emerson's genial abstraction. The Alcotts moved a lot, since A. Bronson Alcott frequently squandered their money on high-minded schemes. But the family's tale is well told at **Orchard House** (399 Lexington Road; 978-369-4118). This Alcott family home is the house described in *Little Women* with the throat-catching fondness that only loss can engender. It's more modest than Emerson's abode, and nearly a century and a half later the sagging floors and roofline speak of the family's diminished economic circumstances. Behind Orchard House stands a simple shack that aspired to be something more: Bronson Alcott's Concord School of Philosophy. Orchard House is open April through October, Monday through Saturday from 10:00 A.M. to 4:30 P.M. and on Sunday from 1:00 to 4:30 P.M. From November through March, the house is open Monday through Friday from 11:00 A.M. to 3:00 P.M., Saturday from 10:00 A.M. to 4:30 P.M., and Sunday from 1:00 to 4:30 P.M. Adult admission is $7.00.

The individual shops of Concord village have changed since the days of Emerson and Alcott, but in many ways it is still the same deeply rooted small town that nourished an intellectual revolution. Main Street and its environs are the kind of lively commercial walking streets that have disappeared in so many towns. Stop in to restock your classics at **The Concord Bookshop** (65 Main Street; 978-369-2405), with separate sections for contemporary and historic local authors. You might also visit **Lacoste Gallery** (25 Main Street; 978-369-0278) to see a broad selection of fine contemporary crafts.

DAY ONE: afternoon

LUNCH

Guida's Coast Cuisine (84 Thoreau Street; 978-371-1333) strikes a more worldly pose, presenting a palette of flavors and ingredients that conjure up chef-owner Guida Ponte's roots in the Portuguese islands of the Azores. This sleek restaurant is located upstairs at the Concord Depot, which has interesting shops on the ground level.

You'll probably want to sit in the airy front room that overlooks the commuter rail platform, though the mural-decorated back room is romantically intimate. For a light meal, you won't go wrong with Ponte's striking Caesar salad, some of her to-die-for Portuguese bread (half corn flour), and a bowl of the classic kale and potato soup of Portugal, *caldo verde*. If you'd like a little more, ask about Ponte's fish specialty of the day. She is one of the Boston area's most revered seafood cooks.

The Other Louisa May Alcott

Pressed for money late in life, Louise May Alcott taught herself to write with her left hand so that she might put in twice as many hours at the writing desk. Curiously enough, her left-handed output was as different from her right-handed as night from day—tales of blood and thunder, satirical essays, gothic romances. Scholars later discovered that she had been writing and publishing such works for years under pseudonyms. For a glimpse of the flesh-and-blood Louisa May, take turns reading aloud the thriller Behind a Mask *or* A Woman's Power *by "A.M. Barnard."*

After lunch, it's a short drive to **Sleepy Hollow Cemetery,** leaving Concord Center and traveling northeast on Bedford Street (Route 62). Enter at Pritchard Gate (second entrance on the left) and follow the signs to Author's Ridge, where there's a small parking area. Up on the ridge to the right you'll encounter the graves of Ralph Waldo Emerson (marked with a rugged boulder), Henry David Thoreau (a minuscule marble tablet), Nathaniel Hawthorne (two stones, at head and foot) and Louisa May Alcott (a small, conventional headstone). Their family members lie all around them, reminders that they were not just names from American literature but persons who walked in the world beside those they loved. Look carefully for small offerings left by admirers—handfuls of smooth pebbles on Emerson's stone, a hemlock cone for Thoreau. Alcott's grave is aflutter with small flags, tributes to her service as a nurse during the Civil War. On the ridge as you drove up is the grave of Daniel Chester French, the sculptor best known for the seated Lincoln in the Lincoln Memorial. His grave is usually scattered with pennies.

Henry David Thoreau prided himself on his lack of property, and little material evidence of his life survives. To round out your visit to Concord, visit his beloved **Walden Pond**. In 1845, Thoreau went to live on a woodlot owned by Emerson next to Walden Pond. He stayed for two years, keeping a journal of his thoughts and his encounters with Nature and society—a journal he tinkered with for seven more years before *Walden* was published in 1854. Walden Pond is managed by the state ($2.00 parking fee), which limits the number of visitors at any time to 1,000. It's a popular spot for swimming, boating, and fishing, but we suggest that you ask the rangers for directions and hike to the site of Thoreau's cabin. The foundation of his chimney marks the hearth of his home, which was moved from the spot and later torn down. Above the house site are stumps of some of the 400 white pines planted by Thoreau and felled in the great hurricane of 1938.

Thoreau left Walden voluntarily because, he wrote, he had other lives to lead. But his parting words may suit a couple as well as they did a recluse: "I learned this, at least, by my experiment; that if one advances confidently in the directions of his dreams, and endeavors to live the life which he has imagined, he will meet with a success unexpected in common hours. . . . If you have built castles in the air, your work need not be lost; that is where they should be. Now put the foundations under them."

FOR MORE ROMANCE

Concord's rich literary history is also revealed in a number of other sites, including the **Concord Museum** (200 Lexington Road; 978–369–9609; open Monday through Saturday 9:00 A.M. to 5:00 P.M., Sunday noon to 5:00 P.M.; adults $7.00), which has Emerson's study and the world's largest collection of Thoreau artifacts; **The Old Manse** (269 Monument Street; 978–369–3909; open mid-April through October, Monday through Saturday 10:00 A.M. to 5:00 P.M., Sunday and holidays noon to 5:00 P.M.; adults $6.00), a Revolutionary-era home (it overlooks the North Bridge battle site) where Emerson wrote his first great book, *Nature*, and where, later,

Nathaniel Hawthorne spent his honeymoon; and the only home ever owned by Hawthorne, **The Wayside** (455 Lexington Road; 978-369-6975; open May through October, Thursday through Tuesday 10:00 A.M. to 4:30 P.M.; adults $4.00), where Louisa May Alcott wrote her first published works and where Hawthorne came home from Europe to live until his death.

Nashoba Valley Apple Picking

T HE APPLE IS THE FRUIT OF LOVE—even allowing for the troubles Eve and Adam encountered on their fruit-picking expedition. But put aside the tales of the Garden of Eden. The owners of the orchard *you're* visiting are very congenial toward pickers. So for a day outside the city when the air turns crisp and the sun acquires that golden slant seen nowhere but in New England in fall, we suggest you head for the hills—or, more exactly, to the Nashoba Valley.

PRACTICAL NOTES: Although September is best for this day trip, it can be added on to other Boston itineraries from mid-July until the end of October. For a full winery tour and tasting, go on a Saturday or Sunday. Fruit picking begins at Nashoba Valley Winery with raspberries; the apples start ripening at the end of August.

DAY ONE: morning

Your day out of the city begins with a 35-mile scenic drive through the farmland that was America's first fruit bowl. You're following the footsteps of Leominster, Massachusetts, native son John Chapman, better known as Johnny Appleseed. The legacy of this horticultural missionary persists in the orchards west of Boston. Head west on Route 2 by getting on Memorial Drive, which follows the Charles River in Cambridge. Continue west for 11 miles past Concord to Route 126. Turn left (south) past Walden Pond to Route 119 west. This road continues through rolling orchard country past

*R*omance
AT A GLANCE

♦ *Follow in the footsteps of Johnny Appleseed as you drive through the scenic orchards and farmlands of the **Nashoba Valley,** America's first fruit bowl.*

♦ *Tour the wine-making operations of the **Nashoba Valley Winery** (100 Wattaquadoc Hill Road, Bolton; 978–779–5521) and sample the fruit wines, a revival of a venerable regional tradition.*

♦ **Picnic on the winery grounds** *with crackers, local cheeses, and the winery's own fresh apple cider—all available on the premises.*

♦ **Pick your own fruits** *to take home—from raspberries in mid-summer to peaches, pears, and apples into the autumn. No Adam and Eve jokes, please!*

I–495 to the town of Bolton. Turn left at the blinking light. In one-quarter of a mile you'll come to **Nashoba Valley Winery** (100 Wattaquadoc Hill Road, Bolton; 978–779–5521). It is open daily from 11:00 A.M. to 5:00 P.M., with tours and tastings on Saturday and Sunday. The proprietors don't mind if guests arrive before the winery opens, so spread out a newspaper on the picnic tables out front and enjoy the quiet country morning. Once someone arrives, ask permission and you can stroll through the trees laden with fruit.

The farm dates from the nineteenth century, and some of the trees in the fifty-five-acre winery orchard to the 1920s. But the bounteous landscape you see now was the dream of Jack Partridge, who moved his winery operations here in 1983 and created plantings of peaches, plums, cherries, raspberries, blackberries, and more than eighty varieties of heritage apples with an eye toward selected fruits and apple strains that could make the best fruit wines.

New England is still in the midst of a winery boom that began in the 1970s after the industry had disappeared during Prohibition. Early attempts to make wine focused on super-hardy grapes, but Partridge did some historical research and found that Massachusetts had once had a flourishing fruit wine industry, which he set about reviving. In the ensuing decades, Nashoba Valley Winery has confounded the skeptics with a line of table and dessert wines that have won a number of awards.

After a casual stroll through the grounds, go inside for a tour of the wine-making operation from the initial pressing through fermentation to aging in wood or stainless steel and finally to bottling. When Partridge sold the business in late 1995, his original wine maker, Larry Ames, returned to the fold to oversee production. At the conclusion of the tour comes a tasting of four or five wines from a light apple wine to a luscious dessert wine of peach or raspberry. With luck, your tasting will include the winery's newest product, Nashoba Cider—a traditional English-style, mildly effervescent hard cider.

DAY ONE: afternoon

LUNCH

After the tasting, you can select some locally produced cheeses—the Westfield Farm chèvre and the Smith's Farmstead smoked gouda are good bets—from the winery's store cooler along with some crackers and a piece of fruit for a classic farm picnic. The shop also sells the Nashoba Valley wines and cider, some of them chilled in the cooler. On the way in, you may have noticed the lovely green lawns beneath aged maples close to the road. Lean back together on a broad maple trunk and enjoy.

When you're done, sign in to pick your own fruit. You'll find peaches, plums, and blackberries (thornless!) from late August through mid-September, super-sweet

The Taste of a Sweet Name

Apple trees don't breed true— every seedling diverges (sometimes wildly) from its parent stock. So before the advent of professional nurseries, New England could boast thousands of apple varieties, many of them bearing names that reflect this fruit's sensual qualities. Among the New England heirloom apples are American Beauty, Chenango, Cox Orange Pippin, Duchess of Oldenburg, English Beauty, Fameuse-Snow, High Top Sweet, Maiden's Blush, Malinda, Northern Sweet, Opalescent, Peck's Pleasant, Salome, Sops of Wine, Sutton Beauty, Sweet Winesap, and (named by an orchardist who had found his true love) Westfield- Seek-No- Further.

heritage raspberries in late July and again in late September, and apples through the longest season of all. Apple picking begins with Gravensteins in late August, progressing through McIntosh, Cortland, Macoun, Red Delicious, Baldwin, and finally, in early October, Golden Delicious. Many of these varieties, by the way, were first developed within a hundred miles of this orchard.

Although most of the apple trees are grafted onto dwarf or semidwarf stock, Nashoba Valley provides pole pickers. Keeping you off ladders and limbs is good for your health and their liability insurance. Pole picking produces a lot of "drops," but the bruised fruit, with archetypal Yankee thrift, simply feeds the wine presses. Don't be in a rush. You could pick your quota in minutes, but wouldn't you rather tarry a while in this garden spot before you have to drive back east of Eden?

ℋ Foliage ℋike in the Blue ℋills

EW ENGLAND'S DRAMATIC FALL FOLIAGE isn't just an up-country phenomenon. You can drink in the full palette of fall colors with picturesque views and grand panoramas at the largest of the Metropolitan District Commission parks, the Blue Hills Reservation. Just 18 miles from downtown Boston, the reservation is covered primarily with stands of hardwood forest that produce a succession of fall colors from the first reddening of the sumacs and swamp maples to the final solemn bronzes of the mighty oaks. The reservation is laced with 125 miles of trails, ensuring a surprising level of privacy in a preserve so near the urban center. As the two of you make your way through a woodland glade to emerge at an open outlook, you'll have the distinct pleasure of having earned your views—together.

PRACTICAL NOTES: Although public transportation can deliver you within a mile of one hiking trail, driving to the Blue Hills Reservation will give you more choices. MDC rangers advise wearing sturdy footwear and carrying water, a first aid kit, and a trail map. Bring a picnic lunch; chances are good that your hotel will pack one for you. You may also wish to bring binoculars—this is bird migration season—and a camera.

DAY ONE: morning

From Boston take the Southeast Expressway, veering south on the combined I–93, I–95, and Route 128 to exit 3 (Houghtons Pond).

As you come off the ramp, turn right and continue 0.6 mile to a stop sign. Turn right onto Hillside Street and drive past Houghtons Pond and park across from the State Police stables. **The Blue Hills Reservation Headquarters** building, up the hill on the left, is open Monday through Friday from 8:30 A.M. to 5:00 P.M. Even if the rangers are occupied or the office is closed, you can get a trail guide ($1.00) and some helpful brochures at the information center on the porch. If the rangers are around, ask for pointers on where to find the best foliage. Fall color is not a static display; it's an organic process that changes day by day. But, says MDC park ranger Maggi Brown, "You really can't go wrong. It's all so pretty." Since you have brought your own picnic lunch, plan on eating at trailside when you're hungry. Just be sure to carry out any trash.

Start out with an easy warm-up hike around the perimeter of **Houghtons Pond.** This scenic hike is marked with yellow dots on the trees. Begin by walking from the bulletin board at the main parking area down to the pond and follow the dots. Even at a dawdling pace, it takes only about a half hour to make the circuit. Now that the main swimming and boating season is over, the pond acquires an easy tranquility that attracts herons back to its shallows and to Marigold Marsh, which adjoins Houghtons Pond on the east side. Watch carefully and you might see a blue heron stalking sunfish fingerlings. Much of the pond is surrounded by swamp maples, which turn a bright scarlet beginning in mid-September, as well as by the dappled yellow leaves of alder and birch. On a still day with the golden cast of light for which New England is famous, it might be hard to tell where the foliage ends and its reflection on the pond surface begins.

The **Ponkapoag Trail** circles the reservation's largest and most remote body of water, Ponkapoag Pond. The walking is easy, but the full 3.75-mile circuit might take longer than you'd care to spend, so we suggest doing a partial loop that will reward you with a look at a fascinating ecosystem and a view of a road vaulted by an overarching canopy of sugar maples. Retrace your drive and cross the highway to a small parking lot right on the Blue Hill River. A green-blazed trail leads down toward the pond. Take the right fork. As you descend a gentle hill you'll be entering wetlands (the first area to turn color in fall), but the trail is dry. Directly across from the YMCA camp (about 0.3 mile) is the entry to a half-mile boardwalk that crosses a great "quaking bog," so named because if you were to step on it (don't!) the land would quiver. This time of year it undulates with rich reds and russets as the foliage of cranberry bushes ripens and the cotton grass turns golden. Stay on the boardwalk, as this is an extremely fragile environment. Look closely. You'll be able to kneel down together for a close examination of various insect-eating plants, including the pitcher plant and both round-leaf and spatulate-leaved sundews.

Retrace your steps on the boardwalk and continue your walk for about a half mile on what is now called the Redman Farm Path until you come to intersection 5175. (All the trail and road intersections in the Blue Hills Reservation are numbered to make navigation easy.) The road off to the right is the aptly named Maple Avenue. You'll have spotted it at a distance anyway, for few trees turn such splendorous colors in the fall as sugar maples. This lowland area south of the hills has been intensely farmed since the seventeenth century, resulting in the meadows that now hold the 36-hole Ponkapoag Golf Course. Farmers often planted their access roads with sugar maples along both sides so that they could drive a sleigh down a single path to collect maple sap in February to make maple syrup. These trees are nineteenth-century successors, and they create an interlaced canopy of red and gold in fall. We hope you remembered the camera.

DAY ONE: afternoon

You'll have to work a bit harder to reach the greatest foliage vistas all along the **Skyline Loop,** which takes you between the ranger station and Great Blue Hill, the highest peak on the Atlantic coast south of Maine. The trail begins behind the ranger station, and the first 500 feet can be truly daunting as you follow the blue blazes straight up Hancock Hill on a path distinguished chiefly by a criss-cross tangle of tree roots. In fact, the roots provide very solid footing. So take the beginning easy, concentrating on the stillness of the woods. When you reach the top, you've achieved the ridgeline of the Blue Hills chain. Although you'll still be going up and down after this point, none of the ascents or descents will be this steep until you've completed the circuit and descended Houghton Hill to emerge behind the state police stables.

Packing for a Picnic

Poet Omar Khayyám offered the quintessential prescription: "a loaf of bread, a jug of wine, and thou beside me in the wilderness." To make a more complete repast, we'd add a hard cheese, some fruit, and perhaps a handful of chocolate chip cookies.

The rewards of this 3-mile loop, which will require between two and two and a half hours, are worth the exertion. Once you hit the highlands, you'll feel on top of the world. At the open areas near the peaks, watch the sky closely. Throughout late September and into October, you're likely to spot migrating raptors. Red-tailed hawks, merlins, and sharp-shinned hawks all make this region part of their flyway, and the fish hawks—principally ospreys and golden eagles—also ride the ridge thermals. You may even see a peregrine falcon or two on its way south from Maine. (If you're real hawk fanciers, call the Blue Hills Trailside Museum to inquire about the raptor-banding programs offered for two days in late September: 617-333-0690.)

Hawks or no hawks, when you reach **Great Blue Hill** (635 feet above sea level) you can climb the Eliot Observation Tower (named for Charles Eliot, father of Boston's park system that grew into the MDC) for views that stretch a full 80 miles on a clear day. That distant peak to the northwest is Mount Monadnock in New Hampshire. To the east, the Boston Harbor Islands are laid out like a necklace on the sea's blue velvet. And due north, Boston's own towers beckon—a metropolis on the edge of what feels for all the world like wilderness. But perhaps the most spectacular view is not what lies in the distance, but the patchwork of leafy color in the mid-ground and your beloved just feet away.

FOR MORE ROMANCE

For another maple-lined lane, drive to **Brookwood Farm,** which was only recently donated to the MDC and annexed by the reservation. Instead of turning down Blue Hill River Road, continue straight and watch for a somewhat overgrown driveway about a half mile on the left. This former sheep farm represents a vanished way of life in this increasingly urbanized area. You'll see faded red farm buildings and overgrown meadows no longer cropped by sheep. But the best part is a quarter-mile drive lined end to end with sugar maples. Ranger Maggi Brown calls it "a little bit of Vermont in downtown Milton."

Another great way to see the Blue Hills is from the saddle. You can make advance arrangements with **Paddocks Stable** (1010 Hillside Street, Milton; 617–698–1884) for guided trail rides at $30 per person per hour. You can ride until dusk, and the operators will help you select trails suited to your abilities.

A Cross-Country Outing

OSTON IS BEAUTIFUL IN THE SNOW, but the white stuff tends to melt away when a warming wind blows in off the ocean. But just a few miles inland, the blanket of snow tends to stay put. This day trip takes advantage of winter just outside the city, where an excellent cross-country ski track, with its own snow-making equipment, meanders along the banks of the Charles River. After skiing, you can look for gifts and mementos at one of the area's better antiques shops before concluding with a robust Northern Italian meal created by one of the area's legendary chefs.

PRACTICAL NOTES: Cross-country skiing involves exercise in a cold environment, so clothe yourselves accordingly in light layers. You'll need a car to reach all the activities. Cross-country season near Boston is short—mid-December through February. If in doubt about the snow cover, call ahead.

DAY ONE: morning

After a hearty breakfast at home (lunch will be a light snack), get on the Massachusetts Turnpike westbound and take exit 15, staying in the left toll lane to exit toward Route 30 west. At the top of the exit, turn left and cross the highway, proceeding a half mile to the **Weston Ski Track** (Park Road, Weston; 781–891–6575), which opens at 9:00 A.M. on weekends and 10:00 A.M. on weekdays. The ski track, operated by the same people who run Charles River Canoe and Kayak (see "A River Runs Through It: Boating on the Charles")

Ro**m**an**c**e
AT A GLANCE

♦ Get out of the urban center into a winter snowland to ski cross-country in set track on the rolling landscape of the **Weston Ski Track** (Park Road, Weston; 781–891–6575).

♦ Court serendipity as you browse the tables and cases of about one hundred dealers in antiques and collectibles at the **Massachusetts Antiques Cooperative** (100 Felton Street, Waltham; 781–893–8893).

♦ Tuck into a hearty Northern Italian-style dinner with robust wines at **Tuscan Grill** (361 Moody Street, Waltham; 781–891–5486), where chef Jimmy Burke's fame lures even downtown Boston gourmets to the suburbs.

is on the Leo T. Martin Golf Course on Metropolitan District Commission land. (The MDC is the regional authority for parklands in and around Boston.) When cold weather arrives, the rolling landscape of fairways and greens becomes a stupendous cross-country trail system of about 15 kilometers when Mother Nature cooperates. As long as temperatures are low enough, the staff makes snow for a two- to three-kilometer area, which is also lit until 10:00 P.M. on weeknights, 8:00 P.M. on Friday and Saturday, and 6:00 P.M. on Sunday. The entire course is groomed and set daily.

Since the course is still within the meteorological influence of the ocean, there's a fair bit of melt-and-freeze. This factor makes for rather fast conditions, but the easy terrain keeps it from becoming too difficult. If you arrive early in the morning, you'll enjoy newly tracked snow. The trail fee here is a very reasonable $11. You can rent gear (skis, poles, and boots) for $10. If you've never skied before, a package that includes a lesson, equipment rental, and trail fee comes to $29.

In addition to waxless skis, the center also rents (and offers lessons on) skate skis, which require more skill and balance but can be very fast, especially on slick conditions. Skate skis require a different motion—rather like pavement skating on in-line skates—but mastering the technique opens you up to a whole new level of exhilaration. The center also rents sit-skis for wheelchair users.

The Weston Ski Track has a small snack bar where you can pick up a cup of hot chocolate and energy food such as candy bars. Alas, there's no other place to eat—but you'll make up the calorie deficit at dinner.

DAY ONE: afternoon

By early afternoon you will have exhausted the trails at Weston, so turn in your gear and hop back in the car to drive a short distance to Waltham. Return on Park Road the way you came, going all the way to the end. Turn right and get in the middle lane, continuing through the stoplight to the entrance for 1–95 north. Exit 20E (marked ROUTE 20 EAST – WALTHAM) is the first exit from I–95. Turn right at the end of the ramp and follow the road into downtown Waltham. Turn right at Moody Street and right again onto Felton Street.

You'll be backtracking on this one-way street to reach the **Massachusetts Antiques Cooperative** (100 Felton Street, Waltham; 781–893–8893). With about one hundred dealers, this group shop looks smaller than it is until you realize that one room leads to another and that some cases are tucked into a tiny cellar and a larger loft. Few dealers specialize here, which makes browsing both harder and more fun, since you never know which case might contain a piece that will interest you.

DAY ONE: evening

DINNER

After you've poked around Massachusetts Antiques Cooperative until you're satisfied, lock your booty in the trunk and return to Moody Street by turning right at the nearest street to get back to Main Street. Moody Street is known around Boston for the quality and number of shops that specialize in home decorating supplies— tiles, carpets, plumbing fixtures—but your real reason to return (unless you're determined to see the latest in high-fashion bathrooms at Brickman's) is the **Tuscan Grill** (361 Moody Street, Waltham; 781–891–5486; moderate) between Spruce and Walnut Streets.

This storefront trattoria lives up to its name, with sumptuous and smoky food going straight from the exposed kitchen to several small tables along an exposed brick wall. Chef Jimmy Burke, something of a legend in Boston culinary circles, is apt to change the menu whenever he feels like it, but you can count on rich and startling risottos (artichokes, shrimp, and lemon basil, for example),

Some Massage Basics

You both may feel a little stiff after today's workout—but what better excuse to share a massage at the end of the day? Two basic techniques will help you work out the kinks: effleurage and friction. Effleurage consists of long, soothing strokes applied toward the heart using the palms of your hands to cover as much skin as possible. It relaxes large muscle groups. Friction strokes are usually applied in slow, circular movements to an area the size of a quarter using fingertips and knuckles.

To break down muscle spasms, begin with a half dozen effleurage strokes in the general area and then switch to light friction strokes on the whole spasm area, using the pads of your fingers. Slowly make the circles smaller while pressing harder. Then make a few strokes across the spasm site, then up and down. Perform a few effleurage strokes and repeat the cycle as needed.

mouth-watering pastas (such as his chard and ricotta ravioli in sage-parsley sauce), and magnificently grilled meats. You've probably worked up quite an appetite, so go ahead and splurge on the grilled beef tenderloin with gorgonzola potato gratin and Chianti beef glaze. To drink? Try a Spanna or a Gattinara—both made from the Nebbiolo grape and haunted by overtones of sweet cherries or blackberries. As you probably know, cross-country skiing burns more calories than almost any other form of sustainable exercise, so you can afford to indulge in dessert as well.

For More Romance

Another good day-trip ski center about forty minutes from Boston is **Great Brook Farm Ski Touring Center** (1018 Lowell Street, Carlisle; 978-369-7486). Hours, rates, and terrain are similar to those at the Weston Ski Track, but the inland location makes snow cover more likely. To reach Great Brook, continue west on the Massachusetts Turnpike to I-495. Take I-495 north to Route 4 in Chelmsford. Turn right on Route 4 and proceed to Lowell Road.

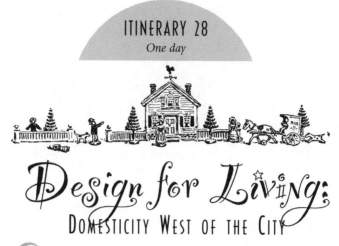

ITINERARY 28
One day

Design for Living:
DOMESTICITY WEST OF THE CITY

SOMETIMES IT REQUIRES WIDE OPEN SPACES for domesticity to come into full bloom. This daylong sojourn ventures west of Boston to the tony ex-urb of Lincoln, a community populated by many Harvard and MIT professors and the senior partners of large Boston law firms and brokerage houses. Yet for all that resident money, it's a surprisingly modest landscape, with few gaudy estates. The residents of Lincoln seem to understand (for the most part) that living well is far superior to merely living large. You'll get a peek into the private life of the Gropius family (Walter was one of the fathers of modern design) as expressed in their private home, and spend several hours wandering the fantastic, sometimes gently surreal landscape of the DeCordova Sculpture Park. Dinner will also be a work of art, but with an Italian theme, in nearby Waltham.

PRACTICAL NOTES: This itinerary is best undertaken during the summer months when the Gropius House is open to visitors from Wednesday to Sunday (hours are very limited at other times), and the grass of the sculpture park is green and inviting. Bring a blanket to spread on the grass in the DeCordova Sculpture Park. And be sure to make dinner reservations as far in advance as feasible for Il Capriccio (781–894–2234).

DAY ONE: morning

You'll be spending most of the day on small country roads, but to get to the countryside, first follow the Massachusetts Turnpike westbound to exit 15, where you should take Route 128/I-95 north

*R*omance
AT A GLANCE

♦ *Bauhaus design guru Walter Gropius might have championed spare boxes for public buildings, but he made his private family home in Lincoln a comfortable delight. See how a design genius lived at the* **Gropius House** *(68 Baker Bridge Road, Lincoln; 781–259–8098).*

♦ *After enjoying a sprightly and healthy lunch at the* **Cafe @ DeCordova,** *tour the rolling, park-like grounds of the* **DeCordova Museum and Sculpture Park** *(51 Sandy Pond Road, Lincoln; 781–259–8355).*

♦ *Sample the contemporary Italian cuisine of chef Rich Barron and the astounding selection of Italian small-estate wines at* **Il Capriccio Ristorante e Bar** *in nearby Waltham (888 Main Street, Waltham; 781–894–2234).*

for a few miles to exit 27, Trapelo Road. Take the westbound (Lincoln) side of the exit and proceed along Trapelo Road for about 2 miles to what passes for a major intersection in bucolic Lincoln. Five roads converge here, and the handsome stone town library is on the immediate right. After stopping, continue straight across the intersection to Sandy Pond Road. The entrance to the DeCordova Museum and Sculpture Park comes up in about one-half mile on the right. But continue to the next intersection, veering left onto Baker Bridge Road.

There's a delightful simplicity about place names in Lincoln. Sandy Pond Road goes past Sandy Pond, so named because its shores are sandy. Baker Bridge Road goes to a village area built up around a bridge constructed by a man named Baker, proprietor (we presume) of nearby Baker Farm.

A short distance on the left you will see the sign for the **Gropius House** (68 Baker Bridge Road, Lincoln; 781–259–8098). This museum house is owned, maintained, and shown by the Society for the Preservation of New England Antiquities. But unlike most SPNEA properties, the Gropius House is hardly an antiquity—it was built in 1938. The house is open for tours June through mid-October from Wednesday to Sunday. Tours, which cost $5.00 for adults, are given on the hour, with the first tour at 11:00 A.M. and the last at 4:00 P.M.

Most of us have experienced one of those awful house tours—either in person or on television—in which some terribly competent

Experimenting
to Get it Right the First Time

One of the joys of a good relationship is that you frequently find yourselves in tune with each other. And when your moods click, it seems that all's right with the world. One of the DeCordova's artistic strengths is a medium that shows just how this magic can be accomplished: the monoprint, which fixes an artistic vision in one unique image. But creating that image is not as instant as printing it. The artist lays down pigment on a smooth surface and then begins to experiment and embellish and adjust and manipulate. When it all comes together as a single harmonious moment, the artist rolls paper over the surface and makes that one enduring print. Like coordinating your moods, it seems effortless but might take considerable effort to achieve that effect.

woman or some supercilious man waves you through room after room, demonstrating fussy decorative touches with the insinuation that you either lack the cleverness or the means to accomplish something similar in your own home. Not here.

Walter Gropius didn't believe in gilding lilies, nor was he a particular fan of building on past designs. As the founder of the Bauhaus in Weimar, Germany, shortly after World War I, Gropius led a legendary group of architects and designers who effectively created the blueprint for modernism. The central tenet of their design credo was that every new product—a building, an automobile, a chair—should be approached freshly without reference to previous forms and designs. Moreover, the Bauhaus designers embraced modern materials and construction techniques.

Not surprisingly, Gropius had no love lost for the Nazis who took over his country, so in 1934 he quietly slipped off to England and, three years later, accepted a position as professor of architecture at Harvard University, where he remained active as an architect until his death in 1969.

But even an architect needs someplace to live, so Gropius gratefully accepted the donation of this lovely Lincoln site and set about designing a nest for himself and his wife and teenage daughter. Completed in 1938, the house practices what he preached about the embrace of industrial lines and materials with surprisingly comfortable results. Throughout are radical innovations—glass bricks, acoustic plaster, cork and rubber flooring—that had never been used in domestic architecture before but have become home-design clichés in the ensuing years.

Yet the Gropius House feels as though you could move right in and be at home immediately—from the neatly hidden drawers and pocket-door closets of the bedroom to the sleek furniture of the living room to the recessed spotlights over the dining table. Sixty years after it was built, and seventy years after many of the furnishings were designed, it still appears sleekly contemporary. You'll wish you could slip into one of the original cantilevered Barcelona chairs by pal Mies van der Rohe or take a breather in one of the original tubular, chrome-plated metal chairs created by Marcel Breuer. It's a tribute to the enduring classicism of Bauhaus design that most of the Gropius House furniture is still in production.

Although Bauhaus designers have been maligned for depersonalizing space, it's clear in this home that Gropius carefully crafted private spots for each member of the family: a dressing table for his wife, a writing desk for himself, an arrangement of overhead shades for discreet sunbathing on the second-story deck, a separate outdoor staircase to give their teenage daughter some privacy but watch her comings and goings. The house is enduring proof of Mies van der Rohe's two most famous observations: "Less is more" and "God is in the details."

DAY ONE: afternoon

LUNCH

Backtrack now to the **DeCordova Museum and Sculpture Park** (51 Sandy Pond Road; 781–259–8355). The museum is open Tuesday through Sunday from 11:00 A.M. to 5:00 P.M.; adult admission is $6.00. The Sculpture Park is open for free every day during daylight hours. Pay your admission and head upstairs to the **Cafe @ DeCordova,** open Wednesday through Sunday from 11:00 A.M. to 4:00 P.M. It's set up so you can help yourself to sandwiches (smoked turkey, ham, and brie), order a hot entree like Thai chicken noodles or lemon shrimp couscous, pick up a piece of cake and a drink, and then either settle in at a few tables amid some cheerful contemporary artwork or go outside. If the weather permits, "outside" is the better choice, as you can squeeze in together at a little cafe table under the trees on the Sculpture Terrace to enjoy your repast. Look one way and you'll see the latest terrace installation. Look the other, and the blue sweep of Sandy Pond stretches out at the bottom of a long green bowl. The DeCordova's location atop a hill affords long, dramatic views of the landscape.

Like the Gropius House, the DeCordova is a marvel of the new. The central building, now obscured by mid-1990s additions and renovations, was converted from a country manse in 1910 by Julian DeCordova, who collected modern art until about 1930, when he gave the entire estate to the town. Eight years later (the same time that the Gropius family moved into their new home) it opened as a museum. By 1951, the focus had settled on contemporary art with a New England association, and several buildings on the grounds were made into workshops for art and sculpture classes—modernism in the grass, as it were. Several buildings are still used for classes, and one has become the excellent **Store @ DeCordova,** which sells more materials for art-making than most museum shops. The store also carries an excellent line of artists' jewelry, hand-painted scarves, witty weather vanes, and a whole range of gift items made by artists.

The museum's exhibitions place particular emphasis on photography, one of the most modern of artistic expressions. The medium is the fastest growing portion of the permanent collection, and, at any given time, at least one photography show is available for viewing. Unlike some museums, which sprawl all over the countryside, the DeCordova's galleries are arranged vertically, sloping up a long hill. One wall of the staircase looks out through glass at the garden-like grounds, so don't be in a rush to get from floor to floor.

When you've finished touring the galleries, take some time to enjoy the thirty-five-acre sculpture park. About sixty massive sculptures are sited throughout the park. Pick up a map at the front desk before leaving the museum so you can find some of those that are more camouflaged than others. It is striking how well modern art blends into rolling landscape. Take, for example, the lovely and elegant piece called

Three Lines. George Rickey's three slender spears of stainless steel wave and bob in the wind with every passing breeze. And mind you, they move like tall grasses and trees, swinging on their vertical axes, thanks to Rickey's clever use of counterweights.

As you stroll around the campus (it feels like an idyllic college campus in many ways), you'll encounter art that mimics life and some that mimics nothing but itself. Stop near the studios to interact with one of the few sculptures that you are encouraged to touch, Paul Matisse's *The Musical Fence*. This construction of aluminum sounding bars and reinforced concrete functions as a giant double xylophone, with corresponding tones at each end of the sculpture. See if you can pick out the notes to "your song." Work on your harmonies.

You don't have to spend every minute looking at art, of course, since you so wisely brought along a blanket to spread out on the grass. Catch some rays. Spend some time staring at each other. While away the afternoon as only lovers can.

DAY ONE: evening

DINNER

Return to Route 128/I-95 and drive south to exit 20E, which is marked ROUTE 20 EAST–WALTHAM, following the signs toward the center of town. After 1 mile, you will be on Main Street. Keep a sharp lookout on the right for **Il Capriccio Ristorante e Bar** (888 Main Street, Waltham; 781-894-2234; moderate), where you have wisely made an advance reservation for dinner.

We say "wisely" because this brilliant little restaurant, owned and operated by Rich Barron, is consistently rated as one of Boston's great restaurants, and it isn't even in the city. The unpromising blank exterior gives way to a warren of small rooms inside, made apparently bigger by the liberal use of mirrors and dividers. Chances are good you will have an intimate little nook to yourselves to enjoy the sumptuous northern Italian fare.

Out-of-Town Sleepovers

Salem When It Ruled the Waves

THE DAYS OF SAIL STILL TWEAK our imaginations with the adventure of exotic ports, but there's no need to book an ocean voyage to recapture that spirit. Only 17 miles from Boston, Salem dominated the American trade with the Far East in the late eighteenth and early nineteenth centuries, sending ships to Macao and Manila, to Ceylon and Shanghai. These sleek vessels sailed home laden with pepper and tea, silk and porcelain, and their captains returned with fat purses. Much of the spirit of that time lingers in Salem's grand houses, museums, and public spaces. Spend a few days together with the ghosts of these Yankee traders in a city steeped in the romance of faraway places and maritime derring-do.

PRACTICAL NOTES: Salem's busy season for visitors is skewed by the city's association with witchcraft, making lodging scarce during October.

DAY ONE: morning

After breakfast at home, strike out for Salem. The most direct route from Boston is to take the Expressway north from downtown, then pick up Route 1 for about 16 miles to Salem—a short distance but a major shift from urban bustle to a small-town pace. Plan to check in late morning at **The Salem Inn** (7 Summer Street, Salem; 978-741-0680 or 800-446-2995; $129-$275), a group of three historic buildings, each with its own pleasures and charm. The West House (actually, a group of three circa-1834 town houses opened up to one building) is the quirkiest of the lot, with rooms ranging from

*R*omance
AT A GLANCE

♦ Stay at **The Salem Inn** (7 Summer Street, Salem; 978–741–0680 or 800–446–2995), choosing a "honeymoon suite" with fireplace and double whirlpool tub in the elegant Curwen House, built in 1854.

♦ Savor the subtly flavored dishes of the refined **Museum Café** (East India Square, Salem; 978–745–9500) that reflect the city's history as America's leading spice trader.

♦ Visit the **Essex Institute** campus (East Indian Square, Salem; 978–745–9500) to visit historic houses and examine exquisite Colonial and Federal furniture from Salem's past.

♦ Visit the extraordinary collections of the **Peabody Museum** (East India Square, Salem; 978–745–9500) and the **Salem Maritime National Historic Site** (174 Derby Street, Salem; 978–740–1660) to grasp the danger and romance of the China Trade.

♦ Dine on exceptional New American cuisine—accompanied by a fine selection of European and American wines—at the candlelit **Grapevine Restaurant** (26 Congress Street, Salem; 978–745–9335).

♦ Visit the **House of the Seven Gables** (54 Turner Street, Salem; 978–744–0991), the house that inspired the Gothic tale in Nathaniel Hawthorne's "Romance" by the same name.

quiet and fairly small quarters overlooking the back patio garden to giant suites suitable for a family of six. This is the only building of the three with a contingent of smoking rooms. The Peabody House, two buildings away, consists of immense family suites that could make a good base for a week of touring the region. But for a romantic getaway, our preference runs to the Curwen House at 313 Essex Street, which has a no-smoking, no-children policy. You're a three-minute walk from breakfast in the basement of the West House, and these rooms wear their 1854 character well. First and second floors are graced with immense windows and towering ceilings, while the short-but-wide windows of the third floor provide a sense of cozy intimacy. For a combination of fine appointments and peace and quiet, we like the left rear corner rooms—113, 213, and 313. These are "honeymoon suites" with queen canopy beds, working fireplaces, and double Jacuzzi tubs (in addition to a tub-shower).

Walk down Church Street, which turns into Brown Street, to reach the broad, tree-lined Common, one of New England's prettiest town greens. You might want to stroll around its perimeter to marvel at the houses that surround it, a veritable catalog of Georgian and Federal architecture. On one corner you'll see a stern-looking bronze of Roger Conant, founder of Salem in 1626. Then follow Hawthorne Boulevard 1 block to Essex Street. The combined Chamber of Commerce and Salem Maritime National Historic Site **Visitor Service Center** (2 New Liberty Street; 978-740-1650) is right off Essex Street. Pick up a map and check hours for guided tours of the waterfront buildings conducted by National Park Service rangers.

DAY ONE: afternoon

LUNCH

Before you set out exploring, stop for lunch at **The Museum Café** (East India Square; 978-745-9500) in the Peabody Essex Museum. The "café" part of the name is misleading, for this bright room of formal tables with linen tablecloths and a light midday menu of salads, pastas, fish, and chicken dishes is no coffee-and-sandwich cafeteria. As you sit surrounded by portraits of sailing ships, try the scallops in a saffron broth with capellini for a taste of the sea spiked with an exotic flavor from the spice trade.

The **Peabody Essex Museum** (East India Square; 978-745-9500) was born of the merger of two older museums within a block of each other on Essex Street. The Essex Institute recounts the county and domestic history; the Peabody Museum focuses on the glory days of world trade. The two museums are open year-round Tuesday through Saturday 10:00 A.M. to 5:00 P.M., and on Sunday from noon to 5:00 P.M. From April 1 through October 31, Monday hours are from 1:00 A.M. to 5:00 P.M. The library at Essex Institute and the entire Peabody Museum also remain open until 8:00 P.M. on Thursday. Adult admission is $10 for two days.

Begin your visit with the **Essex Institute** campus. The Institute opened in 1799, making it one of the oldest continuously operating museums in America. A broad, winding staircase leads to the main exhibition galleries. Salem was clearly a boomtown for portrait painters in the late eighteenth and early nineteenth centuries, as everyone with some money had his likeness and those of his

The Courting Candle

As you venture through the historic homes of the Peabody-Essex, you'll notice a curious lighting device in many of the front parlors. It appears to be a candlestick in which the candle is inserted deeply into a coil of flat metal. On the side is a lever by which it can be lowered or raised. At first glance you might think this candle lamp is an ingeniously thrifty Yankee device that snuffs a candle automatically if the householder falls asleep reading. Ingenious it is, but the design has nothing to do with thrift. When a young man came courting in Salem, he and the object of his affections were permitted the privacy of the front parlor, but once the courting candle went out, he had to leave. A father, it is said, would keep the candle short for a suitor he didn't like, but would raise the candle high for a prospect of whom he approved. Reproductions of the courting candle, available in the museum gift shop, are popular modern engagement gifts in Salem.

family limned in oils and framed in gilt. The portraits of Salem movers and shakers share the Andrew Oliver Portrait Gallery at the head of the stairs with excellent examples of eighteenth- and nineteenth-century furniture, much of it by cabinetmakers from Salem and nearby towns on Massachusetts' North Shore.

The interior gallery, divided with a mezzanine, tells many different tales of local history, including the origins of Parker Brothers, the Salem amusements company made famous by its board game *Monopoly*. But the most striking exhibits are three period rooms created in 1907 by the Essex Institute's pioneering curator, George Francis Dow. The 1750 kitchen and circa 1800 bedroom and parlor were among the first museum installations in America to re-create domestic environments to give visitors a better understanding of the past. These charming rooms are only an introduction to the rich domestic history captured by the museum, which also has a number of historic homes on its grounds. Guided tours of these buildings are included in the admission.

Two of the Essex Institute houses sum up the swelling wealth of the town. The **Crowninshield-Bentley House,** a Georgian manse built in 1727, is an early home of the prominent Crowninshield family (of whom you will hear more). The **Gardner-Pingree House** is an imposing Federal-style monument to mercantile wealth built in 1790 and greatly augmented in 1820. The contrasts between the two homes are instructive—pewter and wood on the dining table soon give way to porcelain and crystal. You could say that good taste made Gardner's fortune. In 1798, he sold his clothing store and sent sailing ships to India and Sumatra to bring back black pepper and other spices.

The **Peabody Museum** was founded by Salem's true adventurers: the captains and supercargoes (the chief commercial officer on a trading ship) who had ventured beyond either the Cape of Good Hope or Cape Horn, thereby qualifying for membership in the Salem East India Marine Society. Members were required by the charter to collect "natural and artificial curiosities" on their voyages.

The museum emphasizes trade with the Far East, including a collection of model ships engaged in that commerce. One instructive exhibit shows the entire process of creating Chinese export porcelain—which ships took on as ballast, in many cases. Several pieces from the early twentieth century remain in their ingenious packaging, designed to withstand the tossing and turning of a voyage halfway around the world.

The Peabody's Crowninshield Gallery features America's first seagoing pleasure yacht, a vessel called *Cleopatra's Barge*, launched by George Crowninshield in 1816. A former Revolutionary War privateer (that is, a pirate sanctioned by the American government) and merchant sailor, Crowninshield spared no expense in creating his luxury retirement craft. A full-size reconstruction of the wood-paneled salon is festooned with displays of the ship's great Mediterranean cruise of 1817, completed two months before the owner's death.

DAY ONE: evening

When you return to the inn, settle into the parlor to recuperate from your forays into distant ports and the distant past. As you sip glasses of sherry that you have poured from the decanter in the front hall, you can contemplate the domestic pleasures (like this house) attained through risk and deprivation on the high seas. It was not uncommon for a couple to be separated for a year or more as he sailed out to seek a fortune and she kept the hearth for his homecoming.

DINNER

The bright decor and lively food of the **Grapevine Restaurant** (26 Congress Street; 978–745–9335; moderate; reservations essential) will replace your thoughtful mood with one of celebration. Sunny yellow walls are covered with colorful contemporary prints, and the candlelit small tables create an air of intimacy. The menu emphasizes sure-handed combinations of strong flavors. A wide selection of pastas suggests an Italian cuisine, but dishes like the roasted pork loin stuffed with black olives signal that the kitchen is distinctly New American. A good selection of wines by the glass and an even better selection of about sixty bottles, split evenly between red and white, complement the cooking nicely.

DAY TWO: morning

BREAKFAST

Breakfast at the Salem Inn is a buffet in the basement of the West House at 7 Summer Street. Fresh muffins, croissants, and sweet rolls are offered, along with fruit, juice, and cold cereal for a low-key but healthful start to the day. On a nice morning, you can take your meal to a table in the garden patio in back of the house to contemplate the fountain and listen to the birds as you eat. When you've finished, set out for Derby Street on the waterfront to tour the **Salem Maritime National Historic Site.** Ranger-led tours begin at the orientation center at 174 Derby Street. The site is open daily from 9:00 A.M. to 5:00 P.M.; 9:00 A.M. to 6:00 P.M. during July and August. Adults pay $3.00.

Although only a handful of wharves remain from more than fifty during Salem's heyday, the infrastructure of international trade still exists here on the waterfront—the warehouses, the greatest of the wharves, the all-important Custom House, and the rich homes of shipowners.

One Park Service tour takes you through an early home of Elias Hasket Derby, who became America's first millionaire by the time of his death in 1799. With American ships barred from British ports after the Revolution, Derby and his in-laws, the Crowninshield family, cast their sights farther around the globe, opening up India, China, and the Russian Baltic ports to New England shipping. In 1786, Derby's ship *Grand Turk* was the first Salem vessel to venture beyond the Cape of Good Hope, bringing home tea, silk, spices, and cassia. It opened an era of such extensive trade that many in Asia believed "Salem" to be a sovereign nation. Ironically, Derby never went to sea himself, although he designed many of his ships. Part of his genius was to invent the supercargo post—sending a clever trader aboard ship to "trade on my behalf as best you can."

As the goods poured into Salem, the little port was contributing as much as 12 percent of the revenue to run the American government. These taxes were levied as customs, and the handsome 1819 **Custom House** filled the Federal coffers. Salem's mercantile importance began to decline by mid-century, but not before one of the port's most famous native sons had his turn in a patronage post at the Custom House. From 1846 to 1849, Nathaniel Hawthorne served as "surveyor of the port," and you can visit his office on the first floor. When a new political administration came to power, Hawthorne was suddenly deprived of his pension. But Sofia, his wife, had been secretly saving money to buy him time to write—she believed he had "scarcely tapped genius." Hawthorne settled on a subject provocative enough to sell, creating *The Scarlet Letter*, which proved to be an immediate commercial and literary success.

DAY TWO: afternoon

LUNCH

Stop for fried clams or a lobster roll at **Derby Fish and Lobster** (215 Derby Street; 978-745-2064) before moving on to a bit more about Hawthorne at **The House of the Seven Gables** (54 Turner Street off Derby Street; 978-744-0991), the structure that inspired his second "romance," as Hawthorne called his book-length fictions.

The dark house looks little changed since Hawthorne described it almost 140 years ago: "Halfway down a bystreet in one of our New England towns stands a rusty wooden house, with seven acutely peaked gables. . . ." The house, originally constructed in 1688 and added onto several times, was owned by Hawthorne's second cousin, Susannah Ingersoll. The writer was a frequent visitor and expressed great fascination with Salem's older houses as symbols of an earlier, darker time in the city's history. The rooms are like portraits—not exactly a perfect likeness of the people who lived here, but containing enough of their characteristics so that you can animate the rooms with your imaginations. Another building on the grounds is the modest house where Hawthorne was born and lived until his father died when Hawthorne was four years old. Amid the buildings is a fine example of a classic Salem flower garden, which, like the rest of the city, looks out to the sea. The House of the Seven Gables is open daily. Tours are offered from 10:00 A.M. to 5:00 P.M. From January through March, the house opens at noon on Sunday. Adults pay $8.00.

FOR MORE ROMANCE

Somewhat removed from other attractions, **Chestnut Street** is an amazingly intact collection of fine houses from Salem's wealthiest days early in the nineteenth century. Federal architecture here had more room to sprawl than in Boston, so local architect Samuel McIntyre (a student of Charles Bulfinch) defined a country-baronial version of his master's rational orderliness. Only the occasional Greek Revival portico grafted onto the entrance suggests that subsequent owners found anything they wanted to change.

Salem's long association with witchcraft has mutated into an enterprising New Age commerce in all matters occult. If the spirit moves you, there's no shortage of places to have your fortune told through the Tarot, palmistry, and even crystal balls. We foresee an intensely happy love life, a long sea voyage to distant shores, and subsequent wealth beyond your dreams. . . .

Sweet Seclusion on Old Cape Cod

APE COD IS A MYTHIC PLACE in the American imagination—where Patti Page's silky voice forever extolls summer indolence in "Old Cape Cod" and the distant figure of John Kennedy stalks an endless beach lost in his thoughts. Sand and sea and saltwater hay . . . lobsters and clams and the freshest of cod.

But there are at least two distinct Cape Cods: the endless summer of freckles and swimsuits and beaches uninterrupted by stones that characterizes the Outer Cape (see "Provincetown by Ferry") and the more measured, salt-tanged Upper Cape, where the colonial settlers farmed as much as they fished and the land is in less danger of washing into the sea. The Outer Cape buzzes with adrenaline. But the Upper Cape, closer to Boston, is more like a great conversationalist, finding new ways to charm at every turn. Destination: Falmouth—our idea of perfection on the Upper Cape, with short, sandy beaches and a postcard-perfect historic town green.

PRACTICAL NOTES: Falmouth is spectacular in June. Accidents of geography and ocean currents combine to make this piece of the Cape a veritable flower garden, with rhododendrons and azaleas and beach roses. The same itinerary also works in October because Falmouth stays warm long after most of New England has begun to chill; it's also the season for the colorful cranberry harvest. At either time, the roads are less congested, the lodgings and restaurants less crowded, and the beaches almost deserted. Bring your bathing suits.

Romance AT A GLANCE

◆ Unpack your bags and move right into the spacious but cozy confines of "Suite Seclusion," a private cottage behind the gingerbread Queen Anne–style **Palmer House Inn** in historic Falmouth (81 Palmer Avenue, Falmouth; 508–548–1230 or 800–472–2632).

◆ Sit back at generously sized tables to enjoy contemporary gourmet cuisine in a picturesque setting amid Ralph Cahoon paintings of seafarers and mermaids at the **Coonamessett Inn** (Jones Road and Gifford Street, Falmouth; 508–548–2300).

◆ Whiz along the easy trail of the **Shining Sea Bike Path** through the bayberry and marsh grasses of conservation land en route to Woods Hole.

◆ Soak in the sunset over **Old Silver Beach** on Buzzards Bay. Watch the horizon together closely and you might be able to join the select ranks of people who have actually seen the elusive "green flash" of the last ray of sunset.

◆ Set anchor for a culinary masterpiece dinner on the marina behind the glass wall of the splendid **Regatta of Falmouth-by-the-Sea** (Scranton Avenue, Falmouth; 508–548–5400).

◆ Not every delectable meal has to be a big bash. Picnic on the beach with steamed lobsters and stuffed quahogs from **Green Pond Fish'n Gear** (366 East Menauhaut Road, East Falmouth; 508–548–2573).

DAY ONE: afternoon

Drive down Route 3 from Boston. At the Sagamore traffic circle, follow Route 6 west to Buzzards Bay, where you'll pick up Route 28 south over the Bourne Bridge. Route 28 skirts the western edge of Cape Cod until it makes a 90-degree turn directly through Falmouth Center, the largest of the town's eight villages. (Like most Cape Cod towns, Falmouth covers a lot of territory.)

An hour and a half after leaving Boston you'll pull in at **The Palmer House Inn** (81 Palmer Avenue, Falmouth; 508–548–1230 or 800–472–2632; rooms $90–$199; cottage $165–$225), a lavishly decorated Queen Anne Victorian just off the Falmouth Center town green. If you have made reservations for it in advance, innkeepers Joanne and Ken Baker will have "Suite Seclusion," a stand-alone cottage behind the main inn, ready for you. Suite

Seclusion includes a sitting room, a bedroom with king-size bed, a fireplace, a Jacuzzi area with mood lighting on a dimmer, and a little kitchen with a microwave oven but no stove (so you won't feel compelled to really cook). It also has a small refrigerator just right for chilling a bottle of champagne.

You can pick up that champagne in the village center, a short walk away, at **John's Liquor Store** (729 Main Street; 508-548-2287). The store stocks a range of New England regional wines; we recommend the steely, crisp sparkling chardonnay from Westport Rivers. A few doors down (just follow your noses), drop into **Ghelfi's Candies of Cape Cod** (878 Main Street; 508-457-1085) for mouth-watering truffles to accompany the bubbly. On the way back to your room to stash both in the refrigerator, walk up to the end of Academy Lane to the **Chamber of Commerce Information Center** (508-548-8500 or 800-526-8532) for a Falmouth map and a copy of "A Walk Through Falmouth History," the local historic walking tour.

Spend what remains of your afternoon strolling in the village. Along the postcard town green, the white Congregational church has a Revere bell, and the broad lawns next to St. Barnabas Church are the scene for the Strawberry Festival in late June in a town renowned for its berries. At the end of the Main Street shops, you'll find Shore Street, which is true to its name. Saunter down to the end, passing pleasant little houses set back on shady lots, until—in about ten minutes—you arrive at the bright light and long vistas of **Surf Beach**. On a clear day, you can make out the island of Martha's Vineyard. Take off your shoes for a long walk in the beach sand. If you want to take a plunge, the waters of Vineyard Sound are typically about 10 degrees warmer than those on the other side of the Cape in Cape Cod Bay.

DAY ONE: evening

DINNER

In the seventeenth and eighteenth centuries, Falmouth was a well-to-do town, and this colonial-era wealth is reflected in the **Coonamessett Inn** (Jones Road and Gifford Street; 508-548-2300; expensive). The inn's capacious dining room has a superb New American menu and a remarkable display of artwork by local primitive Ralph Cahoon. Cahoon's imaginative paintings of mermaids and sailors in idealized nineteenth-century settings often sold for $200–$300 a decade ago; by 1994, one canvas fetched $77,000. The rule of thumb at the Coonamessett is to opt for one of the evening's fish specials. Dessert awaits back in Suite Seclusion.

DAY TWO: morning

BREAKFAST

Join the less secluded Palmer House Inn guests for a sumptuous breakfast in the dining room of the inn. Savor your Swiss eggs in puff pastry or perhaps a plate of French toast—the Bakers prepare a sweet entree one day, a savory one the next.

You'll want to walk off your heavy meal, and Falmouth's just the place to do it. Take out the historic walking-tour map you acquired yesterday at the Chamber and set off. The route begins at the Old Burying Ground on Mill Road, where in 1705 Desire Bourne claimed the first grave in this Succanesset Plantation settlement. Many of the older stones are engraved with the years, months, and days of the person's life—for these hardy settlers, every day counted. There are gravestones without graves (for sailors lost at sea) and graves without stones (for bodies washed ashore).

As the tour continues toward the town green, it wends past a virtual gallery of American domestic architecture, including the home at 16 West Main Street where Katharine Lee Bates was born. Falmouth folk may be the only ones who recall that she penned "America the Beautiful." Never mind that she moved away when she was twelve; she's still celebrated as a local girl who made good.

DAY TWO: afternoon

LUNCH

You'll be done in time to walk down a block to the very casual **Laureen's** (170 Main Street; 508-540-9104), a combination bake shop, cafe, and gourmet grocery store, for a lunch of soup and salad or the pasta of the day. Laureen's doesn't boast any special decor—just the conventional Formica tables—but the staff is upbeat and cheerful, and you'll feel that way, too.

Walk back past the Town Common to rent bicycles from **Corner Cycle** (115 Palmer Avenue; 508–540–4195). Reservations are suggested. Each bicycle rents for $8.00 for the first hour, $14.00 for two to five hours, and $18.00 for five to twenty-four hours. Several bike paths share the Falmouth roads, but the **Shining Sea Bike Path** (as in "from . . . to . . .") is a "rails-to-trails" conversion. Far from autos, it traverses a nearly flat 3.5 miles between Falmouth and the village of Woods Hole. No need to be in a hurry, as there's plenty to see if you're observant. You can stop at Trunk River Beach for another fix of ocean, or pause at a marshy inlet where swans and songbirds congregate. You may want to have binoculars handy to look for the source of a trilling bird song.

The path ends in **Woods Hole,** the embarkation point for ferries to Martha's Vineyard and Nantucket. Blending the best of Camden, Maine, and Cambridge, Massachusetts, Woods Hole is a nautical spot with an academic bent, due to researchers from the Marine Biological Laboratory and the Woods Hole Oceanographic Institute. The **WHOI Exhibit Center** (15 School Street; 508–457–2000, ext. 2663) maintains quaint, if low-key, historical exhibits. The short films (including an underwater tour of the wreck of the *Titanic*) are fascinating. The center is open Memorial Day to Labor Day, Monday through Saturday from 10:00 A.M. to 4:30 P.M. and on Sunday from noon to 4:30 P.M. A $2.00 donation is requested. When you've seen enough, swagger through the Woods Hole streets with a nautical roll to your stride and toss back a brew and oysters at **Shuckers** (91A Water Street; 508–540–3850).

Be sure to return to Falmouth Center in time to pick up the car for a drive to **Old Silver Beach** (Quaker Road, North Falmouth, off Route 28) to watch the sun go down over Buzzards Bay. West-facing beaches are uncommon on the East Coast, and few offer such a long vista over water. Old Silver is one of the few spots where you may be able to see the elusive phenomenon called the "green flash."

DAY TWO: evening

DINNER

You'll make a full evening of the dining adventure awaiting you at **Regatta of Falmouth-by-the-Sea** (Scranton Avenue at the head of the Falmouth Marina; 508–548–5400; reservations suggested; expensive). The Regatta is a great surprise—worlds apart from the kind of casual eateries you usually encounter on a harbor. In this case, you can enjoy a beautiful view (reserve a window table) as well as excellent service and imaginative food. The cuisine is New American in the best sense—firmly rooted in local tradition (the lobster and corn chowder is deceptively complex) but with accents from the Caribbean, the Mediterranean, and Asia. The wine list is long and deep. If you opt for the lamb, let the sommelier suggest an appropriate Rhone wine, maybe a Gigondas. With the fish, a Pouilly-Fuissé is perfect.

The Green Flash

The "green flash" is the first or last glint of the sun seen under perfect conditions of no pollution or clouds. It is a sudden, intensely green ray of light that many people never see in their lifetimes. The view from Old Silver Beach, especially under weather conditions encountered in June and October, offers one of the best opportunities to observe this rare phenomenon.

DAY THREE: morning

After breakfast at the Inn, swing the car down Shore Road past Surf Beach, keeping to the shoreline whenever the road offers an option. Shore Road becomes Nobska Road, which is, together with Shore Road, the long, scenic route to **Nobska Light**. This picturesque lighthouse, like all the New England lighthouses, is automated now but still has the poignant charm of an outpost on a bluff. Ships can see the light from 17 miles out to sea, and you can see about as far in return. Pull off the road and walk on the seaward side for great views over the beaches out to sea. *Hint:* The best photograph is taken from uphill, above the lighthouse looking down. You won't be able to get the whole light into the frame unless you have a wide-angle lens or step way back.

LUNCH

By now you will have discovered that the seaside air and light have an intoxicating effect. There's no better way to end your visit than with a casual lobster picnic from a local institution: **Green Pond Fish'n Gear** (366 Menauhaut Road, East Falmouth; 508–548–2573). Order some of their famed chowder, stuffed quahogs (a local specialty), and a steamed lobster or two and settle down on a boulder on the beach across the road. If you really want to make like the locals, roll up your sleeves and pants and splash around in the salt water to rinse off after your repast.

FOR MORE ROMANCE

The west side of Falmouth offers fascinating driving and, occasionally, walking vistas. Using your town map, head west and then wind your way slowly up the coast toward the village of Buzzards Bay.

The **Cahoon Museum of American Art** (Routes 28 and 130, Cotuit; 508–428–7581) features the work of Ralph Cahoon and other, mostly modern, painters. It is open February through December on Tuesday through Saturday from 10:00 A.M. to 4:00 P.M. A donation is requested.

The Regatta of Falmouth-by-the-Sea has a sister restaurant, the **Regatta of Cotuit** (Route 28, Cotuit; 508–428–5715; expensive), more geared to land than sea, practically across the road from the Cahoon Museum.

Provincetown by Ferry

WHO WOULD THINK A ONE-TIME FISHING TOWN at the knuckles of the fist of Cape Cod could be such an inspiration? Provincetown is a village of extremes—extremes of light, of land, of water, and of social expression. Perched on 4.5 square miles of sand and dunes, it is America's oldest continuous art colony, attracting the likes of Edward Hopper and Robert Motherwell to paint and Eugene O'Neill and Stanley Kunitz to write. Part of Provincetown's appeal is the light, diffuse and ubiquitous from the salt spray that cocoons this knob of land from every side. And no small part of the attraction is that Provincetown embodies summer with a sinuous sensuality like the taste of salt on your lover's skin. A frankness about sexuality is part of the local ethos, which makes P'town a poor choice if you're bothered by other people's amorous orientations but an exhilarating locale if you're not.

PRACTICAL NOTES: Sunblock and a broad-brimmed hat are wise precautions in Provincetown, since cool sea breezes mask the heat of the intense summer sun. This itinerary must be done mid-May through early October to take advantage of high-season transportation. Make dinner reservations in advance of your visit since would-be diners vastly outnumber restaurant seats in Provincetown in summer. Read on to discover our suggestion for the most romantic spot in P'town.

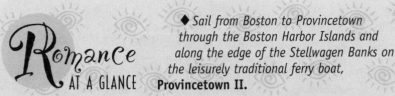

Romance AT A GLANCE

♦ Sail from Boston to Provincetown through the Boston Harbor Islands and along the edge of the Stellwagen Banks on the leisurely traditional ferry boat, **Provincetown II.**

♦ Set yourselves up in your cheerful and bright room at the **Beaconlight Guest House** (12 Winthrop Street, Provincetown; 508–487–9603 or 800–696–9603), an in-village B&B with an English country manor feel and a resident golden retriever.

♦ Peruse the visions of Cape Cod light in the **art galleries** on Commercial Street and stop off for a bite to eat at **Pucci's Harborside Restaurant & Bar** (539 Commercial Street, Provincetown; 508–487–1964), an artist's hangout.

♦ See the sun dip below the horizon as you bounce over the dunes of Cape Cod National Seashore with **Art's Dune Tours** (508–487–1950 or 508–487–1050).

♦ Enjoy some of Cape Cod's most acclaimed fine dining with a candlelit dinner in one of the tiny rooms of the **Martin House** (157 Commercial Street, Provincetown; 508–487–1327).

♦ Kick off your shoes and socks and perambulate down the long sandy strand of **Herring Cove Beach;** you'll be the model of human intimacy in a vast natural setting.

DAY ONE: morning

You'll be sailing at 9:00 A.M. on the *Provincetown II* from the World Trade Center Pier. Get your tickets in advance from **Bay State Cruise Company** (Long Wharf; 617–748–1428; $30 round trip). You'll find long-term parking nearby if you arrive by 8:45 A.M. or so.

The ferry offers two open decks lined with benches for sightseeing and one enclosed deck below, where breakfast is served once the ship is under way. The $6.25 buffet breakfast is a good value and helps pass the time. (The voyage lasts three hours.) But you may not want to head straight to the table, as the first half hour of sailing is a narrated cruise through the Boston Harbor Islands. (See "On a Desert Island in Your Dreams.") When you begin to cross Massachusetts Bay, you'll be on the far edges of the Stellwagen Banks, known both for its schools of fish and as a feeding ground for summering whales.

DAY ONE: afternoon

When you dock at 12:30 P.M. at MacMillan Wharf in Provincetown, you'll be met by your hosts, Stephen Mascilo and Trevor Pinker, who will whisk you up the street to your room at **The Beaconlight Guesthouse** (12 Winthrop Street; 508-487-9603 or 800-696-9603; $105–$185). British professionals who fell in love with Provincetown and took over the Beaconlight in 1994, Stephen and Trevor have renovated and redecorated to give the interior the feel of an English country manor house. Every room is distinctive, but the most romantic is easily the Cape Ann Suite, with its rich red walls and bright yellow swags and drapes. The room has its own outside entrance, a canopied king-size bed that faces a log fireplace, and an intimate sitting area.

LUNCH

You'll spend the afternoon getting a feel for the historic and contemporary Provincetown art scene. Rather than walking along the main drag, Commercial Street, from the center of town, begin at the east end and work your way back. Stroll down Bradford Street (with lighter crowds) as far as Hancock, and then cut down to have a bite to eat at **Pucci's Harborside Restaurant & Bar** (539 Commercial Street; 508-487-1964). The lunch fare is fairly standard—sandwiches, seafood, soups—but this is a spot where many artists hang out when the muse is uncooperative. Eavesdrop on their conversations for a little insight into the town's character.

For a sense of history stroll down to look at 571 and 577 Commercial Street, where Eugene O'Neill and John Dos Passos, respectively, lived and wrote. Then head back toward town, stopping in the shops and galleries that catch your eye.

Between Cook and Bangs Streets you'll encounter Provincetown's artistic institution, the **Provincetown Art Association and Museum** (460 Commercial Street; 508-487-1750). Established in 1914, the Association has enrolled virtually every artist who has lived and worked in Provincetown over the years, including Edward Hopper, Marsden Hartley, Milton Avery, and Robert Motherwell. The museum exhibits both established and "emerging" artists as well as treasures from its permanent collection. It is open daily from noon to 5:00 P.M. and from 8:00 to 10:00 P.M. in July and August. Check the bulletin board for openings and receptions and pick up a free *Provincetown Gallery Guide*. Admission is by a suggested donation of $3.00.

Close by and across the street (445 Commercial Street) is the home occupied by Milton Avery and his family. A pair of interesting contemporary galleries pop up in the next block as well: the **Rice-Polak Gallery** (430 Commercial Street; 508–487–1052) and the **UFO Gallery** (424 Commercial Street; 508–487–4424).

Turn off Commercial at Pearl Street to the **Fine Arts Work Center** (24 Pearl Street; 508–487–9960), where artists have had studios since 1914. Check to see if there's a show hanging in the gallery. Robert Motherwell worked in the red barn on this property and in 1962 painted one of his *Elegies to the Spanish Republic*, now hanging in the Metropolitan Museum of Art in New York.

Close by is the even older **Cape Cod School of Art** (48 Pearl Street; 508–487–0101), founded in 1899 by Impressionist painter Charles Hawthorne. The school still carries the torch for American Impressionism—perfectly understandable given the luminous qualities of landscape at the end of Cape Cod. Check to see if instructors at the school will be offering a painting demonstration during your stay; they sometimes paint an entire landscape from start to finish.

Return to Commercial Street and continue toward town. You'll soon pass the **Provincetown Heritage Museum** (356 Commercial Street; 508–487–7098), which has a number of paintings amid the antique fire equipment, fishing artifacts and marine gear. It is open daily Memorial Day to Columbus Day weekend from 10:00 A.M. to 5:30 P.M.; admission is $3.00. Next you will come upon the **East End Gallery** (349 Commercial Street; 508–487–4745), one of the well-established galleries showing contemporary work.

At some point in the afternoon you should make a reservation with **Art's Dune Tours** (Standish and Commercial Streets; 508–487–1950 or 508–487–1050) for Art Costa's "sunset dune tour," which costs $15 for each of you and departs ninety minutes before sunset (call for times). Art started giving these tours back in 1946 with a 1930s Ford woodie with balloon tires. These days he has a fleet of six Chevrolet Suburbans and a half-century-plus track record of respect for fragile environments as well as a half century plus to hone his anecdotes. The tour will touch on some sites you've seen

(O'Neill's house), then swing up to the shore north of Provincetown, site of many a shipwreck over the years. When the sun begins to dip into the ocean (sometimes it's so big and red we expect it to hiss), you'll be standing on Race Point Beach.

DINNER

This little town has the lion's share of fine dining on the Outer Cape, but possibly the most romantic spot available is in one of the small dining rooms scattered through the 250-year-old **Martin House** (157 Commercial Street; 508–487–1327; moderate to expensive), at which you have made your reservations. Chef Alex Mazzocca emphasizes a New American style with many international influences and a whole-hearted commitment to local products. So you're likely to find the sweet-sour flavor of tamarind added to your dish of littleneck clams, or grilled frisée as one of the accompaniments to plump, delectable Wellfleet scallops. Desserts by pastry chef Sarah Dinsmore are delight-ful turns on old favorites. For example, her "lemon tart" is a short-bread topped with lemon curd and a golden brown puff of meringue.

DAY TWO: morning

After a predictably delicious fresh-baked breakfast at the Beaconlight (frittata, fruit breads, chocolate muffins—whatever the innkeepers are inspired to make that day), walk down to the Town Wharf to catch the **Beach Shuttle** ($1.25), P'town's answer to inad-equate parking. The bus makes the rounds between town, beach, and highway lodgings every hour from 8:00 A.M. A few minutes later, you'll be at **Herring Cove Beach**, which has bathhouses should you wish to change into swim attire. This dune-backed sandy beach is one of our favorites for long walks. Kick off your shoes and socks and meander along the water's edge on this tame side of the peninsula that faces back toward the mainland. As the wind blows in your hair, you might feel just a little silly because the scene is so familiar from bad movies and television commercials. Forget about it. Media types like this shot because it evokes human intimacy in the face of benign but powerful nature. You're not watch-ing the scene—you are the scene.

Even long walks on the beach have a limit, so return to town for some final sightseeing, including **The Pilgrim Monument** and **Museum** (Bradford Street; 508–487–1310). Open daily from 9:00 A.M. to 7:00 P.M., the monument commemorates the first landing of Pilgrims in 1620, where they decided Provincetown was too unprotected and moved on to Plymouth. The 255-foot tower, the tallest granite structure in the United States, provides a panoramic view of the entire Cape across the bay to Plymouth. The museum records major periods in Outer Cape history: a whaling captain's quarters and the Pilgrims' *Mayflower* on the day of arrival in the New World. There is something rather touching about a wide-open, hedonistic town like Provincetown laying claim to an austere Pilgrim heritage. The most intriguing exhibits relate to P'town's legendary fishing history. Admission costs $6.00.

DAY TWO: afternoon

LUNCH

Even with an explosion of chef-crafted cuisine in P'town, a few old standards can't really be improved. For clam chowder by which to judge all others, we suggest stopping in for lunch at **The Lobster Pot** (321 Commercial Street; 508–487–0842), an old-fashioned ultracasual seafood restaurant run by people who know their fish.

This Be the Food of Love

Folklore claims that many foods have aphrodisiacal attributes, a proposition supported in a general way by the Encyclopaedia Britannica, which points to "the psychophysiological reaction that a well-prepared meal can have upon the human organism. The combination of various sensuous reactions—the visual satisfaction of the sight of appetizing food, the olfactory stimulation of their pleasing smells and the tactile gratification afforded the oral mechanism by rich, savoury dishes—tend to bring on a state of euphoria conducive to sexual expression." Outer Cape Cod happens to be one of the richest areas in the world for the foods most often cited as aids to love: shellfish. So enjoy that bowl of mussels and brochette of scallops. Cape oyster season opens in August, ahead of the usual September opening in Chesapeake Bay.

You might want to revisit a gallery to purchase an etching to hang at home as a permanent reminder of P'town, the place where summer dwells. The ferry back to Boston begins boarding at 3:15 for a 3:30 P.M. departure.

For More Romance

If you'd like to eke out a few more hours in Provincetown, you should avail yourselves of the express ferry service ($40 per person round trip), which takes only two rather than three hours. Moreover, the express ferry leaves Boston at 8:00 A.M. and departs Provincetown at 6:30 and 7:30 P.M.

Of course, the best way to extend your Provincetown romance is to stay another day. If so, plan to rent bicycles from **Provincetown Bikes** (42 Bradford Street; 508–487–TREK) to explore the trails in the Cape Cod National Seashore, which abuts Provincetown. Get the best of both worlds—the traditional reverence for good fish and a contemporary culinary panache—by dining at **The Dancing Lobster** (371 Commercial Street; 508–487–0900; inexpensive to moderate), which begins seating at 5:30 P.M. (no reservations).

RECOMMENDED ANNUAL EVENTS

JANUARY–MARCH

Anthony Spinazzola Gala. Variable date from late January to early February; World Trade Center; (617) 344–4413. This black-tie evening offers samplings from the city's best restaurants.

Chinese New Year. Late January to March depending on lunar calendar; throughout Chinatown; (617) 482–3292. Celebration includes parade, lion and dragon dances, and firecrackers.

FEBRUARY

Beanpot Hockey Tournament. First two Saturdays of February; Fleet Center; (617) 624–1000. Boston College, Boston University, Harvard University, and Northeastern University hockey teams vie for Boston supremacy.

MARCH

New England Spring Flower Show. Mid-March; Bayside Expo Center; (617) 536–9280. Oldest annual flower exhibition in the United States. (See "Hearts and Flowers: A Celebration of Spring.")

APRIL

Patriots Day Parade. Third Monday; downtown and North End. Parade begins at 9:30 A.M. at City Hall Plaza and concludes at Paul Revere Mall for a reenactment of Paul Revere's Midnight Ride.

Boston Marathon. Third Monday; from Hopkinton, Massachusetts, to finish line in Copley Square; (617) 236–1652. The world's oldest marathon attracts spectators and runners from throughout the world.

MAY

Walk for Hunger. First Sunday; 20 miles through the city; (617) 723–5000. One of the oldest and largest pledge walks in the country.

Ducklings Day Parade. Second Sunday; Boston Common; (617) 426–1885. Retraces the route of the ducklings in Robert McCloskey's classic children's book *Make Way for Ducklings.*

Boston Brewers' Festival. Mid-May; Bayside Exposition Center; (617) 825–5151. About one hundred brewpubs and craft breweries from around New England display their wares.

Hidden Gardens of Beacon Hill. Third Thursday; Beacon Hill; (617) 227–4392. Self-guided tour of gardens that cannot be seen from sidewalk.

Lilac Sunday. Third Sunday; Arnold Arboretum; (617) 524–1717. More than 400 fragrant lilacs are in bloom from deep-red to palest white.

Annual Street Performers Festival. Late May; Faneuil Hall Marketplace; (617) 338–2323. This four-day festival features fifty of the world's top street performers outdoors in the market area.

JUNE

Scooper Bowl. Tuesday, Wednesday, and Thursday of first full week; City Hall Plaza; (617) 632–3300. One of the largest ice-cream festivals in the country.

Bunker Hill Weekend. Weekend before June 17; Charlestown; (617) 242–5641. Costumed reenactors, drills, firing demonstrations, tours of Bunker Hill Monument.

Bunker Hill Day Parade. Sunday before June 17; Charlestown; (617) 242–2646. Local residents are out in force for the parade from the foot of Bunker Hill, around the Monument, and down to the militia training field.

Dragon Boat Festival. Early June; Charles River on Cambridge side; (617) 441–2884. Teams race intricately carved and painted boats on the river from JFK Street to Western Avenue to commemorate the life of Chinese poet-patriot Qu Yuan.

JULY

Boston Harborfest. Week that includes July 4; waterfront and downtown; (617) 227–1528. A variety of events, including a Chowderfest and fireworks skyconcert, celebrate Boston's marine heritage.

Boston Pops Annual Fourth of July Concert and Fireworks. July 4; on the Esplanade. The Pops presents several other free concerts on the Esplanade during July; (617) 266–1492.

Bastille Day Street Dance. Friday before July 14; Back Bay; (617) 266–4351. Street festival with food and dancing in the French style. (See "Laissez Les Bon Temps Rouler: Bastille Day in Boston.")

Religious Festivals. Mid-July through August; North End; (617) 635–4455. Weekend festivals with parades, music, and food honor patron saints from the Old Country.

Festival Betances. Third weekend of July; South End; (617) 927–1700. Music, dancing, food, sports, and other events honor Puerto Rican patriot, Dr. Ramon Betances.

AUGUST

Civil War Encampment. First weekend; Georges Island, Boston Harbor; (617) 727–7676. More than 300 people in period costumes recall the fort's history as a Civil War prison.

August Moon Festival. Mid-month; Chinatown; (617) 479–7558. The streets are lined with food vendors and arts and crafts displays, while out-door stages showcase Chinese opera, martial-arts demonstrations, and the traditional lion dance.

SEPTEMBER

Art Newbury Street. Third weekend of September; Back Bay; (617) 267–7961. Galleries host open houses with exhibitions and refreshments.

South End Open Studios. Third full weekend of
September; South End; (617) 426–5000. The area's
largest concentration of artists welcome visitors to
their studios. (See "The Artist's Touch.")

OCTOBER

Fort Point Arts Community Open Studios. Third
weekend of October; Fort Point neighborhood of
South Boston; (617) 423–4299. More than one
hundred artists in twenty-three buildings open
their studios to visitors. (See "The Artist's Touch.")

Head of the Charles Regatta. Next-to-last Sunday
in October; Charles River, Cambridge; (617)
864–8414. The largest single-day rowing event in
the world.

NOVEMBER

Brickbottom Artists Open Studios. Open studios
the weekend before Thanksgiving; Somerville
Avenue, Somerville; (617) 776–3333 for information, (617) 776–3410 for driving directions. (See
"The Artist's Touch: Two Autumn Weekends.")

DECEMBER

Crafts at the Castle. First full weekend in
December; Back Bay; (617) 523–6400. High-quality
juried crafts exhibition geared to holiday shopping.

Reenactment of the Boston Tea Party. Sunday
closest to December 16; downtown and waterfront; (617) 338–1773. Patriots dressed as Indians
proceed from Old South Meeting House to Tea
Party Ship and Museum to reenact the dumping
of tea in Boston Harbor.

First Night. December 31; throughout Boston;
(617) 542–1399. City-wide, arts-driven New Year
celebration takes place in fifty indoor and outdoor
venues. The concept has spread to more than 130
other cities, but Boston remains first and, we
think, best. (See "The Right Foot: First Night.")

Special Indexes

ROMANTIC RESTAURANTS

Restaurant price categories in this index, represented by one to three dollar signs, reflect the cost of an appetizer, an entree, and dessert for each person. Under "Tea and Desserts," the cost indicators are only for tea and a dessert. The approximate price for each category is indicated in the following key:

Inexpensive ($): Less than $20
Moderate ($$): $20 to $40
Expensive ($$$): $40 and up

New American

Anago ($$), 65 Exeter Street, 86, 89

Biba ($$-$$$), 272 Boylston Street, 130, 133–34

Bob the Chef's ($$), 604 Columbus Avenue, 50, 51

Bristol Lounge ($$), Four Seasons Hotel, 200 Boylston Street, 163, 164

Clio ($$$), 370 Commonwealth Avenue, 98, 100

Gallery Cafe and Patio ($-$$), Royal Sonesta Hotel, 5 Cambridge Parkway, Cambridge, 56

Harborside Grill ($$), Harborside Hyatt Conference Center & Hotel, 101 Harborside Drive, 139

Harvest ($$$), 44 Brattle Street, Cambridge, 40, 43

Icarus ($$-$$$), 3 Appleton Street, 122

Library Grill at the Hampshire House, The, ($$), 84 Beacon Street, 4, 9

Martin House ($$-$$$), 157 Commercial Street, Provincetown, 223, 226

Museum Cafe ($$), Peabody Essex Museum, Essex Street, Salem, 208, 209

On the Park ($-$$), 315 Shawmut Avenue, 122

Pravda 116 ($$), 116 Boylston Street, 117, 120

Salamander ($$-$$$), 25 Huntington Avenue, 38

Salts ($$), 798 Main Street, Cambridge, 55, 57

Scullers ($$), Doubletree Guest Suites, 400 Soldiers Field Road, 142, 144–45

Stephanie's on Newbury ($$), 190 Newbury Street, 168

29 Newbury Street ($$), 29 Newbury Street, 118

Traditional American

Charley's Eating & Drinking Saloon ($-$$), 284 Newbury Street, 67

Coonamessett Inn ($$$), Jones Road and Gifford Street, Falmouth, 216, 217–18

Durgin Park ($), 340 Faneuil Hall Marketplace, 11, 13

Grog ($), 13 Middle Street, Newburyport, 174, 176

Henrietta's Table ($$), Charles Hotel, 1 Bennett Street, Cambridge, 40, 44

Oak Room ($$$), Fairmont Copley Plaza Hotel, 138 St. James Street, 86, 92

Parker's Restaurant ($$), Omni Parker House, 60 School Street, 15

Brew Pubs

Boston Beer Works ($), 61 Brookline Avenue, 50, 81–82

Brew Moon ($–$$), 50 Church Street, Cambridge, 76, 79

Cambridge Brewing Company ($–$$), 1 Kendall Square, Cambridge, 81

Commonwealth Fish and Beer Co. ($), 138 Portland Street, 76, 78

John Harvard's Brew House ($), 33 Dunster Street, Cambridge, 76, 80

For Brunch

Brew Moon, 50 Church Street, Cambridge, 76, 79

Brown Sugar Cafe, 129 Jersey Street, The Fenway, 53

Café Fleuri, Hotel Meridien, 250 Franklin Street, 156, 160

Golden Palace, 14 Tyler Street, 102, 107

Harborside Grill, Harborside Hyatt Conference Center & Hotel, 101 Harborside Drive, 139

Henrietta's Table ($$), Charles Hotel, 1 Bennett Street, Cambridge, 40, 44

House of Blues Gospel Brunch, 96 Winthrop Street, Cambridge, 109, 113

Hungry i, 71 Charles Street, 37

Liberty schooner *Clipper*, 24

Library Grill at the Hampshire House, The, 84 Beacon Street, 4, 9

On the Park, 315 Shawmut Avenue, 122

Parker's Restaurant, Omni Parker House, 60 School Street, 15

Chinese

Golden Palace ($), 14 Tyler Street, 102, 107

Wisteria House ($-$$), 264 Newbury Street, 67

Continental

Café Suisse ($$-$$$), Swissôtel Boston, 1 Avenue de Lafayette, 103

Copley's Grand Cafe ($$-$$$), Copley Plaza Hotel, 138 St. James Street, 90

Hungry i ($$), 71 Charles Street, 37

Ritz Roof, The ($$$), Ritz-Carlton, Boston, 15 Arlington Street, 134

Delis, Cafes, and Sandwich Shops

Au Bon Pain ($), Faneuil Hall Marketplace, 29

Bruegger's Bagel Bakery ($), 2050 Commonwealth Avenue, Auburndale, 58

Cafe @ DeCordova ($), 51 Sandy Pond Road, Lincoln, 201

Café Paris ($), 19 Arlington Street, 69

Café 300 ($), 300 Summer Street, 124

C'Est Bon ($), 110 Mt. Auburn St., Cambridge, 113

Garden of Eden ($), 577 Tremont Street, 122

Gardner Café ($-$$), Isabella Stewart Gardner Museum, 280 The Fenway, 95, 98, 146

Laureen's ($), 170 Main Street, Falmouth, 218-19

Museum Café ($), Museum of Fine Arts, 465 Huntington Avenue, 89, 99, 161

Museum Café ($), The New Museum at the John F. Kennedy Library, Columbia Point, 149, 152-53

Rudi's ($), 30 Rowes Wharf, 70

Tavern on the Water ($), 1 Pier 6, Charlestown Navy Yard, 23

Winter Garden ($), 222 Berkeley Street, 34

Classic French

Brasserie Jo ($$), Colonnade Hotel, 120 Huntington Avenue, 95

Café Fleuri ($$-$$$), Hotel Meridien, 250 Franklin Street, 156, 160

Sandrine's ($$), 8 Holyoke Street, Cambridge, 156, 159

Sel de la Terre ($$$), 255 State Street, 26, 31

Torch ($$), 26 Charles Street, 4, 7

New French

Ambrosia on Huntington ($$$), 116 Huntington Avenue, 95, 97

Aujourd'hui Restaurant ($$$), Four Seasons Hotel, 200 Boylston Street, 163, 168

Café Louis ($$-$$$), 234 Berkeley Street, 35

Federalist ($$$), 15 Beacon Street, 130, 132

Hamersley's Bistro ($$$), 533 Tremont Street, 122

Les Zygomates Bistro & Wine Bar ($$), 129 South Street, 125

L'Espalier ($$$), 30 Gloucester Street, 35–36

Maison Robert ($$–$$$), 45 School Street, 11, 14, 156

Sonsie ($$), 327 Newbury Street, 36

Indian

Tanjore ($), 18 Eliot Street, Cambridge, 40, 41

Irish

Kinsale ($$), 2 Center Plaza, 149, 151

Traditional Italian

Mamma Maria ($$–$$$), 3 North Square, 26, 28

Maurizio's ($$), 364 Hanover Street, 32

New Italian

Artù ($$), 6 Prince Street, 26, 31

Davio's Cafe ($–$$), 269 Newbury Street, 67

Figs ($–$$), 42 Charles Street, 6

Galleria Italiana ($$$), 177 Tremont Street, 102, 105

Giacomo's ($$), 355 Hanover, Street, 32

Grapevine Restaurant ($$), 26 Congress Street, Salem, 208, 212

Il Capriccio Ristorante e Bar ($$), 888 Main Street, Waltham, 199, 203

Papa Razzi ($$), 271 Dartmouth Street, 91

Pignoli ($$$), 91 Park Plaza, 163, 164

Pomodoro ($–$$), 319 Hanover Street, 26, 27

Tuscan Grill ($–$$), 361 Moody Street, Waltham, 195, 196

Villa Francesca ($$), 150 Richmond Street, 32

Mediterranean

Casablanca ($$), 40 Brattle Street, Cambridge, 109, 112

Rialto ($$$), The Charles Hotel, 1 Bennett Street, Cambridge, 109, 112

Pan-Asian

Brown Sugar Cafe ($), 129 Jersey Street, The Fenway, 53

Pho Pasteur ($), 8 Kneeland Street, 136, 138

Thai Dish ($-$$), 259 Newbury Street, 67

Portguese

Guida's Coast Cuisine ($$), 84 Thoreau Street, Concord, 180, 181

Seafood

Anthony's Pier 4 ($$), 140 Northern Avenue, 19, 20

Barking Crab ($), 88 Sleeper Street, 19–20

Daily Catch ($$), 261 Northern Avenue, 21

Daily Catch/Calamari Cafe ($-$$), 323 Hanover Street, 32

Dancing Lobster ($-$$), Marina Wharf, Provincetown, 228

Derby Fish and Lobster ($), 215 Derby Street, Salem, 213

Green Pond Fish'n Gear ($), 366 Menauhaut Road, East Falmouth, 216, 221

Legal Seafoods ($$), Prudential Center, 166

Lobster Pot ($), 321 Commercial Street, Provincetown, 227

Pucci's Harborside Restaurant & Bar ($$), 539 Commercial Street, Provincetown, 223, 224

Regatta of Cotuit ($$$), Route 28, Cotuit, 221

Regatta of Falmouth-by-the-Sea ($$$), Falmouth Marina, 216, 220

Shuckers ($), 91A Water Street, Woods Hole, 219

Union Oyster House ($$), 41 Union Street, 154

Spanish

Iruña ($$), 56 John F. Kennedy Street, Cambridge, 111

Tapeo ($$), 267 Newbury Street, 62, 67

For Tea and Desserts

Bristol Lounge, Four Seasons Hotel, 200 Boylston Street, 163, 164

Café Fleuri Dessert Buffet (Saturday afternoons September through May), Hotel Meridien, 250 Franklin Street, 156, 160

Finale, 1 Columbus Avenue, 102, 106

ROMANTIC LODGINGS

Inexpensive *(most rooms $175 or less)*

Boston Bed & Breakfast Afloat, Lewis Wharf, 24

Harborside Inn of Boston, 185 State Street, 160

Harvard Square Hotel, 110 Mount Auburn Street, Cambridge, 109

Isaac Harding House, 288 Harvard Street, Cambridge, 45

Newbury Guest House, 261 Newbury Street, 61–62

Palmer House Inn, The, 81 Palmer Avenue, Falmouth, 216–17

Salem Inn, 7 Summer Street, Salem, 207–08

Moderate *(most rooms $175–$275)*

Beaconlight Guesthouse, The, 12 Winthrop Street, Provincetown, 223, 224

Cambridge House Bed & Breakfast, A, 2218 Massachusetts Avenue, Cambridge, 148–49

Charles Hotel, The, 1 Bennett Street, Cambridge, 109, 114

Charles Street Inn, 94 Charles Street, 3–4

Copley Square Hotel, 47 Huntington Avenue, 117

Doubletree Guest Suites, 400 Soldiers Field Road, 141–42

Gryphon House, 9 Bay State Road, 49–50

Harborside Hyatt Conference Center & Hotel, 101 Harborside Drive, 136

Hyatt Regency Hotel, 575 Memorial Drive, Cambridge, 75–76

Inn At Harvard, 1201 Massachusetts Avenue, Cambridge, 39, 40

Omni Parker House, 60 School Street, 10–11

Royal Sonesta Hotel, 5 Cambridge Parkway, Cambridge, 55

Seaport Hotel, 1 Seaport Lane, 18–19

Expensive (*most rooms $275 or more*)

Eliot Suite Hotel, The, 370 Commonwealth Avenue, 94, 95

Fairmont Copley Plaza Hotel, 138 St. James Street, 85–86

Four Seasons Hotel, 200 Boylston Street, 162–63

Hotel Meridien, 250 Franklin Street, 155–56

Lenox Hotel, 710 Boylston Street, 33–34

Regal Bostonian Hotel, Blackstone and North Streets, 25–26

Swissôtel Boston, 1 Avenue de Lafayette, 101–03

XV Beacon, 15 Beacon Street, 130–34

DIVERSIONS

Cabaret
Lizard Lounge, 45

Dancing
El Bembé, 123
Pravda 116, 117, 120
Ritz Roof, The, 134

Tango Rialto, 115
Wally's Cafe, 98

Jazz Clubs
Bob the Chef's, 50, 51
Les Zygomates, 125
Regattabar, 109, 113

Scullers, 142, 144–45

Music Venues
Concerts in the Courtyard
(Museum of Fine Arts), 93
FleetBoston Pavilion, 19, 21
Hatch Shell concerts, 67
Kinsale, 149, 151

Comedy Club
Nick's Comedy Stop, 120

Theater
American Repertory Theatre,
40, 43, 107
Charles Playhouse, 101
Colonial Theatre, 101, 104
Emerson Majestic Theatre, 104, 168
Lyric Stage, 169
Sanders Theater in Cambridge, 169
Shubert Theatre, 101, 105
Wilbur Theatre, 101, 104

Movie Theaters
Brattle Theatre, 112
Harvard Film Archive, 45
Kendall Square Cinema, 81
Stage Two Cinema Pub, 174, 177

Performing Arts
ArtsMail, 101

Ballet Theater of Boston, 168
Bostix, 101
Boston Ballet, 168
Boston Baroque, 140
Boston Center for the Arts, 121
Boston Symphony Orchestra,
94, 97
Firehouse Center for the Arts, 178
Handel & Haydn Society, 169
Huntington Theatre, 107
Lyric Stage, 169
Mobius Art Space, 125
New England Conservatory of
Music, 99
Wang Center for the Performing
Arts, The, 101, 105, 168

Cocktail Lounges and Bars
Aria, 106
Atrium Lounge, 28
Bay Tower, The, 11, 14
Bristol Lounge, 163, 164
Café Budapest, 120
Green Dragon Tavern, 78
Harvest, 40, 43
Julien Bar, The, 157
Oak Bar, The, 86, 89

Parker's Bar, 15

Spinnaker Italia, 79

Cafes
Cafe Graffiti, 28
Caffè Vittorio, 29

Billiard Club
Boston Billiards Club, 50, 51

Observatory/Star Gazing
Gilliland Observatory, 58
Hancock Observatory, 68

Evening Tours
Elegant Touch Carriage Corp., 134

Dinner Cruise
Spirit of Boston, 19, 23–24

Annual Events
Bal Musette, 155, 156, 160
Bastille Day Street Dance
    Festival, 157
Black Nativity, The, 163, 165
Christmas Revels, The, 169
Dragon Boat Festival, 60
First Night, 136–38

Driving, Guided, and Walking Tours
A Walk Through Falmouth History
    (Falmouth), 217
Art's Dune Tours (Provincetown),
    223, 225
Beacon Hill Walking Tour, 5
Black Heritage Trail, 9
Boston Beer Company, 76
Charles River Sightseeing
    Excursion, 55, 56
Charlestown Navy Yard, 21–23

Elegant Touch Carriage Tours, 134

Harvard Yard (Cambridge), 40

L'Arte de Cucinare, North End
    Walking Tours, 32

Salem Maritime National Historic
    Site (Salem), 208, 212

Outdoor Activities
Apple-Picking (Nashoba Valley
    Winery, Bolton), 186
Biking the Cape Cod National
    Seashore, 228
Biking the Emerald Necklace, 62
Biking the Shining Sea Bike Path
    (Falmouth), 216, 219
Bird-Watching at Plum Island
    (Parker River National Wildlife
    Refuge, Newburyport), 174
Bird-Watching in Mount Auburn
    Cemetery (Cambridge), 109
Boston Harbor Islands
    Excursion, 71
Canoeing on the Charles River
    (Charles River Canoe and
    Kayak), 58
Cross-Country Skiing (Weston Ski
    Track, Weston), 194–95
Excursion to Boston Light (Boston
    Harbor Islands), 74
First Day Hike (Blue Hills
    Reservation, Milton), 190
Hiking at the Blue Hills Reservation
    (Milton), 190
Horseback Trail Ride (Blue Hills
    Reservation, Milton), 193
Ice-skating on the Frog Pond
    (Boston Common), 37
In-line skating along Memorial
    Drive (Cambridge), 80

Sailing on the Charles River (Community Boating), 55, 56

Swimming at Herring Cove Beach (Provincetown), 223, 226

Swimming at Surf Beach (Falmouth), 217

Attractions and Historic Sites

African Meeting House, 5

Boston Common, 16, 37, 137

Boston Public Garden, 68

Boston Public Library, 86, 90, 120

Bunker Hill Monument, 23

Castle Island, 74

Copp's Hill Burial Ground, 26, 30

Custom House, 11, 12, 213

Faneuil Hall, 11, 12

Fenway Park, 50, 51

Fleet Center, 76, 79

Franklin Park Zoo, 66

French Library and Cultural Center, 38, 157

Granary Burying Ground, 16

Gropius House (Lincoln), 199–201

Hancock Observatory, 68

House of Seven Gables (Salem), 213

King's Chapel, 17

King's Chapel Burying Ground, 15

Lyman Estate Greenhouses (Waltham), 142, 146

Massachusetts Horticultural Society Library, 146

Massachusetts State House, 8

Mount Auburn Cemetery, 109, 114

New England Aquarium, 20, 137

Nobska Light (Falmouth), 220–21

Old North Church, 26, 29–30

Old South Meeting House, 16

Old State House, 17

St. Stephen's Church, 30

Sleepy Hollow Cemetery (Concord), 180, 182

Symphony Hall, 95, 97, 169

Trinity Church, 34, 86, 90, 139

USS *Constitution*, 22

Walden Pond (Concord), 180, 183

Wellesley College Greenhouse (Wellesley), 147

Woods Hole Oceanographic Institute Exhibit Center (Woods Hole), 219

World Headquarters, First Church of Christ, Scientist, 95

Historic Homes

Emerson House (Concord), 180

Frederick Law Olmsted National Historic Site, 69

Gibson House Museum, 37

Harrison Gray Otis House, 4

John F. Kennedy National Historic Site, 149–51

Longfellow National Historic Site, 111

Nichols House Museum, 4, 6–7

Old Manse (Concord), 183–84

Orchard House (Concord), 180, 181

Paul Revere House, 27

Wayside (Concord), 184

Museums

Busch-Reisinger Museum (Harvard University, Cambridge), 42–43

Cahoon Museum of American Art (Cotuit), 221

Concord Museum (Concord), 183

DeCordova Museum and Sculpture Park (Lincoln), 199, 201

Fogg Art Museum (Harvard University, Cambridge), 41–42

Harvard Museums of Natural and Cultural History (Cambridge), 44

Institute of Contemporary Art, 117, 119

Isabella Stewart Gardner Museum, 86, 91, 95, 98, 142, 145–46

Museum of Fine Arts, 86, 87, 99

Museum of Science, Gilliland Observatory, 58

New Museum at the John F. Kennedy Library, 149, 152–53

Peabody Essex Museum (Salem), 209–11

Pilgrim Monument and Museum (Provincetown), 226–27

Provincetown Art Association and Museum (Provincetown), 22

Provincetown Heritage Museum (Provincetown), 225

Revolving Museum, 124

Sackler Museum (Harvard University, Cambridge), 43

Neighborhoods

Back Bay, 130, 156

Beacon Hill, 3

Charlestown, 21

Chinatown, 106–07

Fort Point Arts Community, 116, 123–24

Harvard Square, 109–11, 159

North End, 25

South Boston, 74, 149, 152–53

South End, 121

Theater District, 103, 168

General Index

A

Adams, Samuel (beer), 77
Adams, Samuel (patriot), 10, 16, 78, 87
Adesso, 165
African Meeting House, 5
African Tropical Forest, The, 66
Alcott, Louisa May, 119, 180–82, 184
Alianza Contemporary Crafts, 167
Ambrosia on Huntington, 95, 97
American Animated Classics, 119
American Repertory Theatre, 40, 43, 107
Anago, 86, 89
Anthony's Pier 4, 19, 20
Antiques at 80 Charles, 9
Arche, 165
Aria, 106
Arnold Arboretum, 65
ART. See American Repertory Theatre
Artful Hand Gallery, The, 166
Arthur M. Sackler Museum, 43
Art's Dune Tours, 223, 225
ArtsMail, 101
Artù, 26, 31
Atrium Lounge, 28
Au Bon Pain, 29
Auburndale Park, 59

Aujourd'hui Restaurant, 163, 168
Australian Outback, 66
Avalon, 53

B

Back Bay, 130, 156
Back Bay Bicycles, 62
Back Bay Fens, 50, 52, 63
Bal Musette, 155, 156, 160
Ballet Theater of Boston, 168
Barbara Krakow Gallery, 118
Barking Crab, 19–20
Bastille Day Street Dance Festival, 157
Bay State Cruise Company, 223
Bay Tower, The, 11, 14
Bayside Expo Center, 142
Beach Shuttle, 226
Beacon Hill, 130
Beacon Hill Spirits, 8
Beaconlight Guesthouse, The, 223, 224
Bella Santé, 130
Belleza, 169
Biba, 130, 133–34
Bill Rodgers Running Center, 13
Bird's World, 66
Birdwatcher of Newburyport, The, 177
Black Heritage Trail, 9

Black Nativity, The, 163, 165

Blue Hills Reservation, 140, 190

Bob the Chef's, 50, 51

Booksellers at 355 Boylston Street,
The, 165

Bostix, 101

Boston Antique Cooperative
No. 1, 9

Boston Ballet, 168

Boston Baroque, 140

Boston Beer Company, 76

Boston Beer Works, 50, 81–82

Boston Billiards Club, 50, 51

Boston Bruins, 79

Boston Celtics, 81

Boston Center for Adult
Education, 38

Boston Center for the Arts, 121

Boston Common, 16, 37, 137

Boston Harbor Islands Ferry, 71

Boston Harbor Islands Park, 71–72

Boston Light, 74

Boston National Historical Park
Visitor Center, 12

Boston Pops, 67

Boston Public Library, 86, 90, 120

Boston Red Sox, 49

Boston Symphony Orchestra,
94, 97

Boston's Bed & Breakfast Afloat, 24

Botanical Museum, 44

Brasserie Jo, 95

Brattle Book Shop, 105

Brattle Theatre, 112

Brew Moon, 76, 79

Brickbottom Artists Studios, 125

Bristol Lounge, 163, 164

Brooks Brothers, 167

Brookwood Farm, 193

Brown Sugar Cafe, 53

Bruegger's Bagel Bakery, 58

Bulfinch, Charles, 3, 4, 5, 8, 12, 30,
40, 119, 214

Bunker Hill Monument, 23

Busch-Reisinger Museum, 42–43

Bussey Hill, 66

Butterfly Landing, 66

C

Cafe @ DeCordova, 201

Café Budapest, 120

Café Fleuri, 156, 160

Cafe Graffiti, 28

Café Louis, 35

Café Paris, 69

Café Suisse, 103

Café 300, 124

Caffè Vittoria, 29

Cahoon Museum of American
Art, 221

Calamari Cafe, 32

Cambridge Brewing Company, 81

Cambridge House Bed & Breakfast,
A, 148–49

Cambridge Information Kiosk, 110

Cambridge Office for Tourism, xiv

Cambridgeside Galleria, 60

Cape Cod School of Art, 225

Casablanca, 109, 112

Castle Island, 74

C'Est Bon, 113

Charles Hotel, The, 109, 114

Charles Playhouse, 101

Charles River Boat Company, 55, 56

Charles River Canoe and Kayak, 58

Charles River Esplanade, 55

Charles Street, 9

Charles Street Inn, 3–4

Charlestown Navy Yard, 21–23

Charley's Eating & Drinking Saloon, 67

Chase Gallery, 119

Chestnut Street, 214

Chinatown, 106–7

Christian Science Mother Church, 96

Christian Science Publishing Society, 96

Christmas Revels, The, 169

Christopher Columbus Park, 31

City Sports, 80

Clio, 98, 100

Clipper, 19, 24

Coach Store, The, 35

Colonial Drug, 156, 159

Colonial Theatre, 101, 104

Commonwealth Fish and Beer Co., 76, 78

Community Boating, 55, 56

Concerts in the Courtyard (Museum of Fine Arts), 93

Concord, 179–84

Concord Bookshop, The, 181

Concord Museum, 183

Constitution, USS, 22

Coonamessett Inn, 216, 217–18

Copley Place, 166

Copley Society, 118

Copley Square, 85–87, 139

Copley Square Hotel, 117

Copley's Grand Café, 90

Copp's Hill Burial Ground, 26, 30

Corner Cycle, 219

Crafts at the Castle, 169

Crane & Co. Papermakers, 167

Crowninshield-Bentley House, 210

Curley, James Michael, statue, 13

Custom House, 11, 12, 213

Custom Shop, 166

D

Daily Catch, 21

Daily Catch/Calamari Cafe, 32

Dancing Lobster, The, 228

Davio's Cafe, 67

DeCordova Museum and Sculpture Park, 199, 201

DeLuca's Back Bay Market, 62

Derby Fish and Lobster, 213

Desana, 167

Doubletree Guest Suites, 141–42

Downtown Crossing, 163

Dragon Boat Festival, 60

Durgin-Park, 11, 13

E

East End Gallery, 225

Eddy, Mary Baker, 119

El Bembé, 123

Elegant Touch Carriage Corp., 134

Eliot Suite Hotel, The, 94, 95

Emerald Necklace, 62, 63

Emerson House, 180

Emerson Majestic Theatre, 104, 168

Emerson, Ralph Waldo, 180–81, 182

Emmanuel Church, 95, 98

Emporio Armani, 167

Escada, 165

Esplanade, 62, 67

Essex Institute, 209–11

Eugene Galleries, 9

F

Fairmont Copley Plaza Hotel, 85–86

Falmouth, 215–21

Faneuil Hall, 11, 12

Faneuil Hall Marketplace, 11, 12, 29

F.A.O. Schwarz, 166

Federalist, 130, 132

Fenway Park, 50, 51

Fenway Victory Gardens, 52

Figs, 6

Filene's, 163

Filene's Basement, 163

Finale, 102, 106

Fine Arts Work Center, 225

Firehouse Center for the Arts, 178

First Church of Christ, Scientist, 95–96

First Day concert, 136, 140

First Night, 136–38

First Night fireworks, 136

FleetBoston Pavilion, 19, 21

Fleet Center, 76, 79

Fogg Art Museum, 41–42

Forest Grove, 59

Fort Point Arts Community, 116, 123–24

Fort Warren, 71, 72

Four Seasons Hotel, 162–63

Fox Island, 59

Franklin Park, 66

Franklin Park Zoo, 66

French Film Festival, 161

French Library and Cultural Center, The, 38, 157

Frog Pond, 37

G

Galleria Italiana, 102, 105

Gallery Café and Patio, 56

Gallery NAGA, 118

Garden of Eden, 122

Gardner Café, 95, 98, 146

Gardner Museum, 86, 91, 95, 98, 142, 145–46

Gardner-Pingree House, 210

Georges Island, 72

Ghelfi's Candies of Cape Cod, 217

Giacomo's, 32

Gianni Versace, 167

Gibson House Museum, 37

Gilliland Observatory, 58

Glass Flowers, 40, 44, 147

Globe Corner Bookstore, 110

Golden Palace, 102, 107

Golden Slipper, 24

Granary Burying Grounds, 16

Grand Procession, 137

Grapevine Restaurant, 208, 212

Great Blue Hill, 192

Great Brook Farm Ski Touring Center, 197

Greater Boston Convention and Visitors Bureau, xiv

Green Dragon Tavern, 78

Green Pond Fish'n Gear, 216, 221

Grog, 174, 176

Grolier Poetry Book Shop, 109, 110

Gropius House, 199–201

Gryphon House, 49–50

Gucci, 166

Guida's Coast Cuisine, 180, 181

H

Hamersley's Bistro, 122

Hancock Observatory, 68

Hancock, John, 10, 16, 78, 87, 119

Handel & Haydn Society, 169

Harborside Grill, 139

Harborside Hyatt Conference Center & Hotel, 136

Harborside Inn of Boston, 160

Harrison Gray Otis House, 4–5

Harvard Bookstore, 110

Harvard Film Archive, 45

Harvard, John, statue of, 40

Harvard Museums of Natural and Cultural History, 44

   Botanical Museum, 44

   Mineralogical and Geological Museum, 45

Harvard Square, 109–11, 159

Harvard Square Hotel, 109

Harvard Yard, 40, 113

Harvest, 40, 43

Hatch Shell, 67

Hatch Shell concerts, 67

Hawthorne, Nathaniel, 15, 180, 182, 184, 213–14

Haymarket, 26

Henrietta's Table, 40, 44

Hermès, 165

Herring Cove Beach, 223, 226

Hidden Gardens of Beacon Hill, 9

HMV, 110

Holyoke Center, 40

Hotel Meridien, The, 155–56

Houghtons Pond, 190

House of Blues Gospel Brunch, 109, 113

House of the Seven Gables, The, 208, 213–14

Hungry i, The, 37

Huntington Theatre, 107

Hyatt Regency Hotel, 75–76

I

Icarus, 122

Il Capriccio Ristorante e Bar, 199, 203

Il Fornaio, 27

Inn at Harvard, 39, 40

Institute of Contemporary
    Art, 117, 119

International Poster Gallery, 119

Irish Imports Limited, 151

Iruña, 111

Isaac Harding House, 45

Isabella Stewart Gardner Museum,
    86, 91, 95, 98, 142, 145–46

J

J. Pace and Sons, 28

Jamaica Pond, 65

James P. Kelleher Rose
    Garden, 52, 64

John Harvard's Brew
    House, 76, 80

John Harvard Statue, 40

John Lewis Jewelers, 167

John's Liquor Store, 217

Jordan Hall, 99

Judi Rotenberg Gallery, 118

Julien Bar, The, 157

K

Kelleher, James P., Rose
    Garden, 52, 64

Kendall Square Cinema, 81

Kennedy, John F., 14, 119, 149–51

Kennedy, John F., Library and
    Museum, 149

Kennedy, John F., National Historic
    Site, 149–51

Kennedy, Rose, 30, 149–51

King's Chapel, 17

King's Chapel Burying Ground, 15

Kinsale, 149, 151

Kitchen Arts, 167

Klein, Robert, Gallery, 118

Krakow, Barbara, Gallery, 118

L

Lacoste Gallery, 181

Laureen's, 218–19

Leather District, 124

Legal Seafoods, 166

Lenox Hotel, The, 33–34

Les Zygomates Bistro & Wine
    Bar, 125

L'Espalier, 35–36

Liberty schooner *Clipper*, 24

Library Grill at the Hampshire
    House, 4, 9

Little Brewster Island, 74

Lizard Lounge, 45

Lobster Pot, The, 227

Longfellow, Henry Wadsworth,
    111–12, 119

Longfellow National Historic
    Site, 111

Lord & Taylor, 35

Louis, 35

Louis Vuitton, 166

Louisburg Square, 5

LouLou's Lost & Found, 167

Lovells Island, 71, 73–74

Lyman Estate Greenhouses,
    142, 146

Lyric Stage, 169

M

Macy's, 163

Maison Robert, 11, 14, 156

Mamma Maria, 26, 28

Mapparium, 97

Marine Park, 74

Martignetti Liquors, 28

Martin House, 223, 226

Massachusetts Antiques
   Cooperative, 195, 196

Massachusetts Horticultural Society
   Library, 146

Massachusetts State House, 8

Maurizio's, 32

Memorial Drive, 80

Memorial Hall, 44

MFA, 86, 87, 99

Mills Gallery, 121

Mineralogical and Geological
   Museum, 45

Mobius Art Space, 125

Mont Blanc: The Art of Writing, 166

Moody Dam, 59

Mount Auburn Cemetery, 109, 114

MPC Caricatures, 13

Mugar Library, 53

Museum cafes
   Museum of Fine Arts, 89,
   99, 161
   New Museum at the John F.
   Kennedy Library, The, 149,
   152–53
   Peabody Essex Museum,
   208, 209

Museum Company, The, 167

Museum of Fine Arts, 86, 87, 99

Museum of Science, 58

N

Nashoba Valley Winery, 186–88

Neforas, Thomas, Photography,
   102, 103

Neiman Marcus, 166

New England Aquarium, 20, 137

New England Conservatory of
   Music, 99

New England Life Building, 35

New England Spring Flower
   Show, 142–43

New Museum at the John F.
   Kennedy Library, The,
   149, 152–53

Newbury Guest House, 61–62

Newbury Street, 35, 61–62, 117,
   118–19, 134, 167

Newbury Street Mural, 119

Newburyport, 173, 176

Nichols House Museum, 4, 6–7

Nick's Comedy Stop, 120

Nielsen Gallery, 119

Nobska Light, 220–21

North End Park, 31

O

Oak Bar, The, 86, 89

Oak Room, 86, 92

Old Manse, 183–84

Old North Church, 26, 29–30

Old Port Book Shop, 174, 177

Old Silver Beach, 216, 219
Old South Church, 139
Old South Meeting House, 16
Old State House, 17
Olmsted, Frederick Law, National
    Historic Site, 69
Omni Parker House, 10–11
On the Park, 122
O'Neill, Eugene, 104, 222
O'Neill, Thomas P., 148, 150
Orchard House, 180, 181
Oriental Bird House, 66
Otis, Harrison Gray, House, 4–5
Out of Town News, 156, 160

P

Pace, J., and Sons, 28
Paddocks Stable, 193
Palmer House Inn, The, 216–17
Papa Razzi, 91
Parker River National Wildlife
    Refuge, 174–76, 178
Parker's Bar, 15
Parker's Restaurant, 15
Paul Revere House, 27
Peabody Essex Museum, 209–11
Peabody Museum, 208, 211
Pho Pasteur, 136, 138
Pierre Deux, 167
Pignoli, 163, 164
Pilgrim Monument and Museum,
    The, 226–27
Plum Island, 177
Polcari, 28

Pomodoro, 26, 27
Ponkapoag Trail, 190, 191
Post Office Square Park, 158
Prado, 30
Pravda 116, 117, 120
Provincetown, 222–28
Provincetown Art Association and
    Museum, 224
Provincetown Bikes, 228
Provincetown Heritage
    Museum, 225
Provincetown II, 223
Public Garden, 68
Pucci's Harborside Restaurant &
    Bar, 223, 224
Pucker Gallery, 119

R

Regal Bostonian Hotel, 25–26
Regatta of Cotuit, 221
Regatta of Falmouth-by-the-Sea,
    216, 220
Regattabar, 109, 113
Repertoire, 132
Revere, Paul, 15, 16, 25, 27, 29,
    30, 78, 87
Revere, Paul, House, 27
Revolving Museum, 124
Rialto, 109, 112
Rice-Polak Gallery, 225
Richardson, H. H., 34, 52, 90, 95
Ritz Roof, The, 134
Riverway, The, 64–65
Robert Gould Shaw Memorial, 8

Robert Klein Gallery, 118
Rodier Paris, 167
Rotenberg, Judi, Gallery, 118
Rowes Wharf, 137
Royal Sonesta Hotel, 55
Rudi's, 70

S

Sackler, Arthur M., Museum, 43
St. Stephen's Church, 30
Saks Fifth Avenue, 35
Salamander Dining Room
    & Satay Bar, 38
Salem, 207–14
Salem Inn, 207–8
Salem Maritime National Historic
    Site, 208, 212
Salts, 55, 57
Salumeria Toscana, 27
Sanders Theater in Cambridge, 169
Sandrine's, 156, 159
Sargent, John Singer, 41,
    88–89, 91, 92
Schoenhof's Foreign Books,
    156, 159
Scullers, 142, 144–45
Seaport Hotel, 18–19
Secret Garden, The, 62
Sel de la Terre, 26, 31
Shaw, Robert Gould, Memorial, 8
Shining Sea Bike Path, 216, 219
Shops at Prudential Center,
    The, 166
Shreve Crump & Low, 131, 165

Shubert Theatre, 101, 105
Shuckers, 219
Skyline Loop, 190, 191–92
Sleepy Hollow Cemetery, 180, 182
SmartRoutes, xiv
Society of Arts and Crafts, 167
Sonesta Hotel, 55
Sonia Rykiel, 165
Sonsie, 36
South End, 121
South End Open Studios, 117
South Station, 123
Southwest Corridor, 66
Spinnaker Italia, 79
Spirit of Boston cruise, 19, 23–24
Spring Plover and Wildlife
    Festival, 178
Stage Two Cinema Pub, 174, 177
Stephanie's on Newbury, 168
Store @ DeCordova, 202
Surf Beach, 217
Swan Boats, 62, 68
Swissôtel Boston, 101–3
Symphony Hall, 95, 97, 169

T

Tango Rialto, 115
Tanjore, 40, 41
Tapeo, 62, 67
Tavern on the Water, 23
Thai Dish, 67
Theater District, 103, 168
Thoreau, Henry David,
    179–80, 182–83

300 Summer Street, 124
Ticketmaster Sportscharge, 75
Tiffany & Co., 166
Toppers, 167
Torch, 4, 7
Tower Records, 110
Trinity Church, 34, 86, 90, 139
Tuscan Grill, 195, 196
29 Newbury Street, 118
249 A Street, 124

U

UFO Gallery, 225
Union Oyster House, 154
Up Stairs at the Pudding, 40, 44
Updike, John, 51
USS *Constitution*, 22

V

Victory Garden, 52, 63
Villa Francesca, 32
Visitor Passport, public
    transportation, xiv
Vuitton, Louis, 166

W

Wadsworth House, 40

Walden Pond, 180, 183
Wally's Cafe, 98
Wang Center for the Performing
    Arts, The, 101, 105, 168
Waterfront Park, 26
Wayside, The, 184
Wellesley College
    Greenhouse, 147
Weston Ski Track, 194–95
Whippoorwill Crafts, 13
WHOI Exhibit Center, 219
Widener Library, 41
Wiggin Gallery of the Boston
    Public Library, 120
Wilbur Theatre, 101, 104
Winter Garden, 34
Wisteria House, 67
Women's Educational & Industrial
    Union, 165
Woods Hole, 219
Wordsworth, 110
World Headquarters of The First
    Church of Christ, Scientist, 95
World of Science, 167

X

XV Beacon, 130–34

About the Authors

PATRICIA HARRIS AND DAVID LYON spent more than fifteen years compiling experiences for *Romantic Days and Nights in Boston*. Over that time they have ventured far and wide as travel writers but keep coming back to the romance of the Hub. They reside in a mid-Cambridge neighborhood with their plain gray tabby cat. If you stand just right in their living room, you can see the Boston skyline.